SWALLOWING A FISHBONE?

Swallowing a Fishbone ?

✴✴✴

FEMINIST THEOLOGIANS

DEBATE CHRISTIANITY

———

Edited by

Daphne Hampson

First published in Great Britain 1996
Society for Promoting Christian Knowledge
Holy Trinity Church
Marylebone Road
London NW1 4DU

British Library Cataloguing-in-Publication Data
A catalogue record for this book is available from the British Library

ISBN 0-281-04949-1

Typeset by Wilmaset Ltd, Birkenhead, Wirral
Printed in Great Britain by
Biddles Ltd., Guildford and King's Lynn

CONTENTS

THE CONTRIBUTORS

DAPHNE HAMPSON is Senior Lecturer in Divinity at the University of St Andrews in Scotland. She holds doctorates in history (from Oxford), in theology (from Harvard) and a master's degree in continental philosophy (from Warwick). At an earlier stage deeply involved in the campaign for the ordination of women in the Anglican churches in Britain, she left the church in 1980 and subsequently came to name herself 'post-Christian'. The author of numerous articles in feminism and theology and of *Theology and Feminism* (Basil Blackwell 1990), her *After Christianity* is being published in 1996 (SCM Press). Daphne Hampson is a frequent broadcaster and lecturer in Britain; she has lectured also in Europe and in the United States and Canada, and she was the founding president of the European Society of Women in Theological Research.

JANET MARTIN SOSKICE is University Lecturer in Theology at the University of Cambridge and a fellow of Jesus College. She holds an MA in biblical studies from the University of Sheffield and a doctorate in philosophy of religion from Oxford. Janet Martin Soskice is the author of *Metaphor and Religious Language* (OUP 1985), she has edited a collection *After Eve: Women, Theology and the Christian Tradition* (Harper Collins/Marshall Pickering 1990), jointly edited *Medicine and Moral Reasoning* (CUP 1994) and published articles in diverse fields in theology, ethics, aesthetics and philosophy of religion. She has lectured widely in Europe, in the United States and Australia and New Zealand. From 1992–4 she was the President of the Catholic Theological Association of Great Britain (the first woman to hold this position) and she is at present a member of the English Anglican-Roman Catholic Commission.

NICOLA SLEE is Director of Studies at the Aston Training Scheme, a national foundation course training candidates for ordination in the Church of England. Since studying theology and educational psychology at Cambridge, she has worked in adult theological education. A lay Anglican, Nicola has taken an active part in 'Women in Theology' and other feminist networks. She has published widely in religious education and feminist theology, including a book, *Easter Garden*, a well-known essay on the parables, articles on the psychology of religious development, poetry, liturgical material and children's books. Nicola is on the management committee of the International Seminar on Religious Education and Values.

JANE SHAW is Research Fellow in Church History at Regent's Park College, Oxford University. She holds a doctorate in history from the University of California at Berkeley and a master's degree in divinity from Harvard. Her research is primarily in the area of eighteenth-century religion and she is currently writing a book on religious experience in Enlightenment England. She also writes and lectures on feminist historical theology, and preaches regularly in a variety of contexts as an Anglican lay woman.

JULIE HOPKINS is an ordained Baptist minister who worked in the pastorate in London and in Cardiff. Since completing her doctorate in theology at Bristol in 1988, she has been Lecturer and Researcher in Feminist Theology at the Free University in Amsterdam. Julie, who has lectured widely in Europe, has written on feminist Christologies in *Vom Verlangen nach Heilwerden* (published by the European Society of Women in Theological Research). Her *Towards a Feminist Christology* (SPCK 1995) will be translated into German and Italian in 1996.

SARAH COAKLEY is Mallinckrodt Professor of Divinity, Harvard University. She holds theological degrees from Cambridge (MA, Ph.D.) and from Harvard (Th.M.), where she first went as a Harkness Fellow from Britain. Before moving back to Harvard in 1993, she had been Lecturer and Senior Lecturer in the Department of Religious Studies at Lancaster, and then Tutorial Fellow and University Lecturer in Theology at Oriel College, Oxford. She is the author of *Christ Without Absolutes: A Study of the Christology of Ernst Troeltsch* (Oxford 1988), the co-editor (with David Pailin) of *The Making and Remaking of Christian Doctrine* (Oxford 1991), and the editor of *Religion and the Body* (Cambridge, forthcoming). Her next book is based on her Cambridge Hulsean Lectures of 1992 and is to be entitled *God, Sexuality and the Self: An Essay 'On the Trinity'*. She served for ten years on the Church of England Doctrine Commission, and contributed chapters to two of its reports (*We Believe in God*, 1987; *We Believe in the Holy Spirit*, 1991).

PREFACE

This book has been many years in the making. Back at Harvard in 1988–89 for the year, I found myself engaged in a lively dialogue via lengthy letters with Nicky Slee. Why was she, and why was I not, a Christian? What were the real reasons, the divergences and differences? What concerned us? As the dialogue progressed I realized that a wider audience ought to be able to see the debate and think the issues through.

I began to talk with other women about writing a book together. Initially I supposed that there should be three Christian and three post-Christian women, for all of whom the interface between feminism and Christianity was an issue. People's responses surprised me. Some did not want to commit themselves; did not even see that the compatibility or not of feminism and Christianity was a vital issue. But I found five women whom I knew, of varied stances, and the book was under way. It was important also from the start that everyone had had theological training at an advanced level. Four of us earn our bread and butter teaching systematic theology at universities; the other two are also in tertiary education. There has been no other such public debate between such a group of women of which I know.

All of us who have participated in this enterprise have been deeply challenged by the feminist issue, however different the conclusions to which we have come. As it has turned out however, everyone other than I is a Christian feminist. That is significant. I have many friends who are spiritual persons and not Christians (or only so in the loosest possible sense of the term) – but almost by definition they are therefore not theologians. The debate as a result becomes somewhat skewed. It is important that anyone reading this book who is not appraised of the circumstances should realize that many women have left Christianity behind them in recent years as they became feminists. They saw no way forward.

What has been interesting in the event is that the debate has cut in all directions, not just between Christian and post-Christian. For example I share with Janet a sense of the importance of the structure of Christian thought as it was worked out in the patristic period; Nicola or Julie want to bypass these questions. While Sarah and I in very different ways wish to found our thought upon religious experience or the life of prayer. Not only that, but there are convergences in the sense that I recognize – and Janet has indicated that she does too – that each other's position represents a logical option of which one can conceive; yet as it stands we are diametrically opposed. There is a range of issues at stake between those who are Christians. I had deliberately invited women to participate who are Roman Catholic, 'high' and 'low' Anglican, and Baptist. But it has been a revelation to see that Christian feminists are, on other grounds, so diverse. We have among us in Julie a liberation theologian, Jane's early drafts were deeply influenced by poststructuralist thought, while Nicola has been formed by narrative theology. It has been Jane who from the start has raised issues about the terms of the debate.

We met together for a twenty-four hour period in a small village half way between Manchester and Sheffield in glorious summer weather in 1990. We do thank the Quaker Community at Bamford, in particular my friend Althea de Carteret, for making that possible. It is to Althea, who is an amateur photographer specializing in women's portraiture, that the photograph of us on the back cover is owed. The occasion was important in giving people the opportunity to get to know one another and it gave us a sense of the shape of the book. We spent one session discussing the preliminary statements which we had each written, recording the discussion for its author's benefit. From then onwards we have had to make do with circulating work by post.

The debate has not always been easy. It was difficult for some people who produced their essays early to wait so long for others to do so and not to feel that their work represented a person they had moved on from. But we persisted in waiting. I think also that I had not fully comprehended that, for many Christians, being a part of the church is so axiomatic that one struggles to articulate how it is that one is a feminist and a Christian. For me, by contrast, leaving the church, and subsequently also Christianity behind me, has been the greatest transition of my life – so I know very well why I have done these things. We have all I think found during the course of the debate that our position is moving all the time. Women in recent years have undergone an extraordinary period of growth and change as they have tackled what feminism means for their spirituality. This process in some way finds its reflection in the text.

The book is decidedly British. We are fortunate, surely, that in Britain we have a long tradition of debating. It is something which, I have come to see, is characteristic of our culture; in a way that it is not for example of North Americans. (Indeed it may astonish North Americans that such a book could be written.)

Nevertheless we have not been insular! It was at Harvard many years ago, when we were both studying there, that I first met Sarah; as indeed at Harvard that I met Jane at a later date. Julie, as a result of having spent a considerable time at a position at the Free University of Amsterdam, is much aware of Continental Christian feminist thinking. Janet is Canadian in origin and indeed is back in Canada writing as we complete this book; while it occurs to me that I wrote my essay in Toronto!

It was at the gathering at Bamford that the title of the book was conceived. We were at table discussing what we should call it. There was fish to eat. Julie choked on a fishbone. Fish. ICHTHUS – the acronym in Greek (being the first letters of the words Jesus Christ God's Son Saviour), which the earliest Christians took as the symbol of their faith. Was to be Christian as a feminist to swallow a fishbone? Perhaps to choke? 'Swallowing a Fishbone?' the book was to be. We added 'Feminist Theologians Debate Christianity' to show something of the significance of the exchange and to describe who we are.

Let me conclude this Preface by quoting from the circular letter (one of the first of many), sent out to those women who comprised the group in formation, describing the project as I saw it.

We are a generation of women, highly intelligent – look at us! – who have had to face something which has never quite been faced by such a group of women before: the question of whether Christianity is viable for us. And this question poses itself not just in terms of 'is it true', which other generations have had to face (though that may be an issue also). It is [moreover] a question for us as to whether Christianity is going to help or hinder us in becoming the whole and mature human persons that we wish to be. That raises a whole agenda, and it is that which will make the book interesting to women (and shock some men). We have all had to struggle with that issue. I think therefore that many women will engage with this book. It might be an eye-opener to any man who picks it up as to where intelligent and committed women are at this point.

We should note the historic moment at which this book is written. Twenty years before I wrote those lines the situation which I described did not pertain.

And now I hand over to Nicky, who, at a time I hardly knew her, told me that she was sitting on the London Underground reading my letters and becoming madder by the minute...

Daphne Hampson
St Andrews

My dear Daphne,

Since this book grew out of our correspondence back in 1988, there is something fitting about you sharing the Preface with me in this way. It is, for me, a clear signal of the uniqueness of this book and a testimony to your vision which lies behind it and your unflagging commitment to a methodology which is genuinely dialogical and collaborative, not only in intent, but also in execution, not merely in the grand sweep but also in the minutest detail.

I well remember the excitement and fascination of our initial correspondence, which, as I recall, started when you sent me the extract from *Theology and Feminism* in which you quoted and discussed my work on the parables, wanting to know whether you had understood my work aright and represented my position accurately. Such an action, I soon came to discover, was typical of your energetic pursuit of truth and academic integrity, as well as your painstaking attention to detail.

We had met only briefly, but quickly our correspondence grew into a lively and spirited debate with one another over the fundamental issues, both substantive and methodological, which divided us, as well as a joyful discovery of points of shared experience and common perception. Your almost disarmingly simple questions compelled me to go back to first principles and ask myself why I remained a Christian, why I could not join you in leaving the church, much though the prospect appealed, how I understood the maleness of Jesus and the indisputable sexism of the Christian scriptures, what I understood by prayer and spirituality ... and so on and on. As I wrestled with your questions, I came to a greater clarity about my own Christian feminist identity and what was, and was not, fundamental to me in this commitment. I think, too, that an occasional question or challenge on my part may have caused you to rethink the grounds of your new position and to articulate your religious convictions in new ways.

The experience of writing this book has continued and widened that process of dialogue in rich and fascinating ways. Much of this dialogue remains invisible in the finished text – I think of the hours you have spent on the telephone talking to one or other of us about our essays and responses, the endless letters, cards and faxes that have kept the Post Office in business for the past five years (these alone would make another book and provide a fascinating running commentary on this one!), not to mention that incredible weekend we spent at Bamford eating, talking and yes, even 'praying' (in Quaker style) together. Yet that invisible dialogue both undergirds and is reflected in the methodology of the book which seeks to take seriously, as few collections of essays do, the dynamism and provisionality of theological reflection, as well as the ideal of feminist friendship.

This is not to say that the process of engaging in dialogue with one another has been easy. Far from it. The cost of the commitment to a collaborative process has been high for all of us, in a variety of ways, and for no one more than you: not only in terms of the hours of painstaking work you have engaged in editing our essays, responses and afterwords, but, more significantly, in terms of the vulnerabilities we have exposed in one another and in ourselves as a result of submitting our most cherished convictions to public scrutiny, analysis and critical debate. You have been puzzled and perplexed by the pain and the paralysis that have been as real a part of the process of this book as the elation, fascination and mutual exhilaration. Yet, on reflection, it seems hardly surprising to me that women who, as you yourself say, find ourselves at a historical juncture within western religious consciousness, and addressing choices which have never existed before now, should do so only with tremendous struggle, conflict and dim awareness of the forces with which we battle, both within and outside ourselves. You yourself claim a clarity about the reasons for your own theological position which I suspect few religious people share. This is partly a comment on the kind of person you are, for whom clear, cool and logical thinking remains paramount. But it is also a comment on the position you have taken up. Having left the Christian church, you have, as it were, crossed a rubicon which the rest of us writing in this book are still, in some ways, attempting to straddle. Your perspective on what it is you have left behind is necessarily sharper than ours who remain in the very place we are trying to describe and map, even as we seek to inhabit it. So, once again, I am not altogether surprised that some of us have found it difficult, slow and unsettling to voice our convictions and to state with clarity where we are and why we stand there.

I am both glad and grateful that you persisted with your vision of a dialogue conducted between feminists of religious conviction. What has resulted is, I think, a book unique in both format and ethos: a book which has not only grown *out* of dialogue and will stimulate further dialogue amongst those who read it, but more fundamentally *is* itself a dialogue in a way that few books manage to be. I hope that readers will take away from this book, not only a deeper and sharper sense of the issues which divide and unite feminist theologians, but a vision of what feminist theological methodology can be and might be like, in universities, faith communities and all places of adult learning. For this, as well as for your commitment to continue in dialogue with the women whose faith you can no longer share, I want to say 'thank you'.

Nicky

Nicola Slee
Aston Training Scheme

ACKNOWLEDGEMENTS

We should like to thank Judith Longman and Philip Law, past editors at SPCK, for their considerable help; and Hannah Ward for such thoughtful copy-editing. Jacky Fleming kindly drew the cartoon to represent our dilemma.

1

ON AUTONOMY AND HETERONOMY
Daphne Hampson

A feminist is a woman who does not allow anyone to think in her place.

Michèle Le Doeuff[1]

For a feminist to be a Christian is indeed for her to swallow a fishbone. It must stick in her throat. To be a Christian is to be placed in a heteronomous position. Feminists believe in autonomy.

The word 'autonomy' has often had a bad press among feminists. This, I believe, owes to a lack of careful definition. Autonomy is what feminism has been about. To be 'autonomous' is to let one's own law rule one: literally in Greek to be auto-nomos (self-law). The word, etymologically, does not mean independence. It need not imply conceiving of oneself as an isolated atom in competition with others. Indeed, that it has come to hold such connotations may tell us much about the male psyche within patriarchy; as though the only way to be oneself, to take responsibility for oneself, were to set oneself up over against others.

No: to be autonomous is to overcome heteronomy. Heteronomy, the law of another ruling one, is the situation of the child. To be an adult is to have come into one's own. 'Enlightenment', said Kant, with reference to the movement of the late eighteenth century, is the 'exit of humanity from its self-incurred minority'. And he continues: *'sapere aude!* (dare to know)'; 'have courage to use *your own* understanding'. Feminism might well be understood as the natural working out of the Enlightenment. Women are those, last but not least, who are able to claim their maturity and to think for themselves. It is this in which feminism consists: women coming into their own and not having to bow to authority. The word Kant uses for immaturity is *Minderheit*, the word for a child under age. That, of course, is how women have been treated – as those not responsible for themselves, who have to look to another. Now women are claiming their coming of age. They are able to take responsibility for who they are.

Far from being disruptive of human relations, the recognition of the full maturity of all adults is prerequisite for the human relationships which we would have. It is only as I am treated as an equal, and conceive of myself as such, that I shall be able to be fully present to others. Our goal must be that persons are centred in themselves and open to one another. Indeed, it may well be that it is not until persons come into their own, come 'to' themselves, that they are able so to respond to others. Feminism is the call for the possibility of mature human relationships. Such relationships can only be predicated upon the acknowledgement of women as adult equals. That is what feminism stands for.

Now Christianity, by definition, is not a religion which can allow for full human autonomy. Heteronomy is built into it. This may appear an unwarranted contention. For surely many Christians do achieve a sanctity and a maturity which is enviable. It may however be that this is enabled by aspects of Christianity which, though central to its ethical code, are not part of its definition. It may also be that humans are capable of attaining to a certain maturity against the grain of a religion which is by nature heteronomous. But for a feminist to be a Christian and also to be true to herself and to her feminist beliefs is, I am suggesting, not possible. Therefore although one may recognize that some human beings have become the people they are within Christianity, one must wish that humanity should move beyond that religion. In practice I note that the women whom I most admire, while they may be profoundly spiritual people, have discarded Christian belief.

In this essay I shall explore why, through its very nature, Christianity is heteronomous. That is to say I shall argue that it is built into the structure of Christianity that a revelation, or God, or that institution which is the church, must take precedence over what one would oneself think. Though there may be Christians who are integrated persons, Christians are not centred in themselves. They are centred on God (such is their conception of God), or on Christ, on the Bible, or bound up with the institution of the church; such that authority lies outside themselves. In no other sphere of life need this be the case in the way in which this is necessarily so within Christianity. Of course one does, frequently and in many spheres of life, look to others or heed their authority. But in relation to other humans one may ultimately take responsibility for oneself. Again humanity as a whole (unless there is a God such as that of which Christians conceive) is autonomous: it does not have to look to anything outside itself as an authority. Christianity, however, is a religion in which it is believed that there has been a revelation.

Am I suggesting that feminists are people who are particularly attuned to these issues? I think I am. The world has been 'male' and it has been easier for men to slot into the religion. They are not to the same extent denying themselves if God is understood as male; if they read a Bible couched in male terms; or if the institution of the church is ruled by men. But for a woman to submit to all this must be the undoing of herself. Moreover it is not, I think, simply that women come up against a predominant masculinity in Christianity which they find alienating. Women have had to struggle to achieve what measure of autonomy they have attained to within a male world. This autonomy comes, then, to be a pearl of great price. They will not easily be persuaded to let go of it in the sphere of their religion. Women, finally, may be less hierarchically inclined: it has often been suggested that this is so. In which case the heteronomous nature of Christianity and its institutions will not be something which lies comfortably with the modes of thinking and acting to which they are predisposed.

Why then need Christianity necessarily be heteronomous? I shall approach this question through three different considerations, but they mutually imply one another. I shall firstly discuss Christianity as a religion of revelation and thereby also as what I name a 'historical' religion. Secondly I shall turn to that conceptualization of God which is western monotheism. Thirdly I shall consider the nature of the institution of the church.

I must, however, commence by defining Christianity. One of the most notable features of recent years has been the tendency on the part of women who seek to find a way to remain within Christianity (perhaps because they wish to stay within the church rather than that they espouse Christian beliefs) to twist Christianity to mean whatever they will. There is a certain dishonesty in this. Perhaps such women wish to say that women are 'sovereign' and no one else shall determine what is Christianity! This is no way forward. Words must mean something. There is no point in understanding by Christianity something which patently it does not and cannot be stretched to mean. I should have thought that part of being a religious person, indeed fundamental to it, is a certain clarity and honesty. To call 'Christianity' that which the term, throughout many manifestations of Christianity, has never meant helps no one.

Christianity is without doubt a 'historical' religion. By that I simply intend that Christians believe there to have been a unique revelation in Jesus of Nazareth, whom Christians name the Christ. Moreover by this term the 'Christ', Christians do not mean (and I think one can safely say have never meant) simply that he was the 'messiah' in the terms in which the Jews conceived of the messiah before Christians used this designation for Jesus. The earliest Christian statement of faith that we have is the acronym *ICHTHUS*, in Greek 'fish' (a peculiarly apt slogan for those who would see themselves as 'fishers of men'). The Greek stands for the first letters of the words 'Jesus Christ God's Son Saviour'. Of none other did those who made such a statement of faith say this.

Those early Christians did not, it should be noted, express themselves in terms of a later Chalcedonian orthodoxy; whereby the second person of a triune God is believed to have become incarnate in Jesus Christ, so that the second person of the Trinity is held to be in two natures, human and divine. It would be too narrow a definition of Christian to say that they alone are Christians who have conceptualized their belief in these later terms. Yet Christians from the start, though not expressing themselves in Chalcedonian terms, proclaimed a uniqueness of him whom they named the Christ. Again, since the Enlightenment the possibility of expressing the uniqueness in which they believe in terms of Chalcedonian orthodoxy has become impossible for many Christians. (Indeed one might read the history of theology since that date as an increasingly desperate attempt on the part of Christians to find some way of speaking of uniqueness which could be accounted credible.)

Thus in wishing to set the bounds of Christianity as wide as possible whilst still involving uniqueness, one is allowing that the positions of, say, Friedrich Schleiermacher or Rudolf Bultmann are validly Christian. Schleiermacher does not think in terms of classical Chalcedonian orthodoxy. But his Jesus has an 'unclouded God-consciousness', unattained by any other. Jesus is conceived to have *Vorbildlichkeit* and *Urbildlichkeit*, which we may translate 'exemplarity' and 'archetype-ality'. He is, we may say, a 'Second Adam'. Likewise Bultmann does not speak in terms of Greek philosophy. Nevertheless his Jesus is again unique. In his case, Bultmann speaks of the resurrection as the breaking in of another world order (for there are patently not resurrections in our world). It is an 'eschatological' event, which thereby opens up a new dimension of meaning for humankind. Now the resurrection is the resurrection of a particular man who died on a cross. This man is thereby lent a uniqueness which no one else possesses. In the case of both Schleiermacher and Bultmann (and I have deliberately chosen those whom we may consider to be, respectively, the greatest liberal theologian of the nineteenth century and the greatest radical theologian of the twentieth century), they find a way, or attempt to find a way, of speaking of Jesus as unique. They know that this is necessary if they are to be Christian.

To hold however that Jesus is a very fine human being (and that is the end of it) and then to say that one is a Christian is evident nonsense. This is not what Christians have believed of their Christ. Of course, one may say in a loose way that one lives in a 'Christian culture' if something of one's outlook is derived from a tradition which owes much to the interpretation which there has been of this man's life and teaching. I do not doubt that, if I were to knock on doors, people would say that they were 'Christian', and that by that they might well mean approximately this. But such a definition will not do in theology. Christians have ever proclaimed the uniqueness of Jesus as the Christ. That is to say – one may put it this way – they have not only proclaimed Jesus' message (his teaching), but they have proclaimed a message, a *kerygma*, about Jesus.

It follows that to be a religious person, one indeed who stands within the western tradition, need not necessarily also mean to be a Christian. One can be theistic without being Christian. One may well judge Jesus to have been a person – from what we know of him – who was deeply in tune with God. One may even think that one may learn from him as to what it means to love God. But these things in themselves do not make one a Christian. One is looking to God (one is theistic), and only incidentally to Jesus. Again, a gathering of people who spoke of God, but while making no particular mention of Jesus, might well be termed religious, but it could not truly be called Christian.

Firstly, then, as will be clear from this definition, Christianity is *per se* a religion of revelation. Christians believe in a particular revelation in Jesus of Nazareth; that is to say within history. This person is held in some manner to be unique. I have argued in my *Theology and Feminism*[2] that such a religion is necessarily biased against women. Let us look at the terms of this argument – for it has often been misunderstood. People say that I am 'interpreting Christianity in a fundamentalist way', or comment that 'Christianity is always changing'. But so to respond is to fail to comprehend what it is that I have said. I have never suggested (as we have seen above, and my position now is no different from what it was when I wrote *Theology and Feminism*) that Christianity is to be restricted to Chalcedonian orthodoxy. Nor have I suggested that Christianity is unable to develop. How could one think that? Christianity has been embedded in human history

in the West. Yet Christianity is not, and cannot be, historical
simply in the sense in which, for example, Marxism is historical.
For Christianity is not just an idea which arose within history and
which bears (as one must surmise does any idea) the marks of the
period in which it arose. Let us put it this way (following Søren
Kierkegaard in *Philosophical Fragments*): in the case of Marxism
one could know nothing of the teacher (Marx) and yet subscribe
to the ideology; in the case of Christianity one has a peculiar
relation to the teacher (or should we now write Teacher?), because
one has ascribed to him uniqueness. Again: Christians do not
simply preach Jesus' message, but a message about Jesus.

Christianity is then 'historical' in quite a different sense than is a
system of ideas which is only that. It looks back to its founder not
simply as incidental but as one who is a revelation, or who brings
a revelation. Jesus' message may be interpreted differently in different ages; Jesus himself may be understood differently in
different ages. We have reason to think that this has been the case.
Indeed Christianity itself as a religion may be formulated in varied
terms. It changed dramatically from what had been the early
Palestinian gospel when Christians found themselves called upon
to explain their faith to themselves and others within the framework of a Greek thought-world. Such development will follow
from the fact that any system of ideas is caught up in history.
Christianity however is not, and never can be, simply something
which unfolds within history (as is, for example, a scientific
understanding of the world which too has passed through differing
paradigms). Christianity essentially cannot take one foot up out of
a particular history. It is rooted in history, because Christians
believe that there has been a revelation at a certain point in
history.

It is this which makes Christianity sexist. Christians look to a
particular point in history. Indeed that point in history becomes in
some way normative for them. That is not to say that Christians
do not change their minds on many peripheral matters; even on
what may be thought not peripheral. They may conclude that they
should ordain women. But they still have to contend that the
ordination of women is what Jesus would have advocated had he
lived today; or the implication of the Christian religion; or that
that which must always have been the corollary of Christian
teaching was obscured in the past through the fact that women
were not equals within the society. Christians can never simply say
that it is unethical to discriminate against persons and that that is
the end of it. They must always make a reference to a particular
past history. Both sides – it is to be noted – in the ordination

debate agree on this; however differently they interpret the past and its implications.

Christianity is sexist because the past history to which Christians necessarily make reference was a patriarchal history. This is not to say that Christians think that they must always act now as people acted in the first century. They may agree that times have changed and, given the different society, women should be treated differently now than they were then. I have no fundamentalist view of Christianity, as though one were to hold that, through the fact that in Jesus' parables only men own land, Christians must conclude that only men should have mortgages today! What I am contending is that through reading this ancient patriarchal literature (for that is what the Bible is) Christians imbibe certain attitudes. Even if rationally they acknowledge that times have changed, at a subconscious level, when from childhood onwards this literature is repeatedly heard in a sacred setting, people gain a sense that it is 'natural' that men should, for example, be the heads of households. The fact that these things are not voiced makes them all the more potent. One may furthermore simply find it offensive in a religious or in any other setting (but more particularly in a religious setting) to hear stories told in which men play all the main roles. Past attitudes are projected into the present. That, indeed, is why Christian feminists wish to rewrite the stories or unearth (or import into Christianity) others which are more acceptable!

But quite apart from the fact that to do so will be to reinforce sexism, to look to a past history is heteronomous. It is to allow that history to exercise some kind of precedence in determining what one should think. At least one factor in the issue as to whether women may be ordained has something to do with a man who lived two thousand years ago. (And the problem here is not that he was a man; though it may be thought to add yet another problematical factor that the teachings or actions of a man should determine what happens to women.) Christians, as I have said, have one foot in history. They can never take that foot out of history. They cannot sit down together and think out *a priori* what it is that they would do. On many current issues of ethics (abortion, homosexuality, divorce, pacifism) Christians have one eye on the past. Indeed, they customarily quickly revert to asking what the Bible says and muster verses on 'their' side in relation to other Christians. This may be done less or more intelligently, but it is still done. Such a religion is heteronomous. Women will always be disadvantaged in this situation, for that history to which Christians refer is the history of a patriarchal age.

So, secondly, I am contending that the concept of God held within western monotheistic religions, including Christianity, is such that the relationship to God on the part of humans must be designated heteronomous. This follows from the nature of the religion. If there is held to be a revelation in history, the corollary is that 'God' must, in some way, be conceived of as transcending history. God cannot simply be understood as immanent in the world. Let us pause to consider this. It would appear to be the case that it is taken for granted that the Christian definition of God is the meaning of the word God; so that any other understanding is almost inconceivable. God is, to most people's way of thinking, other than the world (though in Christ 'He' may 'enter' it). The definition of God is that 'He' is eternal (whereas the world undergoes change within time); that 'He' is the creator (and therefore existed 'before' the world). If one doubts that the language of 'outside' and 'before' is appropriately to be used of God, people say that one cannot be speaking of God.

It is not however necessary to conceive of God in this way.[3] If one's starting-point for speaking of God, that which makes it incumbent upon one to speak of God at all, is that prayer is powerful, or that there is that which one chooses to name religious experience, it by no means follows that the reason for these things (which one may name 'God') is somehow 'outside' the world, even figuratively. God may well be a dimension (and I do not intend to use this word as having mathematical connotations but simply with the common meaning of 'one aspect') of the one reality which is. Nor is this necessarily to equate God with the material nature of the world (pantheism). God is something on which we may draw; peculiarly present, we may think, between human beings. The evidence of God is healing, answered prayer, and more generally perhaps an overwhelming conviction of the fact that, despite the atrocities which humans commit, there is an underlying goodness. So to speak of God is not necessarily to conceive that there is that, a sort of 'being', which transcends the universe.

Christians, however, must hold that God is in some way 'other', for they believe there to have been a particular 'revelation' in history. God is not, to them, simply bound up with the history of the world, understood differently by human beings in each age. In revelation something is given which would not otherwise be present; namely a recognition of the nature of God or a particular knowledge of him. As we have said, Christians cannot forego the revelation in Christ if the term Christian is to retain any meaning. The same is true, if differently so, of Judaism and Islam. Judaism is a religion in which ethics is central; while in Islam there may be a mysticism present. Nevertheless, both religions, like Christianity (but possibly unlike eastern religion) believe in a revelation (if they do not have quite the particularity present within Christianity) and thereby also, as a corollary, in a God who is transcendent of the world. This does not, of course, rule out God being conceived also to be immanent within the world. However, to say this alone is, for these religions, not enough.

Now the relationship to such a God must ultimately always be heteronomous. From the fact that this is the case it does not, of course, follow that in each moment a Christian will make reference to God (though one wonders whether this is not some kind of an ideal). God – Christians will say – has created humans as independent creatures and it is for them to think out creatively and responsibly how they should act in the particular circumstances in which they find themselves. Nevertheless it is the case that God, or the conception of God, is some kind of ultimate authority to whom reference must be made. Christians speak of 'God's will' – with the implication that that should take precedence over the will of humans. They believe in obedience to God. Indeed they speak of worship of God. (One presumably only worships a God who is not simply commensurate with nature or a dimension of this one reality of which we too are a part.) The talk of worship suggests an apartness of God, by extrapolation from the apartness of a monarch to whom one might 'do homage' but whom (in the case of a monarch) one should scarcely worship.

Moreover the vocabulary on which we have embarked is surely significant! It is no chance that God has been known in the Jewish, and following that within the Christian, tradition, as Lord, Judge, King and (within Christianity) Father. These are words which were used for earthly patriarchs, to whom one owed allegiance and obedience. It may be that 'Father' suggests someone who loves and cares, who means well for the child, but it should be remembered that the father was very much the head of the Jewish household. The father is an authority figure; he is one to whom the child looks up. The understanding of God has, in the West, been cast in the form of a human to whom one owes allegiance, one whose will ultimately takes precedence. Given that it is held, within the Christian tradition, that God is supremely known through revelation, God will be conceived of as somehow an 'other' in relation to the self or to humanity as a whole.

It follows that if God is an other and is God, the relationship to God must ultimately, by definition, be heteronomous. One who is other than oneself and to whom one could answer 'no', would, given this model of God, in that moment not be one's God. One

would have denied that God was lord over one's life. (It is interesting what masculinist terms one needs to employ in this
discussion!) Hence the joke embodied in feminist Christmas cards
which show annunciation scenes in which Mary gives a negative
reply to the angel Gabriel. That would spoil the whole story! But it
would represent women's autonomy. To think of saying 'no' to
God is, given the Christian understanding of God, to bring God
down to our level – and to make nonsense of the concept of God.
Of course it may be the case that humans do not obey God. Such
disobedience sets them at odds with God. The whole meaning of
God is that God should be God to an individual or to a society.

The necessary heteronomy of the notion of God within the
Jewish and Christian traditions (and clearly also within Islam) is
classically illustrated by Kierkegaard in his commentary upon the
story of Abraham's near sacrifice of Isaac in his *Fear and
Trembling*. There are, I am aware, different ways of reading
Kierkegaard's own position in relation to Christianity in this
book. But this at least is clear. If Abraham is to continue to have a
God, to allow Jahweh to be God to him, then in the last resort he
has to be prepared to obey him. If he believes it to be God's will,
he must slay Isaac. Now to kill one's son is murder. That is to say
Christianity always has, as an implication, the possibility of a
necessary suspension of what we normally conceive to be the
ethical in favour of obedience to a 'higher' command from God.
We may think it to be an extremely dangerous precedent.
Nevertheless it is the corollary of holding that God is God; that
God is 'higher' than 'man' and is 'He' whom we must obey. It is to
be noted that in Kant's case, by contrast, human ethics must
always take precedence over some supposed will of God. Were this
not to be so, human beings would cease to be autonomous.

I turn then, thirdly, to the institution of the church. The church
may be said to have a derivative heteronomy; derived from the fact
that Christianity is a 'historical' religion in which it is claimed that
there has been a revelation in history, which in turn implies that
God is in some way transcendent of the world and humankind. Let
us again compare Christianity here with other potential forms of
religion. Suppose that God were to be conceived of as a dimension
(as I put it) of all that is. It would follow that there could be no
class of people (those privy to a revelation or to specialized
knowledge of the Scriptures which told of that revelation) who
could exercise privilege in regard to conceptualizing what it is that
God may be. That is to say, it would not be the case that the early
disciples of Jesus of Nazareth, or ministers who had had an
arduous training in the Christian Scriptures, should be granted any

precedence in judging how it is that we should speak of God. It does not follow that we should thereby be landed with an incomprehensible jungle, for persons are situated within a culture (in this case the western tradition) and are, in their thought patterns, formed by their culture. There would however be no benchmark against which notions of God should be measured; so that other understandings were judged to be more, or less, heretical.

It should be noted that it is through the fact that Christianity is a religion of revelation that the church acquires its authority. If, by contrast, it is held that all knowledge of God is present in the world or given with the existence of humankind, then no one human or group of humans is able to tell others how God should be understood. It may of course be that some periods are judged to show a peculiar openness to that which is God. We have reason to think that, within the western tradition, as surely also within the history of other cultures, there have been ages in which such a sensibility has been prevalent. (For example, there have been times when knowledge of healing through prayer has come to the fore.) Again, within any one age, one must surmise, it may well be that there are seers whose lives evidently manifest God. But we need not think of these ages or of these persons as having a knowledge of God which differs in kind from that of other ages or persons. God, whatever God may be, is always and everywhere present. There need not be thought to have been a particular revelation of God in history.

In a religion of revelation, however, there will be teaching authorities; for it will be held that there is a 'truth'. Exactly what that truth is will be variously construed by Christians in different ages and traditions. Christians have not notably agreed here. However, in consequence of the fact that they believe in a particular revelation, all Christian churches have had a notion that there is a peculiar 'truth'. There are designated ways of determining what truth may be. Churches have teaching authorities. They have creeds and other statements of faith. They have councils and synods, perhaps a supreme pontiff. In a church where human authorities play a lesser role (there is no pope), the Scriptures may well acquire the greater authority. In every case there will be some kind of a yardstick against which what it is which may be held within the religion will be measured. This follows directly from the fact that there is thought to have been a particular revelation.

Even the World Council of Churches, which proclaims itself not to be a church, has a statement of faith to which any body of

Christians must assent before they may be a member church of that organization. (It has precisely caused much debate in Britain that the Quakers are a part of the new ecumenical bodies when they have no such creed or other statement of faith and has meant that other Christians have had to acknowledge that they say the same things in a different way. Many Quakers, it should be noted, have been most unhappy about this.) Indeed, it is interesting that the initial statement of the WCC after its inauguration, to which churches which would join must assent, was that it was a body of member churches who acknowledged Jesus Christ 'as God and saviour': a statement which differs little from the original confession of the Christians who held *ICHTHUS* to stand for their faith. This has more recently been replaced by a trinitarian formula.

Now because a church has a teaching authority and a notion of truth (however that truth may precisely be formulated), therefore also Christian worship takes certain forms. Christian worship is not, or not simply, a matter of people coming together in silence and waiting on God. (Again the different position of the Quakers may be noted here.) Christians proclaim the gospel. They expect the Bible to be read. In Christian worship God takes precedence, not the people there present. In many churches the sermon is central. The sermon (given by one person) will expound a biblical passage. In more Catholic churches the eucharist is centre-stage. In this case the eucharist is held to be a manifestation of truth and to have an objective efficacy. Thus it is not that a Christian service takes, as its point of departure, the understanding of God which each person brings with them. The attitudinal stance of the person in church is that of hearing the gospel, of witnessing the eucharist. He or she is there to receive.

It follows, moreover, from the nature of Christianity as a revealed religion, that the Christian church will tend to be hierarchical. There is an inner circle of those who have been ordained to preach the gospel or to celebrate the eucharist. In as much as the church is centred on the Bible, there will be privileged expositors who know the original languages of the Scriptures and can interpret their meaning. Often these people will be granted special functions within the church. Since the church is a historical community, which has had a continuous history since its inauguration in the events surrounding Jesus of Nazareth, one generation will admit the next to membership. Children are baptized. There are 'outsiders' and 'insiders'. Again it is not usual for anyone to baptize (though even in Catholic teaching anyone may do so in extremity, provided they intend to do what the church does). Only certain people may ordain or consecrate. Very often these degrees of privilege extend, for example, to the wearing of particular dress, or to separate seating in the church, or to processing in and out.

Church buildings too portray the nature of the faith to which they witness. There will be special places from which the truth is proclaimed: altar or pulpit. The church is not a discussion group (though there may be discussion). The pulpit is placed 'ten feet above contradiction' as has been said. The altar may be guarded. (Often women have been prevented from entering sacred space.) A classic Gothic church points to heaven, to a truth beyond itself. Indeed the whole action of the eucharist may be said to indicate a reference to that which is other. In as much as people listen to a sermon differently from a talk, they expect that sermon to become the revelation of God for them and not simply to be the preacher's words. The Bible of course is granted a peculiar status. It may be processed in. It is opened and closed at particular points in the service. In a Catholic church, the bread of the eucharist is retained. In all these ways the Christian church proclaims a reference beyond itself; a more absolute truth. It is a truth, moreover, which is conceived to have come to fruition at one point in history; from which the Scriptures and the action of the eucharist derive. There is a profound heteronomy present in the nature of the church.

I think that my point will be clear. Nevertheless, it may be helpful to set off the nature of Christianity by contrasting it with what is different. For I can hear people saying, but does not any institution have officers, even who wear certain costumes (the bar, the universities); do not societies have founding documents, as the Declaration of Human Rights of the United Nations, or the Constitution of the United States; do not all groups of humans look back to their foundation? Again I must reiterate the point that to say such things is to misunderstand the peculiar nature of Christianity. Of course all human institutions exist within history, of course they tend to throw up a hierarchy (or so it would seem), of course they look back to founding documents or ideals. None of these things, however, are thought to be absolute or anything other than the creation of human beings. The difference, as far as Christianity is concerned, is that there is held to have been a revelation in history; truth is as it were given to humanity, or given in its fullness to humanity, at that particular point in time. Therefore, there is a necessary reference to that history and a guarding of that truth. My point being I hope clear, I must move on.

Feminists have of recent years tried to inaugurate a way of being

and of acting which is free of past authorities and in which hierarchical ways of thinking do not prevail. This feminist way of
existing is the polar opposite to what is, I am contending, the
necessary nature of the Christian religion. It is because feminists
have experienced these ways of being and of acting that so much
tension arises between feminist and Christian sensibilities. This
difference is in no way solved by ordaining women: the ordained
women may highlight the difference through acting differently
than, on the whole, do men; or they may feel the tension within
themselves. It must be that many men have not, by the nature of
the case, been privy to the groups and movements, the type of
friendship, in which these new skills and ways of conceiving of
oneself have been prevalent. Therefore it is difficult for them to
understand how wide the gap has become. Or in so far as they
conceive of it, they still think the male world to be the norm. By
contrast, a woman who is a feminist may often be living on her
own time, thinking her own thoughts, construing her own
analysis, while present in the 'male' world in 'male' institutions.

It is important that I try, however inadequately, to describe
something of these new sensibilities in order to point to the difference from what is the norm within Christianity. Far from it
being the case that there is conceived to be a truth which was given
in history, or which has been inherited from the past, feminists
normally hold that in a sense people bring the truth with them. In a
feminist consciousness-raising or other discussion group, women
do not start with some truth 'external' to themselves which has
authority. Rather is each woman encouraged to speak for herself.
Feminists are often attempting to express what has not been
thought before; particularly was this so of the heady days of early
feminism. There is no authority, such as might deny that what she
thinks may be thought; nor yardstick by which she should measure
what she thinks. Ideally feminists listen to one another in such a
way as to draw one another out, that they may allow people to
think what it is they need to think, even that they may surprise
themselves in its articulation. Feminists in the early movement
spoke, picking up Nelly Morton's phrase, of 'hearing one another
into being'.

Again the structure of feminist groups is, correspondingly, very
different from that which seems natural to the Christian church.
There are no leaders, or (in as much as this is a myth for there
must always be leaders) leadership functions differently. It tends to
rotate between different people; there is often no overt leadership
and it is taken for granted that each person may come to speech. In
a typical feminist group the seating will be arranged so that people

face one another or face in to the centre. Even such a small thing as this betrays the difference in structure and in presupposition between a feminist group and the Christian church, where the seating will tend to face in one direction towards altar and pulpit. There will be no 'holy literature'. Feminists abhor, on the whole, special costumes which set people apart. As the group tries to find its way forward together different people will speak. It would seem to be a contradiction in terms for a meeting proceeding along feminist lines to set one person up in a pulpit or its equivalent to give a sermon! Nothing is sacred; neither ideas nor space. (To be 'holy' we should remember is, by derivation, to be 'set apart'.)

People who have become used to functioning in feminist space, both geographical and metaphorical, will find it difficult to revert to hierarchy, order and authority. These latter may often seem to be peculiarly inefficient. Women have become used to being able to express themselves and to listening to others. This kind of attentiveness in particular, in groups which function according to 'male' norms, may seem to be profoundly lacking. People make points rather than trying to come to a common mind. The group may be deeply combative. To say these things is to recognize that feminists have, in the last twenty years, developed sophisticated skills as to how people should interact and an understanding as to what it is that is disruptive of the group. Thus it does not follow that a feminist gathering is without form and order, but its disciplining of itself is very different from the discipline involved in an imposed hierarchy and order. All these things will be familiar enough to any feminist. (They do not always work as they should.) I am simply drawing attention to them in order to highlight the clash with what the Christian church has often been.

Of course there are religious groups which differ from what I have characterized as the Christian norm. It is no chance that many a feminist (as I myself) have been attracted to the Quakers. But then I have suggested that a Quaker group functions more like a feminist group, or vice versa, precisely because the Society of Friends, particularly in its modern form, has taken one long step outside Christianity; indeed that the majority of its members do not subscribe to many of the characteristics of Christianity as a religion of revelation founded in belief in a transcendent God. That Quakers speak of 'that of God in everyone' is another indicator as to how far the different questions of which I have been speaking imply one another. A spirituality in which God is conceived of in these terms fits much better with the ways of interacting to be found in the Society of Friends or in feminist groups. Such groups are much more autonomous; both the Quakers considered as a group in relation to Christian history and in the autonomy which, typically, feminist or Quaker groups allow the individual. Again the Quakers do not have consecrated leaders, but temporary officers. There are no special clothes, nor sacred space.

It does not follow that to adhere to such a religious position is to cut oneself off from the past. One can draw on the past as one will. It is simply that one holds that there can be no particular revelation in history and consequently that there is no religious authority. Such a religion will function in the same way as does any other ideology, system of thought or belief, or indeed as human knowledge functions. Truth, whatever truth may be, is present in and with the world. It is either waiting to be discovered (as in a scientific subject), or it is something (such as in arts subjects) in which each age expresses itself as it will. In the same way, one may see God as a dimension of all that is, present to every age in so far as that age is able to discover that truth. In these circumstances human beings take control. It is they who are at the centre of the picture. It need not follow that one believes that 'God' is no more than the individual. (I put 'God' in quotes here because such an understanding of God is other than that which the term has commonly connoted.) But there is no heteronomy involved. God is one with all else that is.

On hearing that I was to write such an essay, for such a book, a feminist friend aptly commented that it had better be called 'On Extricating Oneself from the Whale'! Christianity does have a whale-like quality in western culture: it would seem to engulf all. Some of us however are extricating ourselves. This may be seen as hugely threatening. We are saying that we do not need to live in a heteronomous relationship to the past, to men, or to a God conceived in men's image. We cannot conceive there to have been a revelation which has been given once and for all in past patriarchal history. This does not mean that we shall not draw on human history, just as in every human discipline there is continuity with the past. So to draw on the past is however very different from belonging to a religion which has a particular locus outside our age in a particular revelation, or beyond ourselves in God. One must hope that men too will be willing to leave the Christian religion behind. For what we must surely desire is a complete world, of men and women, who are able to live in the present. As far however as a feminist is concerned, Christianity is a fishbone which must stick in her throat. It should not be swallowed.

2

TURNING THE SYMBOLS
Janet Martin Soskice

Why do I remain a Christian feminist? I find this question no more difficult than its near relation, 'Why do I remain a Christian?' There are reasons that can be given, life experiences to be related, philosophical arguments to put, but in the end I remain a Christian, and a Christian feminist, because of a deep conviction of the truth of the Christian faith. Feminism has caused me to anguish over actions and attitudes of the churches, it has made me suspicious of various representations of Christian teaching, but not to give up on the Christian faith itself. In any case, such a choice would not be a matter of reasons alone.

'Why are you still a Christian?' is a curious question, akin to 'Why are you still in love?' If I ceased to be in love I might well have a set of explanations to give to friends, or at least myself, but I do not remain in love for *reasons*! This is not to say that there are not reasons for loving someone, but reasons are not the end of it. It is a matter of a whole shared life and way of being in the world. One does not, perhaps unless things are going wrong, wake up in the morning and say 'Yes, today I still love x, and for the following reasons'. This is why the idiom 'to *be* in love' is so accurate.

The disanalogy with the above example is that the Christian feminist cannot help but notice that other women are losing heart and losing faith, and that in some cases they no longer, on their own reckoning, are Christians. Maybe they are post-Christians, maybe they have moved even farther away. This movement is rarely just a matter of reasons either, and each woman has a different tale to tell. It might rather be analogous to finding that some of my friends were emigrating to other countries, all for slightly different reasons but with a strong thread of similarity to them. I would be a cold-hearted friend not to see the strength of their reasoning or their despair, even while not feeling the same course of action is one I should take.

If we discount many other features of what prompts such a move and look more narrowly at intellectual considerations, a major difference between Christian and post-Christian feminists is the extent to which a woman feels that it is Christianity itself which is inherently and irrevocably sexist and destructive for women, and the extent to which she feels that, while the Christian faith has had its sexist vehicles, it is nonetheless capable of being the good news for women. It is from the latter camp that I write this essay. For its purposes, following my emigration analogy, I will call myself a 'stayer-on'.

It seems fairly clear that the growth in Christian feminism relates to changes taking place in women's social, political and educational circumstances in this century.[1] To take just one instance, prior to the Second World War it was difficult, bordering on impossible, for women to study theology in most universities or seminaries. When more women began to study theology in depth they found themselves, not surprisingly, drawing different conclusions than an all-male academy had drawn. A more literate and self-confident female population in general found itself bridling under some of the assumptions in Christian circles. (I remember the first lecture of the first course in theology I ever attended. Our lecturer asked the (predominantly male) class, 'Now which one of you ladies would like to make the coffee this term?') Little things add up over the years to form a bigger picture of an indifferent church. As society changes, a church which does not change begins to stand out. Ten years ago in Britain the use of inclusive language in liturgy might have been 'prophetic'. Now, when inclusive language is the norm in broadcasting and the workplace, almost the only time I hear non-inclusive language is in my own Roman Catholic church.

The debates surrounding the ordination of women over the last two decades, debates which in Britain have been largely within the Anglican context, have had inestimable influence on how Christian women (even non-Anglicans) feel about their churches. It has been made clear that, regardless of personal piety and sacrificial gifts of time and energy, women are still for the most part at the margins of church and theology. The Roman Catholic Church, which could not realistically be expected to move with speed towards the ordination of women, might have shown a greater sensitivity to the pastoral needs of its women and found places for women's voices to be heard, even if without priestly orders.

Small wonder that among many Christian women the questions no longer concern the locating of women within the traditional structures of Christianity. As Sandra Schneiders says, the 'add-women-and-stir' recipe for church reform has not worked.[2]

Critical questions are now being asked about the credibility and relevance of Christianity itself. For instance: how can Christianity be the Word of God if it has been so oppressive to women? In what sense are its institutions divine and in what sense purely a product of the imaginations of men? Schneiders asks:

> Did God, in Christ, ordain women's secondary and subordinate position ... or have male hierarchs distorted the Christian message in their own image? If the former ... then women can only remain Catholics at the price of their self-respect as humans and believers. If, however, the church's patriarchal structure and function is a distortion of the gospel, then Catholic feminists have an enormous and exhausting task on their hands; viz. the radical transformation of the church.[3]

Although she speaks to the Catholic situation specifically, Schneiders' remarks will strike a chord with women from across the denominational spectrum. She brings out clearly the gravity and breadth of the issues feminist theologians are now considering, not simply in the Catholic Church or in the United States, but on a world-wide basis. It is, as she says, a calling from women for a radical renewal and one worthy of the Christian gospel. Despite the radical nature of the changes she would like to see, Schneiders' is a voice from within the mainstream of the church. It is the voice of one who wishes to reform, or transform, rather than abandon; of someone who is 'staying on'.

The progressive disillusionment, bordering on despair, of many Christian women is now well documented. Alive to the insensitivities of their contemporary churches and theologies, women have looked into the Christian past and found it wanting. Institutional Christianity is there seen, as often as not, as opposing moves, such as political enfranchisement, that would grant women a greater involvement in decisions directly affecting their lives. The churches spiritually underwrote a picture of 'woman' and 'home' that made women who wanted or had to work feel guilty and insufficiently Christian. The 'good news' as preached seemed to be much better news for men than for women.

With the realization that 'it needn't be this way' a gap appears. What was formerly precious and rare can now appear lifeless and even antithetical to life. We might call this the 'Natural History Museum Syndrome'. The Christian feminist in this position is like someone who gazes on a beautiful tableau in a natural history museum; here a pheasant, there a fox in some gorse, but all stuffed and under glass. She may remember how it was not to be bothered by the exclusive language, condescending promulgations, with caricatures of female nature and vocations. She may even wish (at some level) that feminism had never come her way and she could still participate innocently in this flawed system. But it is no longer possible to stand in that position of innocence. The question then becomes: what is the way forward?

I am aware that the brief I have been given for this paper affects its substance, for I have been asked to say why I find the position 'feminist and Christian' to be, for me, tenable, and not to describe its difficulties. The paper may accordingly appear a little rosy for I will not even mention many sticking-points. It must also be a personal and interim statement. Issues that concern me now did not do so five years ago, and may not five years hence. I would say, however, that in my case the movement precipitated by feminism has not been straightforwardly one 'away'. In some respects I find that feminism has deepened and renewed longstanding Christian convictions. The rather loosely knit argumentative structure of what follows thus pretty well reflects my sense of being more on a quest for, rather than in possession of, the answers to difficult questions.

I will frame my discussion under three headings: the rejection of faith, the renewal of faith, and the turning of symbols.

I

The rejection of faith. Atheism, it is said, is always a rejection of a particular kind of theism. It is thus more accurate to speak of 'atheisms' plural, rather than 'atheism' singular, for to understand a particular form of atheism you need to understand the particular form of theism it defines itself in terms of, and rejects.[4] Similarly, post-Christian feminist positions (while of course not necessarily atheistic) in many cases are rejections of specific versions of the Christian story, of what we might call 'received Christianity'. Some post-Christian feminist positions are recognizably 'post-Calvinist' and others 'post-Catholic'. Perhaps it would be even better to say that some *arguments* are clearly 'post-Calvinist' or 'post-deist' or 'post-pietist', etc., since the point is not to force individuals into narrow denominational confines but rather to acknowledge that there are very different traditions of theology and piety within what has been the mainstream, and that individuals generally reject the version to which they formerly adhered.[5] It may well be, then, that feminists do well to reject a picture of God as over and against his creation, intervening from on high, compelling us to obey him rather than 'our own best will',[6] but then so does the Thomist tradition reject this picture of God with its deist overtones.

From the pews some women reject, as Christian orthodoxy, versions of the religion which could scarcely be considered so by normal scholarly criteria. For instance, one woman wrote to me of the freedom she felt on leaving her church. She said she now saw it was unnecessary to have a man, Jesus, as the go-between for us and God, and that she could relate directly to God on her own. While sympathetic to her story, I could not help wondering what teaching on the incarnation or the doctrine of the Trinity she had had in her church? After all, many of the great treatises on the Trinity make points not very different from her own. If Jesus is just a man then the Christian story is otiose. Why should we need a man to intervene? How could God be somehow pleased by the death of one man for many? Why would not the sacrifice of a bull do just as well? And if Jesus is 'just a man' then surely his death, however painful and humiliating, is not particularly noteworthy? Many of his disciples suffered worse. It might be a small price to pay to be honoured above all men in subsequent Christian history, and so on. We might say that in this case the woman's Christian instincts were better than the theology she had received. But if one believes that Jesus was not just a man but God incarnate then we do not have 'a man *simpliciter*' intervening between us and God, but God, in divine self-emptying, 'one-ing' the world with God. Nor do we have one man who is a hero. Christ becomes not an obtrusive historical stranger but 'God with us'. The Word incarnate in Jesus of Nazareth is also 'begotten, not made', the One through whom all things were made and thus prior to all human maleness and femaleness.[7]

This kind of metaphysical argument would not cut much ice with Daphne Hampson. Her work makes it clear that she is a 'post-*liberal*-Christian feminist' in that, even apparently when she was happier to be called a 'Christian', she did not believe 'that God could intervene in history, or be revealed through particular events in history, or through a particular person'.[8] Her difficulties in this respect are not specifically feminist, as she is quick to acknowledge, but those she feels attendant on all post-Enlightenment Christian belief. I think her (feminist) criticisms of this version of liberal Christianity are quite devastating.[9] It seems to me that she is entirely correct in saying that, if not in some sense true, then these are by no means 'valuable myths' for women to live by. But then this kind of liberal Christianity was never convincing or appealing to me in the first place. I would happily discard my Christian faith on the basis of Daphne Hampson's arguments if I believed what those liberal Christians believe. Just as I would happily dismiss the 'male human hero' described by the woman who wrote to me of her new-found freedom if that was what I thought Christian teaching about Jesus is, but I do not.

Daphne Hampson is very troubled by 'divine intervention', or rather she is not troubled, she discounts it as a possibility. It is a matter of 'knowledge' she says 'that nature is a complete causal nexus and there cannot be "interventions" of God ...'.[10] But her conclusion is by no means universally held or uncontroversially true. I for one would take issue with it. There is a huge philo-sophical literature on divine activity that demonstrates it to be by no means clear that nature is a complete (in the sense of closed) causal nexus. I would want to distance myself, of course, from what many people seem to mean by 'divine intervention' – that a sort of Wizard-of-Oz god watches things from afar and every so often stirs things with a big stick – but that is a deist picture. However, that God as Creator, eternally present to creation, might raise a man from the dead, or answer prayers does not seem to me to be an impossibility. It would not be 'intervention' because it would be of a piece with God's creative activity. We might not be able to comprehend how God could so act, but this does not eliminate the possibility. We cannot comprehend how something (the universe) could arise from nothing, literally nothing, at the Big Bang and yet most astrophysicists believe, independently of any religious convictions, that the universe did have such an origin.

This is by way of a digression, but it shows the extent to which in the thought of any particular Christian, or post-Christian feminist, other philosophical and theological issues are involved apart from the narrowly feminist. To return to the earlier point, it has always seemed to me that unless Jesus is the Christ, God incarnate, then the whole thing is a waste of time. I take Hampson to be saying: why should we bother about another historical individual who happened to have a cult develop around him? Why, indeed, if Jesus is no more than just another man?

I have been suggesting that post-Christian feminisms are various, and Christian feminisms are various not least because 'traditional Christianity' is not one thing (although perhaps from the pulpits we may have been led to believe that it is) but enor-mously varied. Indeed it is possible to find most of the theological features feminists find desirable (for instance, affirmation of bodily existence, inter-connectedness, concern for the created order, the holiness of the everyday) within the texts of historical theology, although perhaps not without an admixture in each case of less

sympathetic ideas. It is this, in part, which makes it a real question
for Christian women as to whether they can reclaim what is good,
true and beautiful in their traditions, or have no choice but to
surrender the good with the bad.

II

The renewal of faith. Christian feminists are as varied a group as
any other. I am amazed by their vitality and originality. For
instance, Rebecca Chopp in her book *The Power to Speak* gives a
vibrant account of 'the Word as perfectly open sign' which, while
distinctly modern (or post-modern) and ecumenical, is recognizably in the Reformed theological tradition of thinking on the
freedom of the Word. At the most general level we might say that
'stayers-on' are united by this: we are as yet hopeful of the wider
truth of the Christian gospel and its ability to be the gospel for
women. Indeed it is at the crux of this position that if Christianity
is not the 'good news' for women it cannot be good news for
anyone.

It seems to me that many stayers-on are feminists as much
because of their Christian faith as despite it: 'Their experience as
disciples of Jesus makes them aware that what is being done to
them in the name of God is contrary to the will of Christ for his
followers.'[11] From this perspective Christian feminists are pioneers
in church renewal and, in their own minds at least, in the
uncomfortable but not unprecedented position of being Christians
who challenge the churches in the name of Christ.

For instance, I find it painfully inexplicable that the ethical
commitments of my own (Catholic) church, in consort with its
christological dogmas, should not make women's issues a top
priority. Women's issues are not, after all, a frivolous luxury but a
life-and-death concern of nearly one-half the human race. I would
have said 'of half the human race' but have recently discovered the
factual inaccuracy of such a claim. Women are far from making up
a majority of the world's population. Amartya Sen writes:

> It is often said that women make up a majority of the world's
> population. They do not. This mistaken belief is based on
> generalizing from the contemporary situation in Europe and
> North America, where the ratio of women to men is typically
> around 1.05 or 1.06, or higher. In South Asia, West Asia, and
> China, the ratio of women to men can be as low as 0.94, or even
> lower, and it varies widely elsewhere in Asia, in Africa, and in
> Latin America.[12]

Although female infanticide is practised in some regions this is not the significant factor, nor is perinatal mortality. Rather, it is persistent failure to give women and girl children medical care similar to that of men and boys, to give them comparable food and access to what limited social services may be on offer in these regions. The title of Sen's article is 'More Than One Hundred Million Women are Missing', for that is the number by which, if we project from western figures, we find a world shortfall of women. 'These figures', he says, 'tell us, quietly, a terrible story of inequality and neglect leading to the excess mortality of women.' Sexism is not just something that hurts women's feelings: on a global scale sexism kills millions and millions of women and girl children. The sad thing is that one feels that many readers and even many Christian leaders on seeing Sen's shocking title will just turn the page and say 'more bleating on about women'.

How is it that with figures like these, and with the on-the-ground experience of so many of their missionaries, the Christian churches have been slow to condemn sexism, slower even than in condemning apartheid as a heresy? How can we understand this? More pointedly, how can women who have become aware of the pervasive and structural nature of sexism, and its systematic annihilation of women on a global basis, be neutral about the sexism which their own churches not only embody but condone? When it is still implied that feminism is a non- and even anti-Christian movement, that good Christian women ought to have nothing to do with it and that feminism is a self-indulgent distraction from the real needs of the world today, we must ask: what world are these people living in? Not the world of prostitutes in the Philippines, or female slaves in China, or of the terrible female morbidity figures Sen documents. The most charitable explanation of the indifference of many church leaders to feminist issues is grievous ignorance.

For me as a Catholic Christian these ethical issues lead immediately to christological ones. I, too, over the years have been influenced by the debates surrounding the ordination of women. Sometimes I have wondered why they interest me quite so much since I have never (yet) felt any personal calling to ordained ministry, nor do I think the ordination of women, as the introduction of female clerics into the existing structures, would resolve all the important questions about 'women and the church', or necessarily be a substantial change to the *status quo*. Nonetheless, I am seriously troubled by the theological grounds on which, once the issue was raised, women were, and in some churches still are, refused ordination.

An examination of the history of Catholic theology reveals that the ordination of women has never in any century prior to our own been a substantive question. At those very few junctures where the question of ordaining a woman is addressed we find, with remarkable frequency, the argument that women cannot be priests because they are subordinate to men and so could not signify the Deity who is subordinate to no one. In the twentieth century, tact as much as conviction decrees that this unattractive, but traditional, argument is not employed. Official pronouncements of the Roman Catholic Church argue that women are 'equal but different'. Today the main argument is an argument from symbolism: a woman could not in her person 'signify' Christ. This begs many and, by now, no doubt familiar questions. Why should being female be so decisive on this issue? Jesus was a young man when he died, yet elderly priests are held to be able to signify him in eucharistic presidency. Jesus was a Jew, yet Chinese men are not barred from priesthood on the grounds of Chinese-ness. What is so important about being a woman that this feature, of all other human features, makes some people un-Christlike in the relevant sense? One is still told in some quarters that this is a matter of divine dispensation. Women can not be priests but of course they can be mothers and nurturers. A Roman Catholic theologian, writing recently, speaks of the 'basic biological facts' relevant to the question. Men have a stronger bone structure and bigger hands: 'Their more powerful arm muscles enable them to take, literally, a more solid "grip" on the world.' Women are more suited to nurturing and tending, guided more by intuition and feeling, more ready for religious devotion. (Why this last should ill-equip them for priestly ministry is not clear.) Men are more bound to their bodies, more individual, more outgoing: 'Because of the nature of female reproductive organs, women are, to a greater extent than men, "sexual beings".' 'The superiorities of men ... lead to a position of authority, but the superiorities of women to a position of subordination', and so on.[13] This kind of argumentation from a contemporary theologian would be amusing were the arguments not so close to those by which an earlier generation explained the ways in which the 'superiorities of the white man' singled him out to rule over nations of 'jolly but feckless' natives.

Woman's role in this picture of celestial symbolics is to be *not Christ*. The whole order of creation, with its finely balanced symbolism, it is implied (it is even asserted), would be upset by ordaining a woman. It would be like trying to baptize a pigeon.

Infuriating and offensive as the account of 'female nature'

described above might be, the christological questions continue to present themselves to me with force: if women cannot represent Christ, can Christ represent women? Is Christ to be only the saviour of men? The creeds were more careful – *homo factus est* (*homo*, the term for 'human' and not *vir*, the term for 'male human'). The soteriological weight of the doctrine of the incarnation lies in the assertion that God became 'Man', to use the older term, not that God became a male. Consider the arguments of such a one as Athanasius (I preserve the language of the translator):

> And as the incorruptible Son of God was united to all men by his body similar to theirs, consequently he endued all men with incorruption by the promise concerning resurrection. And now no longer does the corruption involved in death hold sway over men because of the Word who dwelt among them through a body one with theirs.[14]

This kind of argument, central to traditional Catholic soteriology, becomes a nonsense if too much stress is put on the maleness of the body of the incarnate Word. 'A body similar to theirs' can only be a human body. There are serious christological dangers involved in tying signification of the Christ too closely to the masculinity of Jesus. To introduce, even inadvertently, a novel bipartite soteriology wherein men can fully signify Christ and women can signify 'very good friends of God' would be theologically indefensible in terms of classical Christology. Churches that do not ordain women need to demonstrate how their ecclesial practice is consonant with their Christology.

III

Turning the symbols. I have said that the arguments over the ordination of women now centre around questions of symbolism, and questions of symbolism are not questions to be taken lightly. Human beings are symbol-using creatures. To speak and to write a language is to participate in a shared symbolic order, a 'world mediated by meaning'.[15] The symbols by which we structure our world have direct and substantive effect on how we act in that world.

Christians do not need convincing of the power of symbolic orderings, and nor yet do feminists. Indeed some of the most difficult problems feminist philosophers and theoreticians are today addressing have to do with this question of how it is we can restructure or challenge a symbolic ordering, of whose 'world' is mediated by whose 'meaning'. What does not seem possible, or even human, is that we will be able to dispense with symbols and symbolic ordering altogether.

We learn much more than a vocabulary when we learn a mother tongue – we learn a world in terms of which we define ourselves and sometimes define ourselves against. We come to understand ourselves, our history and our world in terms of shared narratives, shared values and shared symbols. What do we do then if, as in the 'Natural History Museum Syndrome', we find ourselves to be 'on the outside looking in' to systems of meaning and value that once we uncritically inhabited?

The idea of doing entirely without symbols is impossible; the idea of dispensing entirely with all 'harmful' symbols (of which more below) seems implausible. A third possibility exists, well documented by students of social change, and it is that the symbols may be turned.

Some may recall Paul Tillich's lapidary pronouncements on the difference between symbol and sign. Symbols, he says, unlike signs have 'innate power'. This indeed is the major difference between symbol and sign for Tillich. He writes:

> The sign is interchangeable at will. It does not arise from necessity for it has no inner power. The symbol, however, does possess a necessary character. It can be exchanged, it can only disappear when, through dissolution, it loses its inner power. Nor can it be merely constructed; it can only be created.[16]

According to Tillich, signs are arbitrary, but the symbol – and especially the religious symbol – is accorded a glowering and mysterious presence, 'participating in that which it represents'. But what is not sufficiently manifest when symbols (as necessary) are played off signs (as conventional) in this Tillichian way is that symbols like signs are *arbitrary*. They vary from culture to culture, they shift over time, they turn and they can be turned. Symbols, like languages themselves, are social products and not natural kinds like porcupines or zinc. And even shared symbols are not necessarily univocal.

An older gentleman once came to give a talk on symbolism to the students of the theological college at which I was then teaching. Our college was on the hills above Oxford and our speaker took as his example of a symbol the 'dreaming spires' of that city. These symbolized, he said, the excellence, antiquity and integrity of the university, with its long-standing commitment to knowledge and the church's life, and so on. A glance around the room disclosed some vexed student faces. Our lecturer could not know that in their opinion the 'dreaming spires' were a symbol of privilege, the old-boy network, and the co-option of the witness of the church to the needs of the dominant powers in society. The point is not 'who was right and who wrong?', but rather that for both our guest speaker and these students the spires were symbolic. One could say that in both cases the symbol 'participated in that which it represented', but the students read the symbol in quite a different way. For them the symbol had turned.

To whom then are symbols symbolic, and of what? Our position inside and outside various structures enables us to see certain things, and blinds us to others. Symbols generated within a culture may be perceived variously by different groups, while still recognized as having symbolic resonance for the whole community. It is not always simply a question of seeing better, but of seeing differently.[7]

A South African, a Baptist minister and theologian, told me the following story. He had grown up in a township. His mother worked as a domestic for a white family and every day he waited with excitement for her return, not least because she brought home the stale bread from the white household for her own family to eat. Because of this, bread and 'bread of life' had always seemed to him especially powerful Christian symbols. Some years later, as a young pastor, he was sent to minister in the Homelands. The people (largely women and children, since the men were working far away in the mines) were struggling to survive, almost at starvation level. As Baptists they celebrated the Lord's Supper only monthly, using chunks of real bread. When the pastor passed out the bread to the baptized adults during the service of the Lord's Supper the unbaptized children wept with hunger and frustration. For this pastor, the symbol turned. How can you celebrate a celestial banquet when the people around you are starving?

What is the solution? Do we cease to use the symbol 'bread of life'? In this context or in all? The difficulty is that every symbol, by virtue of the power it has to signify, can be turned to negative application in some circumstances. Is the symbol of the bread of communion contaminated for all Christians because for some it is a counter-sign? And what do we say of the other scriptural symbols to which we are heir: the language of kingship and hierarchy, of war and battles, slavery and deception. Can we purge it? Make it inoffensive? And if so, what are we left with? We face a real danger of *symbol starvation*, a state in which having expunged so much we find ourselves placeless, with no narrative continuity with that which went before.

I have deliberately chosen symbols from within the Christian scriptural legacy which, while difficult for feminists, are difficult not just for feminists, and not just in our generation. You might say that the first Christian to be repulsed by militarism and hierarchies of power in religion as received was Jesus of Nazareth, for a good deal of what he was doing in his life and teaching appears to be a reversal of the symbols – the 'king' enters Jerusalem mounted on a donkey. The 'holy Scriptures' of Jews and Christians are scarcely documents of uplifting tales of worthy folk; murder, deception, incest, war, deceitfulness, all take their place. We cannot ignore this or disguise it. We need not and indeed should not use these horrible tales as contemporary directives, but they witness to something precious to many feminists, a religious concern with particularity. It would be paradoxical if Christian feminists, while wanting to stress the particularity of their own circumstances, should be offended by the historical particularity of these ancient texts.

These holy books also attest to a resilient ability in Judaism and Christianity to transform religion and society by a critique from within, a turning of the symbols. What is high is made low and what is rich becomes poor. It is in this sense that Christianity is a historical religion: not by endorsing the values of one place and period for all time to come, but in being a teleological or eschatological faith, always renewing itself as it longs for and works for the 'coming of the kingdom'.

With regard to the specific question of the turning of symbols, the experience of black Christians in South Africa is more than interesting and one of the best analogues to the Christian feminist's dilemma that I can think of. One might think that if anyone had the right, and even the duty, to reject outright the Christian faith as they received it, it would be the colonized peoples of South Africa. Of his own Reformed church tradition. Alan Boesak writes:

When they introduced slavery and enforced it with the most vicious forms of dehumanization and violence, it was the Bible read through Reformed eyes and arguments from the Reformed tradition that gave them justification for such acts of violence and human tragedy. The God of the Reformed tradition was the God of slavery, fear, persecution, and death. Yet, for those black Christians this was the God to whom they had to turn for comfort, for justice, for peace.[18]

Note that Boesak, and others like him, do not reject their Reformed tradition or its favoured symbols for divine power and rule. Rather, energetic and successful reform has come from those who attempt to retrieve these symbols and turn them to new ends. Calvin's preferred repertoire of metaphors for God – Judge, King, Lord and so on – are transformed in the hands of black Reformed theologians like Boesak, who argue (as in charity we must think some of the early followers of Calvin did too) that if God is my King then no man can be my king, if God is my Lord then no system can rule me.[19]

It would seem that most successful revolutions of thought and practice occur, not when a whole life-world is overthrown and attempts are made to construct a new symbolic order from scratch, but rather when the living symbols of faith are turned to become the tools of a new vision and a new life. In the words of Gregory Baum:

> What counts in any reform movement – or any revolution, for that matter – is to reinterpret the significant symbols that people have inherited and thus regain them and reclaim them as sources for a new social imagination and guides for a new kind of social involvement.[20]

Could Christian feminism effect such a transformation of symbols? Some would say not; the central Christian symbols are too tied to patriarchy. The strategies of Black and liberation theologies, they would argue, afford little solace and certainly the proof of the 'liberative' elements of South African and Latin American theologians will come when we see what they mean for women there, usually the poorest of the poor.

I am hopeful. Some of the most powerful gestures of feminist theologians have been those which transform, sometimes by no more than a phrase, a powerful inherited symbol. Consider the success of Elisabeth Schüssler Fiorenza's choice of title for her book, *In Memory of Her*. The shock of an apparent reference to familiar eucharistic prayers is strengthened when one realizes that the reference is not to Christ but to a woman who, despite Jesus' words, is almost completely forgotten. A similar and effective strategy is employed by Phyllis Trible in *Texts of Terror*. She introduces before the discussion of each of her 'texts of terror' a leitmotif. The recollection of Hagar is prefaced by the statement, 'She was wounded for our transgressions; she was bruised for our iniquities.' As Trible remarks, her intention is to give familiar passages, 'unfamiliar applications. Women, not men, are suffering servants and Christ figures.'[21] The move is thought-provoking. Why in the Christian glossing of the Hebrew Bible should the unjust sufferings of innocent women not be read as prefiguring that of Christ? Is it only the sufferings of men that can fit the template of the Christian saviour? The symbol is turned.

It is that aspect which Daphne Hampson finds most estranging in traditional Christianity to which I find myself continuously drawn – its particularity. Since the Enlightenment, Hampson says, there has been an ill fit between claims for divine intervention and what we know of the constancy of nature. It has become 'difficult to believe that we are in God's particular providence, in the way in which this seemed feasible to those who drew maps of the world with Jerusalem at the centre ...', and further, our 'knowledge today of other world religions has made the claims of Christianity increasingly untenable.'[22] Daphne Hampson wishes to deny that God could 'be revealed through particular events in history, or through a particular person, in a way in which God is not potentially present to us in and through all acts and persons'.[23] She wants to distance herself from a faith which makes one historical period and culture normative for all others, and this she understands Christianity, as a 'historical' religion, to do.

But we are not the first generation to find the particularity of the Christian faith scandalous, nor the first to be acquainted with belief systems of a more abstract and universal appeal. The young Augustine was appalled by the primitive nature of the Christian religion – a reasonable reaction for an educated person of his day. Why should a sophisticated and well-educated citizen of Rome give more than a moment's notice to the unedifying tales of an unimportant provincial people like the Jews? With many elegant metaphysical and moral schemes to choose from, what is to be gained from reading about the immoral antics of provincial nobodies? And yet when Augustine had that mysterious experience in the garden and the incarnation became real to him, everything changed. Once he believed that God had as a human being taken on a human history, he seemed to see that not only the history of Jesus but all human history and each human history was sanctified. A God made present to history was present to Augustine's own history, even when he failed to realize it, and by extension to every human history. He could write the *Confessions*.

The life of the slave girl no less than that of the philosopher or king is seen as the place where God dwells and is revealed in fullness. God is not distant, abstract, but very close and very particular. How are we to account for the spread of Christianity, against the odds, in the ancient world, and for its success amongst the least regarded members of society? Perhaps this affirmation of God with us, intimate to the particularities of even the most disregarded lives, had something to do with it. This has been a precious heritage for women and I, for one, would be loathe to give it up.

3
THE POWER TO RE-MEMBER
Nicola Slee

Is it possible to be a Christian and a feminist at the same time, and if so, how? In answer to this question, I wish to say 'Yes, but only if Christian identity is understood in a sufficiently flexible and dynamic way; only if Christian identity is understood to be open to continual renewal, reformation and transformation; and only if feminism itself is permitted to become an agent of Christianity's own transformation.' It is not as if we are comparing two fixed and unchanging systems, 'Christianity' on the one hand and 'feminism' on the other. Both are fluid, complex and developing traditions whose identity is constantly open to question and revision, and is, indeed, most capable of creative transformation at times of deepest crisis. I do not begin this essay, then, with a prior notion of what it is to be a Christian which is independent of my feminist commitment; rather, my understanding of Christian identity has been shaped and sharpened, at least in part, by feminism itself. The question I am therefore interested in asking is not so much 'Are Christianity and feminism compatible?' but 'Can Christian identity be reconstructed in the light of the feminist challenge, and if so, how?'

For it is abundantly clear that Christian self-understanding cannot remain untouched by feminism. Nothing can be sacrosanct, nothing out-of-bounds to feminist critique, including and most especially religious traditions which have for centuries lent divine credence to the oppression of women. Feminism demands a wholesale revaluation of all sacred myths and traditions in the light of women's contemporary as well as long-buried past experience, a 'splitting open' of world, in Muriel Rukeyser's oft-quoted phrase.[1] Yet this demand that long-cherished understandings be tested, sundered and reforged is not entirely foreign to the prophetic spirit present within religious traditions. Just such a demand for the continual reworking of established meanings is made by Christian tradition in every age and time; and it is women followers who are uniquely placed to fulfil this demand precisely

because they are the ones who have been disenfranchised by the
tradition and are most hungry for change.

I believe that the Christian tradition is indeed capable of the
kind of transformation which feminism requires of it. In what
follows, I wish to propose an understanding of Christian identity
which is both continuous with Christianity's own historical past,
and open to fluid and novel development by feminism in the
present. My argument has three main stages. First, I shall offer a
model of the Christian as one who 'remembers the story of Jesus
in and for their own time'. Having outlined this narrative
understanding of Christian identity, I shall go on to discuss the
problems such a model might raise for feminists. Finally, I shall
suggest a way of reading and remembering the Jesus-story which,
whilst it does not miraculously dissolve the dilemmas women face
in their attempts to read ancient texts and traditions, nevertheless
may provide a key to a positive reappropriation of Christian
tradition.

The basis of this argument will be the proposal that the Jesus-
story is best read as parable; that is, as a story which, through a
range of rhetorical and literary devices, radically subverts the
expectations that readers bring to it, and, by so doing, provokes
the hearer to a narrative reconstruction of the self, God and world.
Understood in this way, I shall argue that the Jesus-story refuses
every attempt at slavish imitation or mere repetition and compels
contemporary hearers to shape and tell a new story of the rule of
God active in their *own* lives and times. Thus it is open to the kind
of creative renewal and reform that feminism can offer it.[2]

I

Human beings live uniquely by and within a network of overlapping and criss-crossing stories. 'To be human is to be in story',
according to Brian Swimme, 'and to forget one's story is to go
insane.'[3] All cultures and civilizations seem to have felt the need to
create and transmit stories as ways of understanding themselves
and their world, as ways of enshrining their most cherished beliefs
and sacred values. Story, we might say, is a fundamental and
primary mode of being in the world.

> Without stories there is no knowledge of the world, of ourselves,
> of others, and of God. Our narrative consciousness is our power
> for comprehending ourselves in our coherence with the world
> and other selves; it expresses our existential reality as story-
> telling and storylistening animals, acting and reacting within our
> particular world context, overcoming the incoherence of the

unexamined life ... We live on stories; we shape our lives through stories, mastering the complexity of our experience through the dynamic of our structured knowing.[4]

If human beings have always lived on stories, nevertheless there is a qualitative difference between the relation of our ancestors to the stories by which they lived and our own. Once upon a time, people lived within a single, coherent and unrivalled narrative framework which functioned as the master-story of an entire culture, upholding and explicating a world-view of mythic proportions. But now all that has changed, and we moderns live, uncertain and uneasy, within a world of fragmenting and competing rival stories, all of which have shrunk to the dimensions of the pocket-size paperback and none of which can command unfaltering allegiance. Our age, as Don Cupitt notes, is characterized by the proliferation of the novel and the short story rather than by the dominance of a single myth or a fixed canon of texts. He writes: 'The body of stories that people live by cannot be held within a single fixed canon. Instead we have now a whole living literature which is being continuously added to and modified as values change.'[5]

Within a post-modernity characterized by such a proliferation of competing stories, religious believers are distinguished by their adherence, either fragile or ferocious, to a particular story or set of stories, which they hold as uniquely significant, illuminative and authoritative. Even though the story to which they are committed may no longer have the world-ordering coherence of unrivalled myth, it still functions in some sense as the root-narrative in the complex network of overlapping narratives within which people today inevitably live. It is this root-narrative which illuminates, questions and orders all the other stories, even while its own narrative focus is constantly subjected to critical scrutiny.

Christians, then, are those who live by and within the story of Jesus; who, in the community of the church, remember and rehearse this story repeatedly in the ritual action of liturgy; who, in preaching, teaching and theological reflection re-read and reinterpret this story and explore its connections with their own, and their community's life; who, in prayer and spirituality seek to discern the pattern of the Jesus-story in the world and live more faithfully in accordance with it; and who, in social praxis and proclamation, protest against every injustice and failure of love which contradicts their reading of the Jesus-story. Christians live by and within this story, because they hold it to be, in some sense, paradigmatic of the God–world relationship. Elizabeth Johnson articulates this basic Christian conviction well when she writes:

> The story of Jesus of Nazareth, crucified and risen, confessed as the Christ, is at the centre of Christian faith in God. In the gracious power of Sophia-Spirit unleashed through his history and destiny, the community of disciples continuously retells and enacts that story as the story of God with us to heal, redeem and liberate all people and the cosmos itself. Good news indeed.[6]

Putting it at its simplest, we might say that *Christians are those who remember the story of Jesus within the community of the church, in and for their own time and in their own lives.* 'Remembrance' here has all the well-rehearsed connotations of the Greek *anamnesis*, encapsulating both the recollection of the past but also its making present, its re-membering or actualizing, in the here and now. Christians recall, repeat and rehearse the 'old, old story', passed on from generation to generation, and, at the same time, reappropriate, retell, revise, refictionalize it in and for their own time. And these are not two separate activities, but one; for there is no way to recall and remember that is not at the same time a reshaping and a revising of what is received. Every act of remembrance is a complex process of selection, interpretation and arrangement of what has been received, in the light of the believing community's contemporary needs, experience and perceptions. This has been, from the beginning, the way in which the Jesus-story was both transmitted and renewed by Christians who perceived in its narrative possibilities endless applications to their own situations and lives.

   Thus, from the beginning, variety and multiplicity in the telling of the story have abounded. There is not and never has been *one* 'story of Jesus', but many stories. From New Testament times onwards, the stories told about Jesus have been at least as remarkable for their diversity as their commonality, and the attempt to recapture a 'core' of *either* unassailable historical fact *or* doctrinal consensus is almost certainly doomed. Thus, to speak of 'the story of Jesus' and define Christians as those who 'remember the story of Jesus in and for their own times', is to employ an inevitably simplified short-hand summary. 'The story of Jesus' must be taken to refer to the complex network of stories told both by and about Jesus which have been preserved by Christian tradition and reworked countless times, not only by theologians and preachers, but also by musicians, artists, novelists, dramatists and poets. Classically, certain versions of the Jesus-story have taken pride of place in the stock of narratives upon which the life of the church has been built: namely, the stories of Jesus told by the canonical Gospels, by Paul and by the other New Testament writers, their doctrinal interpretation and formalization in the creeds, and their ritual expression in the liturgy of the eucharist. Yet whilst these will certainly continue to play a formative role in the shaping of contemporary Christian identity, there is no good reason why other versions of the story may not come to be valued alongside them for the light they shed on our times and needs. When once diversity and multiplicity are understood to be characteristic of the key sources of Christian tradition which were formerly believed to be monolithic, and the notion of a single, coherent 'story of faith' is jettisoned in favour of a plurality of narrative traditions, the grounds for excluding any particular narrative tradition for the 'memory' of the Christian community become much less secure.

By describing the Christian thus as one who 'remembers the story of Jesus', I intend a reading of Christian identity whose chief emphases it will be well to summarize here, though they cannot be argued in detail. First, it is a way of understanding what it means to be Christian which is continuous with the praxis of Jesus, yet open to novel development by successive generations of believers. Whatever we can say with confidence about the Jesus of history, it is clear that story-telling formed a major thrust of his proclamation of the kingdom. Jesus is remembered in the New Testament as the master story-teller who calls others into faith and the kingdom, not by self-proclamation, doctrinal assertion or moral maxim, but by provocative and artful stories. He thus provides a model of narrative creativity which is to be a distinguishing characteristic of his followers.

Second, whilst the model does not down-play the significance of belief in the Christian life, it does not place the centre of Christian identity here. A Christian is one who lives in creative, fruitful relation to the Jesus-story, rather than one who believes certain doctrines about Jesus as the Christ. Such a stance recognizes both the actual diversity of belief represented within the Christian community, as well as the hermeneutical openness of the tradition to multiple interpretation. Clearly, to 'live in creative, fruitful relation to the Jesus-story' assumes a prior commitment to the story which requires some explication. Nevertheless, the defining characteristic of the Christian is the lived relation to the story, rather than a particular set of beliefs about the story. The story invites, indeed compels, theological reflection and articulation, but at the same time resists it, remains larger than any single attempt at explanation, outlives every effort at doctrinal closure.

Thus, and this is the third point, the model affirms and celebrates diversity, plurality and novelty at the centre of Christian identity. There is not one Jesus-story but many, and this is a reason for rejoicing rather than a cause of dismay, for if there were only one story, it would be limited to one particular time and setting, and could not serve the diversity of human needs across time and space which Christians claim it is able to do. There is no neutral, objective or timeless 'remembering' of the story of Jesus, but only a concrete, socially, politically and historically committed reading of the text which serves particular historical needs and interests against others, and must be judged by its historical effects. Yet the welcome embrace of multiplicity and historical particularity need not mean that all meaning is collapsed into the monotonous landscape of absolute relativity. To admit that all human knowing, including the narrative knowing of faith, is finite and revisable does not preclude passionate commitment on the one hand or critical scrutiny on the other. The novel that I am currently reading can command my allegiance absolutely and absorb my intelligence wholly, even though I know it is only one of many available fictions; and if this is the case with regard to the relatively transient commitment a reader gives to a novel, how much greater is the degree of allegiance and intelligent scrutiny we give to those larger stories by which we live our lives. Ruth Page expresses well what such provisional commitment looks like in the christological realm:

> Any portrait of Jesus Christ, and any Christology, is an instance of the use of language for commitment and praxis which will be deconstructible like any text, and hence provisional, and may well be conflictual as well. Yet if this were recognized, it might become possible to *enjoy* multiplicity, as the excess of meaning in the Gospels is worked and reworked into new presentations of Jesus. Moreover, although none of the portraits will be final, it is possible that one of them, or parts from many of them, may so vividly express one's commitment to God in Christ that it gives contemporary meaning and direction to our lives, lives which, after all, are also contingent and provisional.[7]

II

The Christian, I have said, is one who 'remembers the story of Jesus within the community of the church, in and for their own time and in their own life'. Yet it is by no means self-evident how an ancient narrative tradition formulated in a pre-scientific era can serve the complex needs of the modern world. Feminists are not the only ones who find the ancient texts and traditions recalcitrant to their questions and needs. Nevertheless, there are particular problems which must be addressed for women readers who attempt to situate themselves in relation to the 'story of Jesus'.

The first and most obvious difficulty for any female reader of the biblical texts or the subsequent tradition of Christian history is quite simply the glaring omission of women from the story. Within the classic texts of the tradition, women are largely notable by their absence, or, where they are included, marginal to the story, defined almost always in terms of their relation to the male characters rather than in their own right, and generally regarded as infantile or incomplete persons.[8] This may be less so in the New Testament than in its more ancient counterpart of the Hebrew Bible, but, as Elisabeth Schüssler Fiorenza and others have shown, the systematic repression of the memory of women's stories is also clearly evident there.[9] The retrieval of positive images of women which have (miraculously?) managed to survive centuries of patriarchal culture cannot compensate for the terrible injustice of the loss of women's history in Christian tradition, leaving a yawning chasm at the centre of the story which followers of Jesus are committed to remember. The problem goes deeper than this, however, for it is not only the *content* of the texts which has been shaped by patriarchy in such a way as to exclude women, but the construction of the relation between the reader and the text. French feminist theorists such as Julia Kristeva and Luce Irigaray argue that in patriarchal texts the reader is constructed as male and that the only way for females to read the text is to assume the posture of the male, thus forcing women to repress their female subjectivity.[10] Thus, in terms of both *content* and *readership*, the text is predicated on the assumption of the male as norm.

If there are problems for women readers in locating *themselves* within the tradition of the Christian story, there are also problems in relating to the central character of Jesus around which the texts and traditions revolve. There has been a tendency in some Christian feminist circles to draw a sacred circle around the figure of Jesus and, whilst allowing the fiercest criticisms of, say, Old Testament narratives, early church practices, and post-biblical theology, to maintain that Jesus was the 'perfect feminist', untouched by the patriarchy of his day. Such a position cannot be maintained. At the very least, some contemporary readings of the Gospels suggest that Jesus' attitudes towards women were limited by the patriarchal assumptions of his day and that his teaching and life-style were more readily accessible to men than to women.[11]

Even if the story of Jesus itself can be read in ways which are consonant with feminism, as I believe it can, there is something deeply problematic for feminists in the very notion of defining oneself in relation to Jesus, a male subject. This has been put most concisely, and with characteristic verve, by Mary Daly, when she asks: 'Jesus was a feminist, but so what? ... Fine. Wonderful. But even if he wasn't, *I am*.'[12] In other words, feminists do not require justification of their world-view from any male religious authority, and, further, the tendency to look to some such authority for guidance or inspiration is potentially destructive of women's own sense of self. Thus feminists such as Mary Daly and Isabel Carter Heyward argue that Christology typically encourages an unhealthy idolatry, an idolization of Jesus as the one, unique revelation of God, which reinforces women's tendencies towards emotional dependence on men. Instead of finding the God-image within themselves, instead of taking responsibility for themselves and their own decisions, Christology encourages women to look outside themselves to Jesus for guidance and affirmation, and thus to define themselves as the obedient 'other' in relation to the primary, and authoritative, male subject.[13]

III

How, then, is it possible for women to 'remember the story of Jesus in and for their own time' when that story is deeply and pervasively biased against the female reader by its exclusion of women from the tradition, by its presupposition that the reader is male, and by its demand that the reader situate him or herself in relation to the male subject at its centre, Jesus? Clearly, feminism disallows any reading of the tradition which requires the reader's consent to the patriarchal world-view of the text, and struggles for a way of being-in-relation to the story which both delegitimizes that world-view and moreover fuels the vision of an alternative world-order. Here I wish to further my argument by suggesting that there *is* a way for women to read the Jesus-story which does not demand complicity with the patriarchal world-view of the texts but precisely challenges and subverts it. It is important to state that, in so arguing, I am not seeking to downplay or ignore the deep and painful dilemmas women experience in reading patriarchal texts and relating to patriarchal history. There is no feminist 'solution' to the question of Christian identity which will miraculously dissolve the centuries of male bias and oppression enshrined in the tradition or which will recover the lost lives and witness of

countless unremembered women. It is precisely *because* this is so
that we are pressed to find new ways of reading the very texts and
traditions which have marginalized, exploited and victimized
women. I wish to suggest that a clue towards such a re-reading lies
in the parables of Jesus. By reading the Jesus-story as parable, and
Jesus as a 'parable of God',[13] the relation between reader and text
is reconstructed as one of radical freedom, responsibility and
creativity, such that the patriarchal world-view of the text is
overcome in a new fictionalizing of the rule of God in the world.

In order to explicate such a hermeneutic, a brief account of the
nature and function of the parables must first be given. Over the
past few decades, New Testament and literary scholarship have
revolutionized our understanding of the parables of Jesus. From
being understood for centuries as enigmatic allegories of the
spiritual life, biblical criticism at the beginning of this century
proposed an alternative understanding of the parable as a simple,
homely analogy with one clear didactic point, if only it could be
recovered from the text. Both these approaches have subsequently
been superceded by a much more dynamic and compelling
understanding of the parable as language-event which subverts and
disorients hearers' expectations and thus challenges them to make
a decision about the kingdom of God. Sallie McFague provides a
helpful summary of this newer understanding of the parables:

> The parables, brief stories told in the secular language of Jesus'
> time, are extended metaphors that say something about the
> unfamiliar, the 'kingdom of God', in terms of the familiar, a
> narrative of ordinary people doing ordinary things. They work,
> however, on a pattern of orientation, disorientation, and re-
> orientation: the parable begins in the ordinary world with its
> conventional standards and expectations, but in the course of
> the story a radically different perspective is introduced, often by
> means of a surrealistic extravagance, that disorients the listener,
> and finally, through the interaction of the two competing
> viewpoints tension is created that results in a reorientation, a
> redescription of life in the world. A parable is, in this analysis,
> an assault on the conventions, including the social, economic,
> and mythic structures that people build for their own comfort
> and security. A parable is a story meant to invert and subvert
> these structures and to suggest that the way of the kingdom is
> not the way of the world.[14]

Such an account of parable provides a model, I suggest, of the way
in which the larger story of Jesus may be read. The Jesus-story has

all the characteristics of his own parables, and functions vis-à-vis
the reader in much the same way as his parables. Like Jesus'
parables, it is a *mundane, ordinary, human* story, in which the
presence and activity of the kingdom are present by implication
rather than assertion. Like the parables, it is a story which con-
centrates on action, decision and event, within a world of human
relationships, rooting the kingdom of God firmly in the concerns,
decisions and relationships of this world rather than in some
distant or separate metaphysical realm. Like the parables, it is a
story told with a marked economy and vividness of description
and evocation, allied with an absence of explanation or interpretation, such that it is the story itself which holds the meaning,
and the reader is constantly teased into making his or her judgement about it. Like the parables, it is a story characterized by
elements of shock, surprise, extravagance and reversal which
disrupt the horizons of normalcy and compel the reader to come to
decision and judgement. And like the parables, it is a story which
is open to multiple interpretation, thus respecting both the
freedom and the creative imagination of every reader.

Sallie McFague calls attention to three particular features of the
Jesus-story which act as disruptive, destabilizing elements within
the mundane normalcy of this very human story and provide
powerful clues towards a Christian understanding of the God–
world relationship.[15] The first is Jesus' parables themselves, about
which enough has already been said to account for McFague's
claim that they stand as both sign and expression of the radical
destablization of every conventional, hierarchical, oppressive
dualism at work in the cosmos which the kingdom demands.
Although most of the parables themselves do not appear to
address women's lives explicitly, their basic dynamic of reversing
and subverting expectation may be applied by contemporary
women readers to their lives, as I have tried to show elsewhere.[16]

The second feature McFague draws attention to is Jesus' table
fellowship with sinners, which she reads as testimony to the
inclusive character of the kingdom. Jesus situates his ministry and
his stories of the kingdom deliberately within the world of
oppression which was, and still is, the horizon of normalcy for the
poor, for women, for Blacks and for other oppressed groups in our
world. He enjoys table fellowship with 'sinners' (i.e., with those
beyond the pale of the law), calls despised tax-collectors to be his
disciples, shows a special concern for the poor and the socially
vulnerable, and demonstrates a remarkable freedom in his relations with women. He does not so much challenge the injustice of
political, social and sexual oppression directly as assume its brutal

reality as the setting for his own proclamation of the kingdom. Yet the note of extravagance and hyperbole in Jesus' relation to this setting gives the lie to any easy acquiescence with it. He *feasts* and *parties* extravagantly with those beyond the pale of the law, while others more pious are fasting; to a respectable audience of religious leaders he offers as a model of divine forgiveness the lavish outpouring of a prostitute's gratitude; he offends every social sensibility and law of commonsense by proclaiming the poor 'blessed' and the meek 'inheritors of the earth'; he commends the underhand methods of an unscrupulous steward as a model of believing faith. In just such ways, the normalcy of social relations which is taken for granted by his hearers is disrupted and the hearers' position within that world called into question.

The third feature of the Jesus-story to which McFague draws attention as especially revelatory for understanding the God–world relationship is the cross, understood as the epitomy of 'the retribution that comes to those who give up controlling and triumphalist postures in order to relate to others in mutual love'.[17] In the story of Jesus, it is above all the extravagance and the shocking reversal of the cross which disrupts and subverts the expectations that readers bring to it. At the same time, the cross threatens to shatter the normalcy of Jesus' own horizons, especially the horizon of his relationship with 'the Father'. Jesus himself, we might say, is not exempted from the fracturing and dismembering of his own story, and he himself models the process of narrative re-membering which his parables demand of others. In the cross, his trust in and intimacy with the Father is broken, and he is confronted with the radical challenge of his own fractured and subverted human story. Like the implicit challenge of the parables, Jesus must now decide whether he will 'go with' the story, in all its terrible and unforeseen consequences, or whether he will refuse its narrative invitation and stay on 'this side' of the kingdom's unexplored horizons. As parabler *par excellence*, Jesus shows himself capable of the courage and openness which responds wholeheartedly, even *in extremis*, to the crisis of his own broken story, and in doing so demonstrates the way in which a new world of meaning may be born out of the dismembering of the familiar story. The cross disrupts and dismembers Jesus' human story of relationship with God and proclamation of the kingdom. Yet out of his own willingness to 'go all the way' with the story he no longer comprehends, a new and utterly unimagined narrative possibility is created which the evangelists variously and dramatically narrate in the resurrection appearances. The Jesus-story is discovered to have renewed itself, not in unbroken continuity with

what had gone before, but in an explosion of new narrative energy
which leads to the stories of countless others being similarly
remade, renewed and transformed. The ongoing trajectory of
Jesus' own story is now set loose beyond the confines of its limited
historical horizons and taken up in the new narrative of the
church, his body, his continuing presence, his *story*, in the world.

IV

But what does it mean for contemporary readers, and especially
women readers, to read the Jesus-story in this way as parable?
There is no space here to draw out the full implications of my
approach. What I wish chiefly to draw attention to is the consequences such a reading has for the way in which women readers
are invited to situate themselves in relation to the texts and traditions they have inherited from the past. To read the story of
Jesus as parable is not merely to legitimate but positively to
demand a kind of tensile, broken and reforged relation to
authoritative religious texts and traditions, which is the only
possible kind of relation women can maintain with mainstream
religion in our time. In particular, I suggest that to read the story
of Jesus as parable challenges women readers to a radical narrative
reconstruction of our understandings of self, world and God
respectively.

In the first place, it seems to me that the Jesus-story, in so far as
it functions to disrupt and subvert the desire for narrative safety
and closure, turns the tables on women's historical tendency to
define ourselves in relation to an authoritative male subject, and
demands of us that we take responsibility for the creation and
actualization of our own selfhood. That is, Jesus as parabler
refuses to tell us who we are and resists every attempt to make of
him a model to be copied or an authority to be obeyed. As
parabler, Jesus disrupts and subverts the dualism of the subject–
object relation which Daly and others have seen as characteristic
of Christology. He will not be reified as the 'other' upon whom all
our desires can be cast and in whom all our needs can be met: he
slips through the fingers of every attempt to pin him down and
eludes every clinging grasp. The classic instance of such a refusal
of female longing and need is the Johannine story of the meeting
of the risen Christ and Mary Magdalene in the garden (John 20.1–
18). In this story Jesus almost brutally disallows Mary's impulsive
longing to re-establish intimacy and, instead, sends her away to
proclaim her story to the other disciples, and to forge a new life
and a new selfhood out of the broken relationship to the past and
to Jesus. As Elizabeth Moltmann-Wendel writes, it is as if Jesus is

saying 'Grow up, be mature! Accept the grief of parting.'[18] Although the Johannine resurrection story captures this new relation between Jesus and his female followers with great vividness, it is also implied by the resurrection narratives in the other Gospels. In Mark, as in Matthew, the Gospel ends with the women being sent to proclaim that 'he has been raised; he is not here ... he is going ahead of you' (Mark 16.8; Matthew 28.6–7), and in Luke the women are castigated by the young men at the tomb: 'Why seek the living among the dead?' (Luke 24.5). In each case, the old pattern of relationship between the women and Jesus, characterized by intimacy and service, is ruptured and broken, and the women are offered a new narrative beginning, in which to discover a fresh identity in the power of the Spirit.

If the Jesus-story demands of women a reworking of old patterns of relationship and understandings of selfhood, it also, I suggest, requires of women a fresh understanding, a fresh narrative shaping, of what it means to belong to and to live in the world. Just as the story will not tell women who they are or what they must become, so it will not give any easy guidelines for social praxis. The Jesus-story refuses to provide a blueprint for social action on poverty or racism any more than it does for the combating of sexism. It does not work like that. Jesus' preaching and praxis of the kingdom is not and never has been a political manifesto so much as a provocative, disturbing and disorienting vision of the future possibilities inherent in the present moment. Yet precisely because the radical social and political implications of the kingdom are implicit within the story, they depend for their actualization upon the response of the reader. For women readers, this means that it is neither necessary, nor even desirable, that 'Jesus was a feminist' in order for their own political action to be grounded in his story. For one thing, it is sheer anachronism to demand of Jesus that he be a model of modern sexual politics. More significantly, however, the attempt to force Jesus into such a mould would, paradoxically, endanger women's contemporary quest for sexual liberation precisely because it would tend to absolve women from the responsibility of forging their own political commitments. Of course, this does not mean that Jesus' attitudes to and relations with women are unimportant for modern women readers. As Stephen Barton puts it:

> If it could be shown that the teaching of Jesus was irredeemably sexist, that he systematically discriminated against women *per se*, that women were able to respond to Jesus only in hostile ways, and that the qualities for leadership in the early Christian

movement were specific to the male sex only, this would constitute a serious problem for those in the Church today who
wish discrimination against women to end.[19]

Barton however continues to affirm that there is little such
evidence. Thus, we might say with Ruether,[20] Jesus' own praxis
and proclamation of liberation, though it was not explicitly
directed towards the social emancipation of women, is nevertheless consonant with the demands of contemporary feminism,
yet requires translation into the context of sexual oppression in
our own time.

Finally, if it is the case that the Jesus-story read as parable
demands of women a reworking of our understandings of selfhood
and world, it follows that a refashioning of our notions of God is
also implied. Just as the Jesus-story refuses to tell readers who
they are or how they must act in the world, except by inviting
them into the story in order to forge their own narrative decisions,
so neither will it tell us who or what God is or how divinity may
be named and recognized, except by the elusive hints and twists of
the story itself. In the parables, and in the larger story of Jesus read
as parable, God is never named directly but is only to be discerned
within and beyond the frame of the narrative itself as the hidden
horizon of the story. In the story of Jesus, God is, like the modern
novelist, only 'haveable' and 'nameable' within the frame of the
narrative, and the divine identity is at least as much hidden as it is
revealed by the artful construction of the story. Just as parable
insists on the continual narrative re-creation of *self* by the reader,
whose identity is questioned and broken within the world of the
parable, so the larger Jesus-story pushes towards a continual re-
creation of our models of God; and this includes our understanding of the christological identity of Jesus of Nazareth, which
is broken and remade in the cross and similarly fractured and 'remembered' in every contemporary retelling. The Jesus-story, then,
does not pronounce the 'last word' on the nature and name of
God, any more than it provides a blueprint for social reform or a
model of contemporary discipleship. It offers elusive, provocative
hints, nudges, clues towards the locus of God's activity in the
mundane, ordinary events and decisions of everyday life, in the
relationships of welcome, forgiveness and embrace that char-
acterize the kingdom, in the tension between the 'now' and the
'not yet' of the rule of God. But what this means for naming,
knowing and loving God in our own day is left resolutely
unspoken, demanding to be shaped and voiced by those who read
and remember the story of Jesus today.

V

Women whose lives have been shaped by feminism can no longer continue to read ancient scriptural texts and patriarchal traditions in old, established ways. New ways of reading the story of Jesus are demanded, ways which subvert the patriarchal world-view of Christianity and culture, thus creating a space for the construction of a new world-view in which women can play a central, rather than a peripheral, role. Parable, I have wanted to suggest, and the parables of Jesus in particular, may provide a key to such a reading.

The parable, we have seen, functions by beginning with the world of the hearer but then disrupts and destabilizes that world through some element of extravagance, surprise or reversal, forcing a decision on the part of the reader and thrusting the responsibility for completion or closure of the story onto the hearer herself. The parable creates a shared beginning, in which speaker and hearer are united, but it has no 'ending' until and unless the hearer responds. It is essentially open to the future, pivoted towards its own future development in the life and the action of its hearers. So, too, with the story of Jesus, the Christian tradition. It disallows slavish imitation or mere repetition and compels the hearer to take responsibility for its narrative development in her own life and times. Like a parable, the Jesus-story provides a framework of shared beginnings which can only be completed in the hearer's own words and ways. And, like a parable, it refuses every attempt at final closure, demanding to be reread, repeated, rewritten, remade countless times. The story of Jesus naturally spawns a thousand other new stories, stories of the destabilizing, disruptive presence and power of the kingdom in other times and lives, stories which may take as their starting-point the classic texts and traditions, but whose direction and shape will be forged by the needs and experiences of the contemporary narrator as much, if not more than, by the clues and hints from the past.

My argument throughout this essay has brought me to a position close to that set out by Don Cupitt in his book *What is a Story?*[21], though I do not share his non-realist metaphysics. Here Cupitt argues that if Christianity is to survive and speak to the needs of our world, Christians need to exercise a much bolder 're-fictionalizing' of the Jesus-story than we have so far recognized is necessary or have permitted ourselves to do. Thus, he writes:

> Established views of what Christianity is don't allow it enough scope for change for it to be able to survive ... A more literary

view of what Christianity is, however, gives some hope. If you
treat religion as a mythology, a large body of stories, then you
can understand how those stories may be selectively told and
retold with very different morals ... We will never reach a
purely historical, pre-fictionalized Jesus. There is none to be
reached, and we should not even wish to reach such a figure. To
be understood at all Jesus must from the very first be described
in some particular period vocabulary, with its myths and its
values. He is always already, mythicized – so nothing stops us
from re-mythicizing him in our own way. Until we try, we will
not know what the ideal of the holy life might mean today, or
what Christ might mean to us today.[22]

Some examples of what it might mean in practice for feminists to
so 're-fictionalize' the story of Jesus are provided from a number
of different directions. Novelists such as Michèle Roberts and Sara
Maitland have created some glorious re-fictionalizings of biblical
stories from the perspectives of various female characters who are
largely passed over in the text. Such stories allow female readers to
re-create and relate to biblical tradition in quite new ways.[23]
Feminist theologians such as Rosemary Radford Ruether, Isobel
Carter Heyward, Mary Grey and Rita Nakashima Brock have
developed fascinating Christologies which subvert the male
hegemony of classical Christology and thereby suggest new ways
for women to be-in-relation to the Jesus-story.[24] Liturgists such as
Janet Morley and Miriam Therese Winter have created a new
vocabulary of prayer which enables women to address Jesus in
new patterns of relationship as 'elder brother', 'stranger', 'friend'
and even 'mother' or 'sister' in place of the traditional 'Lord and
master'.[25] Numberless small groups of women (and sometimes
men) are forging new patterns of worship and study as they
wrestle with the biblical texts and stories and find a way of reading
women back into those stories, even where they are absent or their
memory largely submerged. Nor – if the parables themselves are
anything to go by – need 're-fictionalizing the story of Jesus in and
for our own time' always require explicit reference back to the
'original' name and doings of Jesus himself. Rather, they hint at a
way of story-telling which works by indirection, paradox and
opaqueness, which points away from Jesus to the secret of the
kingdom present in the lives, concerns and decisions of his followers today. For women to 'remember the story of Jesus in and
for their own times and in their own lives' thus requires a degree of
inventiveness, freedom and daring which we are more than ready
to exercise. Women who, for centuries, have been despised as

'tittle-tattlers' and 'gossips' are reclaiming the dignity and creativity of their vocation as those who 'gossip the good news' of God's presence in our world and thereby renew and reshape the ancient story of Jesus in lively and liberating ways.

4

WOMEN, RATIONALITY AND THEOLOGY

Jane Shaw

> When eating a fish, don't we pick the bones out first?
> Alessandra Lipucci[1]

There are two questions at the heart of this book. First, are feminism and Christianity compatible? Second, can one be both a feminist and a Christian? These questions, though often conflated, are distinctly different: how we answer the first will probably determine how we answer the second. But the second question, which asks whether a woman can be both a feminist and a Christian, is also about female subjectivity: that is, the social, cultural and psychic construction of what it means to be a woman (and a Christian), and, in turn, how we position ourselves as women in relation to the Christian tradition.

While these two questions are integral to the conceptualization of this book, I think that a third, related, question, also about female subjectivity, is suggested by the book's subtitle, 'Feminist Theologians Debate Christianity'. This subtitle advertises the authors as feminist theologians, debating whether we can be both feminist and Christian, and in doing so presupposes that women *can* at least be theologians. In the second section of this article I examine this assumption and argue that, while it may be possible to be both feminist and Christian, it is necessary to interrogate the ground on which we stand as feminist, women theologians. Thus I ask a series of broader questions about the construction of female religious identity through this specific question: can a woman be feminist, Christian and a theologian? Let me turn first to the matter of feminism and Christianity.

I

Any answers to these first two questions, about the compatibility of feminism and Christianity, and whether one can be both a feminist and a Christian, will depend upon an individual's interpretation of what it means to be a Christian and what it means to be a feminist. When we ask whether feminism and Christianity are compatible, we must also ask: whose feminism? whose Christianity? There are multiple feminisms and multiple Christianities. To ask whether feminism is compatible with Christianity is to suggest that Christianity is a thing to accept or reject as a whole; it implies that there is one Christian message. Similarly, it implies that feminism is such a static, whole thing.

The title of this book invites us to ask how, if we are Christian and feminist, we can stand to swallow the bones of the fish – the church itself – which is supposed to sustain and feed us, but which might just choke, if not kill, us. Much to my surprise, I recently heard a talk in which the speaker, political theorist Alessandra Lipucci, used this image of swallowing a fish whole. Lipucci suggested that to accept all the tenets of one 'school' of philosophy (while rejecting all other 'schools') is like swallowing a fish whole: 'When eating a fish, don't we pick the bones out first?' she asked. This image was not only remarkably coincidental, it was also helpful because it suggested to me that no one could accept or reject Christianity as a whole. To do so would imply that Christianity is such a whole, when in fact it is a rich and complex cultural heritage which each of us interprets for ourselves in accordance with our experiences and in the communities in which we live and work. Similarly, feminism has constantly changed over time, and in response to the concerns of the women (and men) who have defined it. We are faced with the reality of multiple Christianities and multiple feminisms – and, thus, multiple truths.

This awareness of multiple truths has been alive in the Christian West for centuries: the inter-confessional warfare and struggles of the Reformation period, followed by the rise of denominations and various theological positions within denominations, has made this abundantly clear. The European 'discovery' of other religions served further to relativize the Truth – with a capital T – of Christianity. Intellectual developments have also frequently been seen as attacks on that Truth too. The Enlightenment questioned revelation and miracles as proofs of Christianity; the work of Darwin, Freud, Marx and Nietzsche and historically based biblical criticism caused crises of faith in the nineteenth century; and the early twentieth-century emphasis on positivism resulted in an attempt to confine intellectual inquiry to supposedly observable facts, a trend which still seems to linger in English theology. This century, the turn to hermeneutics (interpretation) in the German tradition, by philosophers such as Heidegger and Gadamer and

theologians such as Bultmann, has led to an increased emphasis on
the ways in which we *interpret* texts, or, for that matter, any body
of knowledge. It has also led, with the impetus given by recent
work by feminists, Black scholars, and others who have traditionally been left out of the interpretation process, to an emphasis
on the social position of the interpreter: there is a growing
acknowledgement that a person's social, political, cultural and
even psychological context will shape how he or she both selects
and interprets a text or an image.

These intellectual developments have left Christianity haunted
by 'Truth' tests. Theologians, used to appealing to authorities to
support or prove their Truth claims, whether the Bible, revelation,
ecclesiastical proclamation or historical tradition, have been left
bemoaning the 'decline' of such certainty. Multiple truths have
been seen as a problem, not a benefit. As feminists engaged in
debate about Christianity, it seems that we have too readily
inherited this anxiety about 'Truth' tests: hence we have asked
ourselves (and each other) whether Christianity is 'True' for
women, without asking whether that is a question we want to ask,
and without questioning the question!

For example, feminists have, over the last few decades,
repeatedly asked: does Christianity pass the test as liberating for
women or not? As Christianity has had rather a bad track record
in its depiction and treatment of women, many feminists, not
surprisingly, have discussed the negative images of women in
Christianity and their impact on our lives. Post-Christian feminists
such as Mary Daly and Daphne Hampson have regarded these
images as important reasons for leaving Christianity. But such an
approach tends, for example, to lump together notions of Eve as
temptress and the Virgin Mary as impossibly perfect mother,
without any attention to the interpreters or interpretations of
those images, and thus how those images have functioned at
particular moments in history and in widely varying cultures. It is
a deeply ahistorical approach, ignoring the ways in which a sign
(be it textual or visual) can have multiple meanings. A brief look at
some historical and contemporary examples will illustrate my
point.

Many of us in this post-Freudian world, where our sexual drives
are seen as 'natural', would think of asceticism, especially for
women, in rather negative terms. But Peter Brown's important
work on the significance of virginity in the fourth and fifth centuries, the golden age of asceticism in the church, indicates how
liberating the renunciation of marriage and sexual activity may
have been for women who came from bourgeois families: they

were freed from a social system in which they were merely objects of financial exchange and producers of heirs. To convert to Christianity and live in an ascetic community were radical social acts. The ascetic life represented 'the withdrawal of the person from the claims of society'.[2] For women, society's claims were, primarily, marriage and child-bearing.

This historical example throws into relief our own pre-suppositions and illustrates how ideas have different meanings according to the historical and social context in which they were placed. Symbols and ideas mean different things to different people. The varying ways in which different women have inter-preted the significance of Jesus' maleness also illustrate this point. White feminists have argued that because Jesus, the Christ, is a man, Christianity is necessarily oppressive for women.[3] They ask the question: can a male saviour save women? Some have responded to this by imagining the Christ figure as female: the artist Edwina Sandys did this in her *Christa* statue (a female Christ-figure hanging on a cross), displayed in the Cathedral of St John the Divine in New York City in 1984. For some women, this was a liberating symbol. Hampson comments: 'The fact that such a statue could be produced, and was apparently meaningful to women, shows something of women's yearning in their religion in a culture which is now deeply conscious of feminist issues.'[4] For others, the *Christa* image could not be liberating in a culture which is so violent towards women. Margaret Miles writes:

Edwina Sandys' *Christa* illustrates the danger of appropriating the naked female form to present women's experience ... The image startles; it makes vivid the perennial suffering of women. As a private devotional image it may have great healing potential for women who have themselves been battered or raped. Yet as a public image ... the *Christa*, by its visual association with the crucified Christ, glorifies the suffering of women in a society in which violence against women has reached epidemic proportions.[5]

A different answer is given to the same question as to whether a male saviour can save women in the work of the African-American theologian Jacquelyn Grant. She shows us how Christ's *maleness* is a white woman's issue. The Jesus figure has meant something different to women in Black American churches. Historically, African-American Christian women have seen Jesus, writes Grant, as 'the divine co-sufferer, who empowers them in situations of oppression'. They identified with Jesus because they believed

that Jesus identified with them. Grant continues: 'As Jesus was
persecuted and made to suffer undeservedly, so were they.' And
further: 'This culminated in the crucifixion. Their crucifixion
included rape and their babies being sold. But Jesus' suffering was
not the suffering of a mere human, for Jesus was understood to be
God incarnate.' This is quite different from the white woman's
inability to identify with a male saviour. Rather, Jesus is seen as
one who empowers the weak: identification with him is so strong
that 'Jesus Christ becomes black'.[6] Here, then, are clear illustra-
tions of the principle that it matters who is doing the interpreting.

If we look at the work and lives of women, including feminists,
who have decided to remain Christian and have selected as central
to their faith certain liberating Christian texts and images, we see
that they have encountered a related but further problem. They
have tended to ignore the fact that knowledge is linked to power,
and thus the ways in which those more liberating texts and images
have been left behind in the market-place of ideas. Not all interpretations hold equal weight in a given culture. Many of us
have been left out of the interpreting process (or at least the
interpreting process which has been recorded) because of our
gender, ethnicity, class or other social factors. No wonder, then,
that negative ideas about the nature and role of woman have been
prevalent in Christian culture: women have had little say as to
who we are as Christians, as human beings created by God. Who
is able to declare that certain interpretations, or truths (with a
small t) are the Truth is determined by the exercise of power.
Michel Foucault's insights about the operation of power in the
dissemination of knowledge are important at this juncture:

> Truth is a thing of this world; it is produced only by virtue of
> multiple forms of constraint. And it induces regular effects of
> power. Each society has its regime of truth, its 'general politics'
> of truth: that is, the types of discourse which it accepts and
> makes function as true; the mechanisms and instances which
> enable one to distinguish true and false statements; the means
> by which each is sanctioned; the techniques and procedures
> accorded value in the acquisition of truth; the status of those
> who are charged with saying what counts as true.[7]

The following historical examples will illustrate this complex
point about the relationship between power and knowledge.

Throughout the history of Christianity, it is easy to locate
examples of women who have sought out biblical texts which
would allow them a greater role in the church and in society as a

whole. Very often such women have been a part of groups declared heretical, such as the Montanists in the second century (amongst whom there were female prophets); or the Lollards in late medieval England who offered women a chance to teach and preach. Once such groups are declared to be heretical, the force of their more liberating gospel message for women is necessarily eclipsed. Similarly, women have often been prominent in the early days of new and radical Christian sects, but once those sects have become established churches, women's voices and actions have been suppressed. Sometimes when the seat (and, thus, the balance) of political power shifts, women have been offered a chance to speak and act – but a further shift of such power often quickly eclipses the activity of women. The civil war in mid seventeenth-century England (when there was no established church) was a time when many radical Christian groups, such as the Quakers, flourished. Within these groups women taught, preached and played a part in expounding radical religious and political ideas. Once the monarchy and the Church of England were restored in 1660, many of those sects sought respectability as dissenting churches, and the activities of women were curtailed. Similarly, the early days of a church – when it is essentially at odds with the establishment – can witness the prominence of women, a prominence which is later squashed as the church becomes more established.[8]

We can see that it is not so much a question as to whether it is possible to be both a feminist and a Christian. *That* is perfectly plausible, if, for example, certain biblical texts are selected over others; or in certain cultural contexts where the adoption of particular Christian beliefs presents to women the possibility of liberation, over and against a harsher secular reality. Indeed, for many of us this compatibility is more than plausible: a message of liberation is central to the Gospels. Rather, the issue is whether, in any given context, such interpretations of Christianity – as essentially a message of equality and justice for women and men, indeed for people of all ethnicities, classes and cultures – will hold sway in cultures dominated by people for whom such a gospel of liberation is dangerous to their own control of knowledge and retention of power. For example, while many Christians have claimed that a male apostolic succession represents the Truth and have thus excluded women from the priesthood, other readers of the Scriptures, highlighting the prominence of women in the early Christian world and the significance of Mary Magdalene and the other women as the first witnesses to the empty tomb on Easter morning, might argue for the inclusion of women in ministry and priesthood. The historical examples I have already given of groups such as the Lollards, who were declared heretical, or the recent struggle in the Church of England over the ordination of women, indicate that the exercise of power is deeply implicated in the holding and 'exercise' of knowledge.

How then might we begin to establish our varied and various interpretations of Christianity as potentially compatible with certain forms of feminism in a world in which ideas of equality, justice and liberation are marginalized? For those of us who read the gospel as being about justice, and who experience a relationship with God *both* in personal spiritual growth and in building the kingdom of heaven on earth, to begin to answer such questions is an act of Christian faith. The question of the compatibility of Christianity and feminism is not just intellectual, not just political, but cuts to the core of my faith. Do I have enough faith that Christianity is so profoundly about God loving all human beings, and that my task as a Christian is to try to help build a more just society on this earth, that I will endure the ensuing marginalization which occurs both within the church and in the broader society because such belief and action is so threatening to so many people? This is a central faith issue presented to Christian feminists by questions concerning the compatibility of Christianity and feminism. We must claim the truth of the Christian message as essentially liberating for women and all others who have been marginalized, rather than allow the interpretations of those who would like to see us shut up and go away qualify as the only 'real' Christianity.

II

For the remainder of this essay, I shall address some of the implications of this complex compatibility issue by thinking about how Christian women can put our faith into practice in one particular context – the doing of theology. In this key area, women's voices have barely been present. Why have there been no significant female theologians? Or have there been such women? These questions require us to address complex questions about female subjectivity, knowledge and power, and to think through issues (much debated in the last two or three decades) about the cultural construction of gender and questions of authorship. I shall talk here about Christian culture, but my comments may apply to those feminist theologians who have left Christianity behind.

Throughout the history of Christianity *men* have been constructed as capable of speaking and writing about the transcendent. Therefore, men have been theologians. While men have been seen as the bearers and declarers of universal Truths, women have never been seen to speak in universal terms; for women themselves have been defined as exceptions to the universal. (Think here of the debates which still occur around inclusive language in the liturgy, and the oft-made claim that 'man' stands for all human beings.) Women's truths have been seen as partial, while men have remained blind to the particularity of their truth claims, and thus to the partiality of their theological systems.

Therefore women have rarely, if ever, been defined as theologians. Women who have written about religion have been seen as mystics; or when they have engaged with ideas debated by men in the universities, they have been categorized (both then and now) as women of letters or, occasionally, as philosophers, even when their ideas have clearly been about God, God's relationship to human beings and this creation, and matters of faith. Let me give an example. In the seventeenth century, a number of educated women in Europe, but particularly in England and France, engaged with Descartes' philosophy and its impact on Christian theology and the newly emerging science. These women included Anne Conway, whose work influenced Leibniz; Damaris Masham, friend and patron of John Locke; and Mary Astell, the feminist and High Church writer. Their work has either gone unrecognized or has been described as philosophy or literature – even when the work of their male associates, touching on exactly the same themes, was (and still is) described as theology! Because they were women and lay people, it has not been possible for us to think of these women as theologians. In the British tradition, theologians have been university-trained, ordained men. Women were excluded from formal university education until the nineteenth century, and women are only now being ordained in the Church of England, in the latter part of the twentieth century. Women have not, historically, been allowed to speak, in their own voices, as theologians, about God.

Of course women have spoken and written about God, and their talk about God has been recognized as such. But how? Often, such talk has been given legitimacy by others because women have spoken in voices other than their own; that is, they have been seen as vessels of the spirit. There have been many female mystics, and figures like Julian of Norwich and Teresa of Avila have been much glorified, though such glorification should not blind us to the constant testing to which women mystics have been subjected by the church.[9] The history of Christianity in western Europe and the Americas abounds with examples of women channelling the voice of God as prophets, or possessed by the Holy Spirit or spirits.

Women have been attracted to sects and religious denominations which rely on the authority of revelation or the guidance of an inner light, such as the Quakers.[10] Mid and late nineteenth-century England and North America saw the growth of spiritualism and the popularity of parlour seances; the most famous and successful spiritualist mediums were young women.

What appeals to women about speaking in a voice other than their own is that they can find a voice in a culture in which they are not formally allowed to speak publicly, while simultaneously abdicating responsibility for such subversive behaviour. The 'voice' can be said to belong to God, or to a/the spirit: the woman is merely the vessel or the mouthpiece. How conscious these women were of the subversive nature of their behaviour is difficult to assess. But while this practice or strategy temporarily gives a voice to women, it frequently serves to keep in place certain ideals about how women should behave. Women could speak out loud and engage in theatrical behaviour in the seance, for example, but once they left that arena their status rarely changed.[11]

Women have, then, been seen as vessels for an *embodied* experience of the divine, not as people who could *think* about God, or even *think* systematically about such embodied religious experiences. This should not surprise us: in the mind–body split which has been so persistent in western culture, the 'feminine' has been associated with the body, while the 'masculine' has been associated with the mind. 'Reason' has been thought to be a male quality. Conversely, woman has been associated not only with the body but also with nature, and thus with that which must be controlled, analysed and thought about by the reasoning mind. This association of men with reason is especially problematic in our post-Enlightenment world, where reason has been put at the centre of intellectual endeavour. In many ways, the Enlightenment period saw the construction of the Man of Reason *par excellence*: man saw himself at the centre of the universe, coming to under-stand, by his rational faculties, the workings of an ordered world, created by a rational God. This means that, in the modern world, the 'feminine' came increasingly to be associated with the irrat-ional, the body and nature, and was constructed as sharply different from the 'masculine'.[12] (I am writing, here, of the 'feminine' and 'masculine' and of 'woman' and 'man' as socially, culturally and psychically constructed categories, not of truths about women and men.) Furthermore, this occurred at a time when Christian theology was coming to depend more on reason as one of its key premises (as revelation came to be questioned, and as historically based biblical criticism and scientific work cast doubt upon early presuppositions about the foundations of Christianity). Where, then, could there be a space for women to understand themselves – constructed and disciplined as 'feminine' – as rational, theological thinkers?[13]

We need to ask: how can women forge our identities as people of faith who are gendered as female and think about God? How is that possible when our religious experiences and ideas have been read as mystical, as signs of possession or prophecy, as healing gifts, but not as theology? How do we retain all those vital elements of religious experience, profound components of our relationship with God, and at the same time write and speak theologically? In many ways I am asking an old question – how do we relate the life of the mind to the life of the spirit? – but I am adding the twist of gender. Is it possible for women, constructed as 'feminine', to incorporate and embrace all of these elements: the spiritual, the intellectual, and embodied religious experience? More fundamental than the question of the possible compatibility of feminism and Christianity is this complex set of questions about the (in)compatibility of being a woman, a thinker and a person of Christian faith. Let me tell a couple of stories to illustrate *this* 'compatibility' issue.

I recently read Susan Howatch's series of Starbridge novels about the Church of England. The first I quite enjoyed: I found the exploration of the spiritual, psychological and intellectual make-up of these Church of England clergymen very interesting. By the second novel, I was becoming suspicious: where were the women, who might have equally complex spiritual and intellectual lives? Could *they* ever have spiritual directors who would guide them through the complexities of their psychic life, their spiritual growth, their sexuality and their theological thinking? By the third novel, I realized that the female characters were doomed to being good vicars' wives and unsuitable priests' mistresses, cardboard caricatures of women who could be wheeled on and off stage as and when the clergyman protagonist needed to consider his sexuality. By the fourth novel, I was furious: the protagonist of that novel is a woman who has an affair with the local dean, but she is never allowed the spiritual growth granted to that muddled clergyman. At the end of the affair, she is simply married off to an unsuitable vicar and lives unhappily ever after. She is always caught in the aftermath of a 'bad' affair, with little possibility of redemption. As we discover in the fifth novel, she is doomed to being an empty socialite.

Whether Howatch herself is blind to this set of gender differences or whether she is simply portraying realistically the early and mid twentieth-century Church of England does not really matter. The point is that it is the ordained men who are allowed to integrate the life of the mind, the life of the spirit and the life of the body and emotions. As these characters develop their theology, they also work out their attitudes towards their sexuality, their families and their ministry (usually with the aid of a life-changing retreat and an excellent spiritual director). The female characters are mothers, wives, girlfriends and mistresses who are always associated with the body: women's bodies are needed either as bodies with which these important clergymen have sex or as the bodies which give birth to yet more important clergymen. These women are not portrayed as having either spiritual or intellectual depth, let alone as having any integration of these different parts of the self.

The dilemmas and contradictions faced by women who attempt to think about God and practise a Christian faith, in a culture dominated by the sorts of 'feminine' tropes and images present in Howatch's novels, are demonstrated in a short autobiographical piece by Roberta Bondi. She has written of her experience of being a woman, trained as a theologian, asking the 'complex and painful question': 'What is the relationship between the life of the intellect and the life of the spirit?' In college and seminary she realized that there were gender divisions in the attaining and expressing of knowledge:

> The whole scheme of rationality depended upon a hierarchical division of the human race into the 'thinkers' and the 'feelers'. Men were the thinkers, the powerful ones, the objective carriers of the higher powers who thought about the big issues. Women were the feelers, the carriers of emotion, the enemy of rationality, the ones who lived in the realm of everyday, particular experience.

The relationship between her academic study of Christianity and her understanding and experience of God came to be 'far from straightforward'. In a world where 'reason was objective, and universally verifiable, emotion was dangerously subjective'. Emotions and experience – apparently standing in opposition to conclusions arrived at by rational means – had to be discounted. She came to believe 'simultaneously in three mutually contradictory gods'. The first was the Christian God of her Protestant childhood, 'who continued to grip my guilty imagination with threats of love, images of judgement, and demands of belief'. The second was the liberal God of the academic world: civilized, distant, 'the very embodiment of all the supposedly male virtues academics, including myself, admired: rationality, unemotionality, justice, and impartiality'. This God was the 'supreme rejection of "female" emotionality, particularity, partiality and spirituality ... Belief in this God necessarily entailed the repudiation of myself as female.' The third God was 'the almost secret, private God' whom she had begun to encounter in her readings of the Hebrew Bible, a God whom, she knew in an instant, 'delighted in creation, in light, in water and mountains, in fruit-bearing trees and grasses, in water creatures, and slithering things, in wild animals and tame, in men and most important for me, in women like me'.

It was this God that Bondi encountered five years later, when working on her doctoral thesis at Oxford. Having decided, for all intents and purposes, to be a 'rational man', she was burying herself in what she saw as the *academic* christological controversies of the fifth century. While reading a sermon by one of the founders of Egyptian and Syrian monasticism, she 'once again came face to face' with the God she had encountered in the Hebrew texts, and now 'this God was wearing an unmistakably Christian face'. It was the God 'who sees the whole of who we are and who we have been, who understands the depths of our temptations and the extent of our sufferings'. Thus Bondi gradually came to put together the theological, the spiritual and the emotional. 'Slowly, slowly I began to learn that the God of the monks was the God of the Christological texts. Something was happening to me as my heart began to make the connections the university was breaking.' It was a connection which sent her into (temporary) crisis, retreat with Anglican Benedictines in Oxfordshire, and which finally led her to the realization that 'for the teachers of the early church, rational thought – especially about God or about other people – is only rational when it is also loving'.[14]

Bondi's narrative, in its struggle with theological beliefs, academic study and personal issues, the reaching of a crisis and going on retreat in a religious house, and the resulting attempt to bring together the spiritual, emotional and intellectual, has striking parallels with the stories of the male characters of Howatch's novels. And yet, Bondi's is a story which is necessarily inflected by a *conscious* understanding of the constructions of gender which dominate our culture. In sharp contrast, the men of Howatch's novels never reflect upon their 'masculinity' in order to integrate their faith, their experience and their theology: it is a given that as men they can bring these things together.

What, then, can we learn from these stories about how to go

forward as women committed to a spiritual life which integrates both the intellectual and the experiential? Is there the possibility of compatibility? One clear answer is, that in order for there to be any possibility of such compatibility, we must get beyond the rational–irrational and male–female split. If we do not, we shall be caught in a world of 'mutually contradictory gods', as was Bondi when she tried to shape herself wholly as a rational (male) theologian in opposition to the emotional and personal parts of herself. We need to get out of that binary, to *deconstruct* it.

I use the term deconstruction deliberately because I want to see if it can be helpful in this context. Deconstruction has had rather a bad rap in theological circles, both from its enemies and, I would contend, from some of its supporters. Part of a broader movement of recent French thought generally referred to as post-structuralism, deconstruction is a radical reading strategy (employed especially by Jacques Derrida), aimed at reading a text against itself. It symbolizes for many theologians, even liberal theologians, the end of the line, because it seems to imply destruction. Certainly poststructuralism undermines even further the possibility of universal Truths because it shows that not only is the knower or interpreter of knowledge always positioned, but that knowledge, too, is partial. In particular, poststructuralists have shown how language does not simply describe 'reality out there' but, rather, language actually constitutes reality and, in turn, is constituted by that reality. For example, poststructuralists have consistently pointed out that how we think and feel and act, who we become and how we understand ourselves as women and men, as black and white, depends not on fixed universal or 'natural' meanings of the terms woman or man or black or white, but on the meanings given to those terms in particular, time-bound, cultures.

It is possible that such insights could help us 'undo' or deconstruct the rational–irrational, male–female, mind–body sets of binaries. Many Anglo-American feminists would agree with me as to the potentially liberating and political possibilities for feminists of employing poststructuralism: the adoption of poststructuralist thought by feminist theorists in the last few years has been phenomenal.[15] Yet there are others who urge caution in this area, pointing out that such an undoing of the Enlightenment self, such as this work represents, leaves women without such possibility of a 'self' just at the moment when we are struggling to build our 'selves'.[16]

The work of some male theologians, such as Don Cupitt and Mark Taylor, who have adopted poststructuralism, illustrates these hazards for feminists. Their work emphasizes the 'death' of God and the 'death' of the self, with Cupitt, for example, advocating that we become 'self-less' and 'emptied-out' via 'anti-realism'.[17] But neither Cupitt nor Taylor pays any attention to the question as to whose self or whose God has 'died'. Women (and others who have been marginalized) have not been allowed a subject position which would allow them the authority or agency which this 'dying self' apparently had, and thus no official say about who or what God is. Such an approach ignores a central component of poststructuralist thought as it has been developed, especially, by feminist and African-American scholars in recent years: that is, we are always located in certain places and times, and therefore necessarily have views, positions and convictions.

The critique ('death' or 'loss') of the Enlightenment self does not involve pretending that we can be without a 'self'; instead, it challenges the notion that such a self is either universal or natural, providing a heightened awareness of the particularity of that self. The 'deconstruction' of such an Enlightenment self allows us to see how such a self is shaped in culture, and thus to see it as one of many 'selves'. This process of deconstruction is therefore about the production of meanings, rather than destruction or loss. For those who were never constructed as such rational selves – which is just about everyone who is not an educated white man – this 'deconstructive' move potentially offers a liberation into selves who *can* write and speak in ways which have not previously been possible. The 'loss' of the Enlightenment self is a loss for those who have gained by it for so long; it is not a loss for the rest of us, and should not be framed as such.[18] Thus, deconstruction leads many of us not to the end of theology (*pace* Cupitt, Taylor, et al.) but to the beginning.

How then is it possible for women to have a subject position such that we can think, speak and write theologically, and simultaneously have a spiritual life which is healthily connected to the psyche, body and emotions, when the characteristics of woman have been constructed as incompatible with the qualities which constitute an apparently legitimate theologian; that is, male, rational, often clerical, disembodied and supposedly neutral? The poststructuralist critique of an Enlightenment, rational, self is helpful for women (and others constructed as being on the side of irrationality) because it lays bare the ways in which human beings have been constructed as 'female' and 'male', as embodied and disembodied, as feelers and thinkers, as those who experience God in an emotional way and as those who can think and write about God in a systematic way. Such a critique shows that qualities apparently required for the writing of theology are only arbitrarily assigned to men rather than to women, though that arbitrariness is deeply associated with the wielding and retention of power. Who gets to speak and write publicly about God is a political matter; it is about power. Conversely, the association of woman with the body and emotions, whereby our experiences of God are assigned to the realm of mysticism, possession and the like, rather than formal theology, is also at one level arbitrary and at another level thoroughly related to the exercise of power.

Thus, while the question of the possible compatibility of feminism and Christianity seems to me to be a relatively easy one, the practical living out of that takes us into the more difficult terrain of how to rethink our identities as women and men; how to rethink who is a theologian and why. Ideas about gender and God are so deeply embedded in our culture at large, and in our individual and collective psyches, and they are so profoundly related to the exercise of power, that such rethinking entails a greater set of tasks than one might at first think. These matters are already being challenged by what is happening in the world of theology and the life of the church. The last two or three decades have witnessed not only the rise of feminist theology in the USA and Europe, but also the development of liberation theologies in Latin America, Black theologies in the USA and parts of Africa, and Minjung theology in Korea. Such movements represent the *public* articulation of indigenous theological reflection in the face of the predominant idea that theologians are white, educated, rational men, usually from the West. Furthermore, theologians are grappling with issues of suffering and injustice – such as sexual abuse, domestic violence, addiction, the ways in which we neglect people with HIV and AIDS – and are thus beginning to give voice to the previously voiceless from our own communities, while also urging many of us to examine our assumptions and prejudices about the body, sexuality and gender.

Let me take an example of great relevance to my own church. The average Anglican is now black and female. What would it mean for us to make central to the life and mission of the Anglican Church the theological reflections of such women, when the male English clerics who populate Howatch's novels are still seen to be at the centre of the church, even though they are very much in the minority? In what ways would this require us to 'deconstruct' our ideas not only about gender and theology but also concerning race, ethnicity and mission?

I persist in using the term deconstruction because I think that the production of multiple readings of the Christian tradition is a way forward into the rethinking of our identities, such as I see called forth by the gospel message of justice for all humanity. At the heart of Christianity, for me, is the gospel command to love my neighbour as myself, and that means loving and accepting people for who they are rather than who I think they should be. This requires creating the conditions whereby people of both genders and all classes and ethnicities can become their fullest possible selves in relationship with God. And I believe that one of the most remarkable things about Christianity is that it can not only bear the contradictions and complexities of multiple understandings of what it means to be fully human, but that it embraces such multiplicity.

Such a rethinking of and through our identities is necessary if we are not to fall into the kind of crisis which befell Bondi when, in order to write theologically, she tried to take on the male rational subject position and ignored the emotional, the spiritual and the embodied. In this process of rethinking, I do not imagine that we shall arrive at any easy compatibility between feminism and Christianity, and I do not think that that should be our goal. I shall never find myself agreeing with all the church's doctrines and political positions, and yet I can still find myself spiritually nourished and sustained by regular attendance at worship and participation in Christian communities. Furthermore, by suggesting alternative understandings of, and roles for, men and women, in presenting our experiences and thinking about God *as theology*, and in trying to integrate the rational, the spiritual and the embodied, we shall be challenging the 'status of those who are charged with saying what counts as true' (Foucault) in our Christian communities and in the church at large. This is not a comfortable position to be in: the incompatibilities and conflicts may seem impossible at times. But staying with such a stance is a matter of faith if we believe that the gospel calls us to build the kingdom of heaven on earth, to seek justice in all that we do, because God so loved the world that he sent his only begotten Son. And so finally I ask not whether Christianity is viable for feminists, but whether Christianity is viable without feminists and the multiple voices, work and perspectives of other marginalized groups; whether the church can, in good conscience, fail to acknowledge that such work is indeed theology?

5

RADICAL PASSION: A FEMINIST LIBERATION THEOLOGY

Julie Hopkins

In this essay I shall argue that it is possible to hold a Christian feminist position. I realize, however, that for many women this has proved impossible to maintain and I respect their decision to abandon Christianity. I understand feminism as the political movement of women who, by applying an analysis of the inequality of power between the sexes to their culture, society and personal relationships, hope to develop a new female historical subjectivity beyond or on the boundaries of patriarchy.

Christianity is the dominant religion in the West and as such has played a leading role in morally prescribing and symbolically structuring this inequality of power. Thus to find a bridge between feminism and Christianity it is necessary to believe that, on the one hand, feminism cannot succeed in its ultimate goals without grounding its analysis, ethics and praxis in a transcendental dimension of women's experience and, on the other hand, that there is a radical form of Christianity that is in solidarity with those seeking such a divine ground for their lives. I will try to show that feminist liberation theology offers such a pilgrimage into the transcendent dimension of women's lives and experiences. This critical faith rejects the sexist ideology and patriarchal structures of much of the Christian church, past and present, and yet claims continuity with the western spiritual tradition of reflecting upon reality in the light of the symbolic story of the life, death and resurrection of Jesus, the Christian's Messiah (Christ).

To make my argument clear, I shall first discuss my understanding of embodied spirituality and the method of theologizing and praxis which forms the basis of a Christian feminist liberation theology. In the second part of the essay, I shall take the central theme of salvation to demonstrate how women, through reflection upon their experiences of oppression and liberation, can move beyond criticism and deconstruction towards a reconstruction of the heart of Christian theology. I hope to show that it is possible to centre one's life simultaneously in the liberative power of the story of the life, death and resurrection of Jesus and in the contemporary struggle for female subjectivity and for personal and political equality.

To turn first to a consideration of embodied spirituality, which is the hallmark of liberation theologizing. I believe that Christian feminist spirituality is breaking down the boundaries between contemplation and action, between the mysticism of the Subject in God and the political and moral agenda for justice. Women who claim to be church whilst simultaneously rejecting the exclusively male language and androcentric world-view of Christian liturgy, doctrine and morality are women engaged on a pilgrimage into the heart of faith beyond structures and images. Groping tentatively in the darkness for the God beyond male projections, their journey is both a search for authentic subjectivity and a political revolution. Every step towards integrity which they take, in the face of pressure to conform and obey, is a moment of becoming and a political action of dissent. I understand this form of prophetic-mystical spirituality as living daily in a field of creative tension between feminism and Christianity.

This life and spirituality appears from the outside as at best paradoxical and at worst chaotic. Perhaps it is an illogical way of being, suspended between faith and doubt, hope and despair; however, I believe that it has its own internal logic and integrity and can offer a grounding for a creative and transformative life. This life-style of creative tension can be described in various ways. Rosemary Radford Ruether describes it as a dialectical movement between institutional religion and its prophetic edge.[1] She claims that this dialectic is the basic pattern of biblical religion. In this sense Christian feminists are part of a 'prophetic-messianic trajectory' in history. Ruether uses the word dialectic because she wishes to emphasize that God is revealed as acting in history precisely at the points where religious order and tradition and the prophecy of the oppressed clash. But each pole of the dialectic, institutional religion and the prophetic edge, needs the other. It is not a question of 'either/or', but of the tension between the two.

Another way of thinking of creative tension is to compare it with the way in which religious metaphors work. Sallie McFague has shown how the parables and praxis of Jesus may be thought of as metaphors.[2] By metaphor she means the setting together of a familiar image with a less familiar one to create a new experience of reality. Metaphors have the power to shock us by undermining conventional thinking precisely through the creative tension between the two images which they juxtapose. A metaphor can evoke a religious experience which transcends our language; it breaks open reality, disclosing new possibilities. Christian feminists who live and speak in the creative tension between old images of God and new ones are, one may say, living metaphors.

I find that the most useful way to describe the creative tension of Christian feminism is to speak of a paradigm shift. A paradigm in science is both the accepted model of the universe which structures the way in which scientists ask questions and probe for answers and the scientific community which is answerable to the model. Paradigms begin to disintegrate when new approaches to reality undermine the credibility and mind-set of a research tradition. This happened for example to Newtonian physics when Einstein propounded his quantum theory. The shift from one paradigm to another is a long and painful period of readjustment and tension. Elisabeth Schüssler Fiorenza has argued that feminism is a new paradigm; it is developing a new understanding of knowledge (epistemology) and new principles of interpreting reality (hermeneutics).[3] Feminist theory and praxis are now set implacably against the old western paradigm of patriarchy but they are not yet fully independent. It is a time of tension, a shifting of the paradigm.

In a similar way, many liberation theologians from the Third World have spoken of an 'epistemological break' with western forms of knowledge and belief. Sharon Welch, a feminist liberation theologian, has described this in terms of a new understanding of truth.[4] Traditionally in the patriarchal West, truth has been considered an objective reality, to be deduced through reason and logic and then tested empirically. Élite councils of men who wielded power in the church, or science or politics have claimed that their objectivity is God-given, corresponding with metaphysical laws. Welch argues that this understanding of knowledge, far from being value-free, is a strategy undertaken in order to dominate; for so-called objective reality is in fact laden with the presuppositions and prejudices of those who hold hegemonies of power and who project these onto a fictitious universal abstract *tabula rasa*. Welch agrees with the French philosopher Michel Foucault that westerners should give up the pretension of speaking in universal and dogmatic categories and recognize that a just and peaceful future lies with a new epistemology, which she names the 'political economy of truth', in which every group, class, race, sex and religion has the right to name for themselves what is true and liberating. The voices and memories of the silenced, ignored and oppressed are now being heard, demanding a dialogue between different contextual truths, and not the domination of a monolithic positivistic 'truth'. This they say is the only way to achieve honest communication, co-existence and global justice.

How can one give a religious and moral form to this spirituality of creative tension? I should choose Christian feminist liberation theology, which is a method, a way of 'doing' theology. Its starting-point is that women should reflect theologically and act prophetically out of their own experience and context. In practice this is extremely difficult to accomplish because 'woman' as a gender has been socially constructed; she is artificially created through language, upbringing, culture and religion. For a woman to speak with her own voice, to name the world through her own experience and to forge her own historical subjectivity, is the beginning of a new anthropology (the science of the nature of the human being). For a woman to attempt this on her own would be a recipe for madness or despair. This is why so much emphasis is put by women upon the women's movement and the development of feminist analysis in the fields of psychology, sociology, history, literature, the natural sciences and theology. 'Women's Studies' offers a broader and well-researched perspective to ground each woman's personal journey into the unknown.

The need for such a feminist sense of solidarity and knowledge is borne out by my own experience with the Baptist denomination. When I left theological seminary (with a first-class degree and a disintegrated sense of identity and faith) I had no knowledge of feminist analysis or the women's movement. I assumed that there was something fundamentally wrong with me; that I was, in the words of a male Baptist superintendent, 'too neurotic, too radical and a woman'. For a time I lived with the homeless in central London, not so much because I felt a mission to help them, but because I felt one of them, an outcast who did not fit into church or society. Finally, in spite of considerable opposition from the headquarters of my denomination, a congregation in Cardiff invited me to be their pastor. It was the beginning of an extremely happy and fruitful time. This small Baptist church encouraged me to grow and act in my own way, to develop my feminist awareness and links whilst sharing with them in the pilgrimage of faith within the context of the inner city. Together we analysed the political and social situation, developed projects, prayed, studied, celebrated life and mourned the dead. In the back streets of Cardiff I discovered the world where God is revealed, in the meeting of races, classes, rich and poor, Muslim and Jew, mentally ill and 'sane', children and the elderly. My development as a feminist theologian grew out of those years and the vision that I glimpsed there.

During those years of creative tension between my Christian faith and my growing feminism, I began to understand ecclesiology (the nature of the church) in a new way. I have come to share the view of those sociologists of religion who regard the basic communal religious experience as a feeling of solidarity in the light of an awareness of cosmic powers. People bond together through ritual and myth to approach the transcendent dimension of life. This gives meaning to their lives and instills a sense of happiness, comfort and collective power. So, for example, people in a Baptist congregation make a covenant with each other to practise a basic form of democracy and mutual support in order to facilitate a common act of worship. They want to worship together because they believe that, in spite of all evidence to the contrary, God is good and therefore God can save. For Christians, this fundamental belief, and the life-style necessary to underpin it, is encapsulated in the form of a symbolic story about Jesus of Nazareth. At its best, a local church can be a sign within its community that the worship of God is the highest form of human activity and that the renewal of life, society and nature flows from this praxis. At its worst, a local church can, by preaching a gospel of intolerance, absolutism and world-denial, ferment the alienation and breakdown of a fragile neighbourhood.

It could be argued that I have reduced the church to a function which could equally well be fulfilled by a Jewish, Buddhist or indeed Aboriginal tribal community; apart from the story of Jesus of Nazareth there is nothing particularly Christian. Where in my description is the understanding of the priesthood, the sacraments, the gifts of the Spirit or the Word? I would argue that every religious community has a tradition of reflection and practice concerning the means of grace; that is to say, as to how the unmerited love and power of God is channelled amongst us. But if one takes an honest look at the variety of rituals, liturgies, mortalities, structures of authority and sacramental theologies in the ecumenical worldwide church, then one is forced to recognize how culturally and contextually bound these are. Indeed I would go so far as to agree with Ruether when she argues that even our belief in the life, death and resurrection of Jesus is contextually bound.[5] Christian faith belongs to particular historical groups of believers who, through tradition and choice, name themselves followers of Jesus, their Christ. I choose to be part of such a believing community because, for me, the symbolic story of Jesus still provides a gateway into the presence of God, a moral and political agenda and a utopian vision which empowers me as a feminist in a Christian-influenced culture.

I cannot accept that such an understanding of particularity and contextual truth relativizes Christianity to the point of absurdity. I am a woman, white, western, feminist, socialist, Protestant and middle-class. These are particular facts that are not only essential to my sense of identity but also the source of my power. My integrity, spirituality and politics must stem from these components, however much I am also part of a universal order of human beings. If I try to deny or ignore these elements of race, sex, class and religion, I cannot possibly have a standpoint to communicate or begin to share power with someone who is different. A Christian church which wishes to communicate with the wider secular society, or with different ideologies and religions, must first clearly describe its particular context, traditions and beliefs. Also, in theological discourse, how can one talk about universal hopes for salvation and the means of liberation unless one first listens to what this might mean to individuals or groups from a particular sex, culture, income or religious background?

To have the freedom to redefine the nature of the church using these kinds of insights based upon experience finally requires trust in one's own insights and knowledge of the Bible and Christian tradition. I contend that every Christian woman has the right to these mediums of revelation; in other words, every Christian woman can have a prophetic voice. However, she must realize that the dominant forms of her religion, past and present, deny or ignore the reality of the female presence. For example, in Roman Catholic, Orthodox and some Anglican churches, men of different races, classes and cultures may be ordained priest but women may not. The reason for this is not simply a question of custom or cultural influence: it lies in the very construction of Christian symbolism and dogma. This means that, in her prophetic struggle for authenticity, freedom and a theological voice in the church at this time, a woman's female subjectivity is the most important element in her identity. Female experience of, on the one hand, socio-economic, physical and psychological oppression, and, on the other hand, spiritual insight and power is the prism through which feminist theology evaluates the Scriptures, doctrine, Christian history, tradition and contemporary liturgy.

At this point in history one should not assume that the female contribution to theology is complementary to the dominant male tradition. It is not a question of women adding a few insights from their experience of motherhood to smooth off the rough edges in

the Christian diamond. Women have their own culture. Since the
beginning of history (the invention of writing), women have been
denied access to the public culture of education, politics, priesthood, science and philosophy, the ownership of property and the
means of production. The majority of women in the world are still
in this position. Placed in a patriarchal context where, on the one
hand, they are symbolized as physically weak, irrational, dangerously seductive and morally inadequate and, on the other hand, in
practice they rear and educate their children, sustain the basic
household economy and carry the emotional life of their men and
nation, women have developed strategies for survival and alternative knowledges. These age-long cultures of spirituality, ritual-
making, healing practices, practical wherewithal and physical and
psychological staying power are passed down from mother to
daughter, and from woman to woman through the circles and
networks of what constitute invisible oral traditions.

In this short essay I have attempted to outline the epistemological and methodological presuppositions of a western Christian
feminist liberation theology. We have seen that theologizing in
such a way can be creative, liberative and fulfilling, but the path is
a narrow one. I have argued that female power, self-confidence
and a practical spirituality for our times are only possible if
women work together, analyse and reflect together and prophesy
as the church together.

I shall now turn specifically to the theme of salvation. I take this
theme, which is a central one in all liberation theologies, in order
to demonstrate two things. First that reflection upon the experiences of women by women serves to relativize many Christian
doctrines which are based upon male anthropology, knowledge
and power. But also, second, to show how women's experience
opens up positively the possibility of theological reconstruction.
We shall see that within the Christian tradition there are different
interpretations as to what salvation means, and that women have
new insights to offer to every school of thought and practice.
However, it is within the tradition that considers salvation as a
social experience and promise that women can make the most
positive contribution, for they yearn for liberation in their daily
lives.

Every religion promises its believers salvation from and to
something. Over the centuries Christianity has proclaimed a universal salvation from sin, and promised a new eschatological life
with God in Christ through the work of the Holy Spirit. There
have always been different interpretations as to what precisely this
means. One's understanding of salvation depends upon what one

believes to be negative on the one hand, oppressive, perverse or evil, and, on the other hand, positive, liberative, holy and good. Theological streams within Christianity have focused upon three quite different understandings of salvation, which Ruether has named *cosmological, personal* and *social*.[6] We shall see that feminist theologians have serious criticisms of each of these models in their traditional form.

The longing for *cosmological* salvation springs from a pessimistic world-view. The world of nature, the body, materiality, sexuality and the processes of change are considered to be the signs of a fallen and corrupt creation. The ascetical, monastic and apocalyptic sectarian traditions in Christianity witness to the fact that, historically, the church has had an ambivalent relationship to the natural and secular world. Many sought ways to subdue the flesh and to transcend the givenness of existence, in order to live proleptically the first fruits of the pure spiritual life of the New Creation beyond the end of the world.

Personal salvation typically focuses upon the interior and subjective relationship between the sinner and God. God in Christ knocks at the heart of the repentant sinner, offering forgiveness through the cross and promising the grace of the Holy Spirit. The vocation of the Christian is to walk daily with the Lord, abandoning ego and ambition, fulfilling all the commandments of the Bible, raising a God-fearing family and humbly exercising the gifts of the Spirit in the gatherings and worship of the faithful. The sinner, elected and called, is justified by faith now and for eternity.

The vision of a *social* salvation is an integral part of all liberation theologies. Religious 'base communities' and oppressed groups seek for the signs of the kingdom of God in the political and socio-economic world where the poor and exploited struggle to live and celebrate life. Here transcendence is not so much considered as a dimension outside the world or in the heart of the believer, but is grounded precisely in the secular and profane. Living within a revolutionary praxis which continually seeks ever better approximations of the utopian future of shalom (social justice, peace and harmony), a community of faith can transcend structural evils, breaking through boundaries of oppression.

What do Christian women theologians have to say about these models of salvation? Turning first to the Christian teaching about *cosmological* salvation, Ruether contends that our hope for a redeemed cosmos has been perverted into a morbid obsession with a flight from 'the flesh'. This pathological splitting of the mind or soul from the body is rooted in Greek and Christian androcentric dualistic ideology. In other words, everything that men have considered morally inferior or profane has been associated with 'woman' and the private world that she has been forced to inhabit. Embodiment (that is, the nexus of nature, the material, emotion, feelings, sexuality, fertility, giving birth and suffering) has been symbolized as 'the flesh', the inferior world of the female which is to be transcended by the heroism of the spiritual – or rational, or existential, or scientific – male.[7]

To summarize the research of various feminist theologians: it would appear that 'woman' symbolized as Eve has been made responsible for sin in four dimensions according to the western patristic tradition. She is responsible for the fall into sin of humanity (duetero-Paul, Augustine),[8] the corruption and mortality of creation (Jerome, Augustine),[9] the death of Christ (which takes place in order to rectify the fall (Tertullian),[10] and the introduction of heresy into the church (Jerome).[11] If women were considered such a threat to the spiritual sanctity of men it is not surprising that their presence and their movements were restricted by male ecclesiastical authority. Women who have attempted to act upon their own spiritual authority have been persecuted as heretics, witches or harlots. A virgin may be saved if she offers her body up as a living sacrifice to the church and enters into mystical union with Christ her bridegroom. She must however totally efface her femaleness, becoming, in a popular saying of early Christians, 'a man for the Kingdom of God'.[12]

It may be said of all of us living in the late twentieth century that we are aware of the fragility of the earth. Ecologically our planet has reached the eleventh hour. I contend that we can no longer afford to tolerate the western obsession with transcending the givenness of reality, whether it be through science and technology, escapism through entertainment and drugs, religion or political power-games. The time has now come for some plain speaking in theological circles. Christian cosmological pessimism has alienated us from our world and from each other. Androcentric dualism is a false projection upon the creation which is both good and one interdependent whole. The denial of the intrinsic worth of the female body and of sexuality, which is the power of life, has corrupted and perverted our spirituality. If God exists as anything more than an abstract fantasy, then God must be the ground of life, the connectedness between all forms of energy and matter, the Holy Being who is manifested in the universe.

In my opinion, *cosmological* salvation can only be meaningfully discussed in the context of conceptualizing God as embodied, as immanent and in process of transformation. This is the approach of women theologians as diverse as McFague, Ruether and

Jantzen.[13] Since I was a child I have known this God to be revealed in the movement of the sea. I have never been at home with the eternal Father, Lord, King and static Judge, proclaimed so confidently from a million pulpits. As an adolescent I met my God embodied in a human form as Jesus. As incarnate flesh, brother of my blood and bone, eating and drinking with the marginalized and powerless, hanging as a blasphemer on the cross of the world, the image of God in Jesus spoke to my own emerging physicality and sense of morality.

The crucifixion of Jesus contemplated through the prism of the embodied God offers an insight into the suffering God who is vulnerable to chain saws in the Amazon and to the mental retardation of the hungry child. Here is a vulnerable and loving God who feels and is wounded directly by pain and injustice. The presence of this God, who has abandoned the divine freedom of 'I shall be what I shall be' in a loving gamble for the hearts of humanity, is now in jeopardy. For we have exploited the creative life of our God, forgetting that nature, as well as races and cultures, has a history. Isabel Carter Heyward has powerfully argued that we encounter this God not as a transcendental Lord and Master but through the open, transformative, incarnate power of mutual redemption. The vulnerable life-giving presence of God is a creative energy which can flow between us through our passion for justice in all its myriad forms.[14] The redemption of our world is thus a process that depends upon our openness to the Holy Presence between and around us.

When we turn to the Christian proclamation of *personal* salvation, so emphasized in Protestantism, we see that this too has been the subject of serious criticism by women in recent years. Women who are psychologically conditioned and socially restricted to passive, self-denying and self-sacrificing roles have been told that they are sinners puffed up with pride. They have been enjoined to picture Christ dying on the cross in their place, to repent of their selfishness, and to take up their cross daily. Valerie Saiving, Judith Plaskow and Mary Grey have argued that this form of ethics, with its theological legitimation in a transactional atonement theory, is oppressive to women believers.[15] The sin of women, according to Saiving, is not pride but a lack of self-worth; indeed, a lack of a sense of an organizing centre which may be called a self.[16] Many women too readily offer themselves up to someone else, having such weak ego boundaries; they merge symbiotically with children, husbands, pets, the needy, and vicariously with Christ. Questions need to be asked concerning the link between evangelical preaching and ethics and the problems from which so many women suffer in the field of mental health: obsessive guilt, depression, neurosis and masochistic and manipulative behaviour.

Surely the good news that women need to hear on the personal level is that they have a vocation to be special; a God-given right to be, in their own time, space, feelings, words, thoughts, stories and visions. Each woman is unique and grounded in the divine; each woman is a temple of the Holy Spirit and is a full member of the Body of Christ (in other words she can have a messianic function). Therefore a Christology for women cannot begin with the theological presupposition that passive vicarious suffering is good for us, either because God requires it as a moral duty, or because it is a just punishment for sin. In Christian feminist theology God is not a sadist, Jesus did not go humbly to the cross like a lamb to the slaughter, and women do not have to accept physical and psychological abuse with redemptive patience. A Christ who liberates peoples who have for centuries been pacified, whether they be slaves, Blacks, Indians, Aborigines or women, must be a righteous and angry prophet. (Here I am using the term 'Christ' to refer to the individuals in communities who seek to incarnate the redemptive loving power of God.) She or he is the one who proclaims justice and the day of divine favour and is prepared to live and die to light the flame of a new vision of the kingdom of God. Such messianic figures or movements precisely liberate from fear, guilt, passivity and the sins that paralyse the will and prevent new initiatives and creative action.

For Christian women, the clue as to what constitutes messianic identity is revealed in Jesus. From his story we can learn how to be messiahs to each other; how in our time the healing and liberating power of God/ess may flow between us as we seek 'right-relation'[17] and justice for each other. However, Jesus is only one possible messianic role model. Studying at theological seminary, living in a near-fundamentalist environment surrounded by arrogant male ordinands, I remember how Teresa of Avila became for me my messianic mother. Every night I fell to sleep with her prayer on my lips:

> O my God I do not love Thee,
> O my God I do not want to love Thee,
> But O my God I do want to want to love Thee.

This prayer, like the Gethsemane prayer of Jesus, expresses the grace of the Christ who releases redemptive power through being a wounded healer and unconquerable lover of God and humanity.

Finally I want to turn to a discussion of *social* salvation, which plays such a central role in feminist liberation theology. Until the 1960s the vision of a transformed society, freed from the structural evils of poverty, homelessness, domestic violence, rape, discrimination and exploitation, played a very minor role in Christianity. There is a theological tradition, stretching back to Ireneaus, which conceives salvation to be social. However, whenever it has manifested itself in a social movement it has quickly been suppressed by champions of the dominant Augustinian and Lutheran traditions which think in terms of an absolute schism between the profane fallen world and the eschatological kingdom of God. In the nineteenth century, under the influence of optimistic evolutionary theories, Liberal Protestants flirted with utopianism, but their dreams died in the trenches of Flanders. The western churches today are still generally extremely pessimistic about human nature and the ability to bring about just and peaceful political solutions to social problems. They tend to see themselves as islands of grace, sheltering the faithful as they make their way to the City of God. The mainstream churches apparently do not believe that the kingdom will come on earth as it is in heaven.

By contrast, Latin American, Black, African and Asian liberation theologies have a vision of salvation which is both practical and idealistic. Bread and justice for the poor, they argue, is not merely a material matter, it is also spiritual; indeed the dichotomy is a false one! We are what we do, think and create. In the same way, God is the One who acts to save in history and in creation. God, who liberated the Hebrew slaves from Egypt, revealed his identity to Moses as 'I shall be whom I shall be' (Yahweh). Therefore human and divine praxis is liberative action and the work of creating the historical future. There is an idealistic or utopian dimension to salvation: it is never complete, we can always imagine something better. Every attempt to build a better society must be critically and prophetically assessed; the revolution is a spiral that goes on for ever. God comes to us from the future, where all is complete and perfect, and gives us the Holy Spirit as a power and a promise that our efforts to create the kingdom are not in vain.

Christian feminist theology is sometimes considered to be a daughter of Latin American liberation theology. If that is so, then she is now a daughter come of age. Christian feminist theologians have learned that male priests who make an option for the poor do not necessarily address the problems of women, who are the poorest of the poor. Schüssler Fiorenza has argued that women must speak with their own voices, out of their own contexts and experiences; their advocacy stance must be 'the self-affirmation of women' within patriarchal societies.[18] Women cannot rely so uncritically upon the androcentric Bible as their brothers, since it functions for Christian women not only as the source of their vision but also as the legitimation for their silencing and power-lessness. Neither can women embrace so enthusiastically a Marxist ideology in which reproduction is understood as an aspect of production, for in practice under socialism the reproducers of the proletariat (mothers) have far less power and status than their productive husbands and sons.

Once Christian feminists began to reflect theologically and act politically for themselves it became obvious that there is no uni-versal 'woman'; women come from different social, economic, racial and confessional contexts. Therefore there can be no uni-versal understanding of *social* salvation. A white middle-class western woman, for example, is not only oppressed by sexism; at the same time she is structurally implicated in the racial, neo-colonial and capitalist oppression of her Jewish, Muslim, Black and Third World sisters. She must learn, through dialogue, how to act justly towards these sisters. This is an extremely difficult task. Without using the defence mechanisms of denial, projection and guilt, she must be prepared to listen to women who define them-selves as fundamentally different and whose stories of oppression implicate the white sister. Yet precisely because of her experience of sexism, the white woman may lack confidence in herself and so fall prey to guilt or over-assertiveness.

The dialogue on the theological level requires of everyone extraordinary openness and imagination. Now that women theologians throughout the world are gaining the confidence to speak from their own contexts and cultures, the old western epistemology is in disarray. African women, for example, do not think of themselves dualistically or even individualistically. Their traditions are oral not written, their spiritual power is shamanistic and derives from a fourth dimension of invisible ancestors, of which Jesus is the greatest. Whereas, in the West, Christianity is struggling intellectually for its life in the face of secularization, in Africa Christianity is a daily experience of miracles, healings, prophecy, messianic politics, dance, song and prayer. Again, Mercy Amba Oduyoye comments that when African women read the stories of the Exodus they can feel their liberation directly. There is no sense of a time gap: African experience and con-sciousness is, she could say, biblical.[19]

Out of these ecumenical dialogues between female liberationist

Christians who are concerned to reassert the *social* dimension of salvation, there are emerging important new reflections which can play a part in the reconstruction of an inspiring post-sexist modern Christianity. I shall conclude with a brief description of three themes.

First, feminist church historians are reclaiming early Christian history as a period when women disciples, missionaries, prophetesses and ministers exercised spiritual power and promoted social changes. In her reconstruction of the Jesus Movement within Judaism, Schüssler Fiorenza has demonstrated that it practised a form of social egalitarianism.[20] With the spread of the missionary movement into the gentile Mediterranean world, this praxis constituted a threat to the Roman patriarchal order. Women and slaves were inspired to revolt against their roles, and the church found itself under severe persecution for promoting family and social instability. Over a period of three centuries the church struggled to adapt itself to the dominant patriarchal ethos in order to win respectability. The *social* salvation of women was sacrificed by bishops and theologians that they might ensure institutional survival. Finally the religious and social authority of women was declared heretical and the original emancipatory vision of Christianity was reconceived as eschatological salvation mediated through the male hierarchy of the church.

Second, in the discussion concerning Christian morality, it is Christian liberation feminists who are working for a re-evaluation of erotic love. Christian teaching on love, and thus on God who is love, has always focused primarily upon *agape*, which may be translated as objective unmerited love, grace or charity. *Phila*, or friendship, has rarely been addressed in Christian thought and *eros* completely relegated to the duty of procreation or the sublimation of mysticism. Erotic love is based upon the desire for union with the beloved; it presupposes mutuality of power and feeling. The question for liberation feminist ethics is that of whether lovers can morally channel their mutual attraction into mutual respect, justice and connectedness. What are the spiritual, psychological and cultural conditions necessary for sexual love to become the passion which drives personal and social liberation?[21]

Third, feminist liberation theology is developing new approaches to the symbolic essence of Christianity. By refusing to separate the sphere of profane history from the revelation of salvation history, this type of theology places God in the centre of socio-economic life as well as in the natural process of birth, growth, death and transformation. God is incarnate and embodied; thus, even in the midst of the pain and suffering that we must sometimes bear in our passion for justice and life in all its fullness, we participate in the divine reality. Such an image of God makes it possible to reclaim the doctrines of the Trinity and the two natures of Christ from western dualism. Certainly an embodied and suffering God was the original message of Christianity. Certainly, too, the incarnation and the outpouring of the Holy Spirit was understood as the divinization of those who are in Christ; male and female, gentile and Jew, slave and free. Certainly, too, everyone who cared, healed or liberated another was originally understood as being a form of Christ, an *'alter christus'*.[22]

We cannot turn the clock back two thousand years and claim that we are literally walking in the footsteps of Jesus of Nazareth. Nor indeed can we prove beyond doubt what he said and did. The historical consciousness of Jesus as he was in himself, and the historical facts of his life, death and resurrection come to us in narratives told by interpreters from other contexts. The only thing we know for certain is that his name has been connected with a belief; namely that God was revealed in history through a radical prophet, who died on a cross for blasphemy and sedition, that three days later some women and men disciples witnessed him alive, and that later, in the power of the Spirit, they began to preach a new religion which was based upon the faith that God can transform death into life and that those who believe experience the community of a new authentic humanity that is to be equated with the 'Christ'. This is a powerful and radically disturbing symbolic story which continues to inspire messianic movements, cosmic dreams and personal mysticism. I shall only be convinced it is time for Christian women to give up this myth when I can be persuaded that another myth can better satisfy their aspirations for salvation in all its many dimensions and contexts.

In this essay I have tried to address the question: are Christianity and feminism compatible? I have shown that patriarchal Christianity is not compatible with the aspirations of women to be fully autonomous and equal subjects of humanity, but I have also shown that Christianity as a spiritual and social path to the transcendent dimension of life contains within its resources the wellspring of its own reformation beyond sexism. This wellspring has been rediscovered by feminist theologians not only lying buried under the accumulated rubble of centuries of tradition and exegesis but also ever-springing in the hearts of Christian women who still dare to dream and to act upon their prophetic visions. I have described this wellspring as an unquenchable longing for the wholeness of salvation in all its liberative aspects: planetary, personal and above all social. This longing of the spirit is not of course unique to Christian women, but I would argue that it is compatible with the utopian praxis of feminists. Perhaps if we pool our resources and insights we can traverse together this barren wilderness of existence in the western market economy, for the wellspring is a vision, and without a vision the people perish.

6

KENŌSIS AND SUBVERSION: ON THE REPRESSION OF 'VULNERABILITY' IN CHRISTIAN FEMINIST WRITING
Sarah Coakley

In an important passage in *Theology and Feminism*, Daphne Hampson tackles the question of christological *kenōsis*, or 'voluntary self-emptying on the part of the second person of the Trinity'.[1] Citing Rosemary Radford Ruether's view that Jesus' self-emptying offers a challenge to patriarchy,[2] she counters with the thought that 'it is far from clear that the theme of *kenōsis* is the way in which monotheism would need to be qualified in order to bring the understanding of God more into line with feminist values'. She goes on:

> That it [*kenōsis*] should have featured prominently in Christian thought is perhaps an indication of the fact that men have understood what the male problem, in thinking in terms of hierarchy and domination, has been. It may well be a model which men need to appropriate and which may helpfully be built into the male understanding of God. *But ... for women, the theme of self-emptying and self-abnegation is far from helpful as a paradigm.*[3]

What are we to make of Hampson's rejection of *kenōsis* and Ruether's equally staunch – though brief – defence of it? The matter clearly cuts close to the heart of what separates Christian and post-Christian feminism; and hence my focus on it in this volume. Here, in *kenōsis*, it seems, is a Christic 'bone' on which Hampson chokes; for her, female 'autonomy' is a supreme good which Christology can only undermine, not enhance. In contrast, for me, what rightly distinguishes Christian feminism from various secular versions of it must necessarily lie in this disputed christological realm: here, if anywhere, Christian feminism has something corrective to offer secular feminism.

It will be the burden of this essay, then, to offer a defence of some version of *kenōsis* as not only compatible with feminism, but vital to a distinctively Christian manifestation of it, a manifestation which does not eschew, but embraces, the spiritual paradoxes of 'losing one's life in order to save it'. But in order to arrive at the point where I can justify such a 'loss' for Christian feminism (an ostensibly implausible move, one might think), I first have to unravel some semantic and historical confusions about the very meaning of *kenōsis*, a word that has had a bewildering number of different evocations in different contexts in the Christian tradition. Indeed it is a misunderstanding on this score which is partly responsible for the divergence between Hampson and Ruether, as we shall see.

The value of this unravelling task will not, I believe, be merely pedantic. For it is central to what I am attempting in this paper (an essay, after all, devoted to showing why I remain a Christian as well as a feminist) to demonstrate: that the rhetoric of *kenōsis* has not simply constituted the all-too-familiar exhortation to women to submit to lives of self-destructive subordination; nor (as Hampson believes) can it be discarded solely as a compensatory reaction to 'the male problem'. The evocations of the term have been much more complex and confusing even than that; just as the Christian tradition is in so many respects complex, confusing and (as I believe), continually creative. Thus by showing briefly in this piece how New Testament, patristic, post-Reformation Lutheran, early twentieth-century British, and contemporary analytic philosophy of religion discourses on *kenōsis* fail to mesh or concur at crucial points (and even use the term in straightforwardly contradictory ways), we shall be able to make some finer distinctions than those in the exchange between Hampson and Ruether about what form of *kenōsis* would be compatible with feminist interests, and what not. We shall also be able to distinguish, without disconnecting, the specifically christological meaning of *kenōsis* from the more broadly spiritual meaning. Moreover, since debates about christological *kenōsis* distill for us the more fundamental philosophical problem of how, normatively, to construe the relationship between the divine and the human *tout court*, it will be instructive to note how gender preconceptions, or gender anxieties, tend to lurk in this discussion. (To this extent Hampson's passing remarks about gender and *kenōsis* are certainly suggestive, and have yet to be applied to the philosophical dimensions of the issue.)

Finally, I shall enquire why themes of 'fragility', 'vulnerability' or 'self-emptying' have been relatively muted in white Christian feminist writing up till now, when secular feminism, and non-white or Black womanist theology have in a variety of ways tackled these themes more directly. I shall end with a suggestion for 'right' kenōsis founded on an analysis of the activity of Christian silent prayer (or 'contemplation'[4]), an activity char-acterized by a rather special form of 'vulnerability' or 'self-effacement'. My aim here is to show how wordless prayer can enable one, paradoxically, to hold vulnerability and personal empowerment *together*, precisely by creating the 'space' in which non-coercive divine power manifests itself, and I take this to be crucial for my understanding of a specifically Christian form of feminism. Or to put it more boldly and autobiographically: if I could not make spiritual and theological sense of this *special* form of power-in-vulnerability (kenōsis in one sense to be defined), I would see little point in continuing the tortured battle to bring feminism and Christianity together. In this sense, I am not sure that I want to pick the bones out of the Christic 'fish' before I begin; for it could be that in so doing I had removed the backbone that structures the central mystery of Christian salvation. Our first task, then, will be to turn back to the New Testament in search of Paul's meaning of kenōsis. It will be illuminating to discover how little this has to do with Hampson's critique.

I

The word kenōsis does not appear as a noun in the New Testament at all, and the entire debate about 'self-emptying' goes back to an isolated appearance of the verb kenoō (I empty) in Philippians 2.7. To choose to cite one English translation over others here is already to beg significant questions of interpretation; but the Revised Standard Version of Philippians 2.5–11 runs:

> [5]Have this mind among yourselves, which you have in Christ Jesus, [6]who, though he was in the form of God, did not count equality with God a thing to be grasped, [7]but emptied himself [*heauton ekenōsen*], taking the form of a servant, being born in the likeness of men [*anthrōpōn*, i.e., of humans]. [8]And being found in human form he humbled himself and became obedient unto death, even death on a cross. [9]Therefore God has highly exalted him and bestowed on him the name which is above every other name, [10]that at the name of Jesus every knee shall bow, in heaven and on earth and under the earth, [11]and every tongue confess that Jesus Christ is Lord, to the glory of God the Father.

Without in any sense committing the 'genetic fallacy' of presuming that the 'original' meaning of this passage is now binding on us, it is nonetheless intriguing to enquire what the 'emptying' here did connote at the outset. The matter is, however, one of the most convoluted (and disputed) in New Testament exegesis. Since Ernst Lohmeyer's influential analysis of the strophic structure of the passage in the late 1920s,[5] commentators have been virtually agreed that the passage was originally used liturgically as a hymn (possibly in either a baptismal or eucharistic setting); and the probability that the passage therefore represents pre-Pauline material taken over by Paul for his own purposes in this letter complexifies the issue of interpretation at the outset. (For we thus already have a double layer of meaning within the text as we have received it.) Waves of fashion in this century's New Testament scholarship have dictated widely divergent readings of Paul's (and his shadowy forebear's) intent. At one extreme there have been the (mainly German) exponents of the 'gnostic redeemer' theory,[6] who argue, under the influence of 'history of religions' analysis, that Paul has taken over, and modified, a soteriological framework from (what are taken to be) pre-Christian gnostic circles, in which the archetypal *Urmensch*, or 'original Man', descends to earth and simulates human existence in order to impart secret saving *gnosis* to his select followers. According to this view, *some* form of divine (or quasi-divine) 'pre-existence' is assumed for the Christ redeemer, and the 'emptying' connotes his appearance on earth. The emphasis, however, is not on the precise metaphysical speculation of later patristic Christology, on Christ's full and substantial divinity (or otherwise), as in the debates surrounding the Council of Nicaea (325); rather, it is on the mythological rhythm of salvific intervention and release. As Käsemann put it, 'Philippians 2 tells us what Christ *did*, not what he *was*.'[7]

At the other end of the spectrum lies a more straightforwardly ethical interpretation of the passage,[8] with no clear implications at all of Christ's pre-existence. Such an interpretation may at first sight seem surprising, even suspiciously artful, accustomed as we are to reading this passage through the lens of later credal orthodoxy: is not the 'emptying' of v. 7 most obviously seen as a reference to the incarnation? But there are a number of reasons why this alternative reading might seem more consistent with earliest Christianity in general, and Pauline theology in particular. First, the notion of substantial pre-existence does not otherwise feature in (proto-) Pauline settings. Second, the crucial preceding participle clause ('though he was in the form of God'), which triggers our train of thought towards pre-existence and incarna-

tion, may in context more appropriately be read as a piece of
Adam typology (already a characteristic of Paul's Christology in
Romans 5 and 1 Corinthians 15). On this view the 'form of God' is
a reference to the creation of the *human* race; Genesis 1.26–7, after
all, speaks of God creating 'man' 'in his own image'. So now
Christ, as second Adam (also in 'the form of God'), revokes the
penalty of Eden by undoing Adam's primal disobedience. Thus,
third, the 'thing to be grasped', as the RSV has it (the *harpagmon*,
v. 6), becomes quite possibly an allusion to Adam's first sin in
making himself 'like God' (Genesis 3.5, 22), again here recapitul-
ated and reversed in Christ's life and example.[9] We are not on this
view, then, talking about a set of (pre-existent) divine attributes
which could have been held onto by Christ, but instead were
relinquished. Rather, the 'grasping' is a form of moral turpitude
and arrogance that Jesus avoids right from the start of his
ministry. And so, fourth, then, the 'emptying' on this interpretation now denotes not incarnation, but rather the 'servant-like'
example set by Jesus' demeanour throughout his life (with possible
overtones of the Isaianic 'suffering servant'), an 'empty-ing' which
finds its ultimate end in the events of the cross (v. 8). Thus, on this
'ethical' reading, the 'emptying of v. 7 is *parallel* to the 'humbling'
of v. 8;[10] both take place within Jesus' earthly existence, rather
than the 'emptying' being a precondition of the earthly life (as on
the 'pre-existence' reading).

To sketch out these two dominant schools of interpretation of
Philippians 2 in broad outline is to give only a crude account of the
complexity of the New Testament hermeneutical debates on this
passage over recent decades. The two basic views sketched both
have remaining problems, and some scholars have argued that it is
a false move to force a disjunctive choice between them.[11] Debates
continue about the contextual background of the passage: are the
allusions mainly to the Hebrew Scriptures, or to gnostic and pagan
themes? But one striking point of unanimity in the modern New
Testament discussion (amidst all this dissent) has been the virtual
ruling out of a 'dogmatic' or 'metaphysical' reading of Paul's
interests in this passage. It is not, in other words, a prefigurement
of second-century Logos speculation (in the mode of Justin Martyr,
for instance), let alone a preview of fourth-century Nicaean
orthodoxy (which takes the Son to share all divine characteristics
with the Father in advance of the incarnation). Rather, *if* 'pre-
existence' (of a sort) is implied here, it is of a 'mythological' or
soteriologically oriented kind, as in gnostic redeemer narratives;
and it is this *narrative* structure which the Philippians are being
asked to enter into, to make their own 'mind' (v. 5).

This ostensibly 'anti-dogmatic' tenor of the New Testament discussion of *kenōsis* contrasts forcibly with discussions of Philippians 2 in other circles, as we shall see, especially the contemporary analytic philosophy of religion writing on the matter (which appears strangely ignorant of the New Testament debates). And yet, despite the conscious preference of many twentieth-century New Testament scholars for existential rather than metaphysical categories, we may, I suggest, nonetheless detect ways in which concern about 'incarnation' and the 'two natures' problem has (more or less covertly) fuelled their concerns and fashions, whether in criticism or redirection of traditional patristic options. To expose this rather buried dimension of the New Testament hermeneutical question will also prove illuminating in relation to our central, feminist concern (though, tellingly, I can find no explicit feminist analysis in the voluminous New Testament secondary literature concerning Philippians 2 itself).

Of the two broad tendencies in New Testament interpretation of Philippians 2 I have described, the first, influenced as it was by 'history of religions' methodology, and thus anxious to locate earliest Christology within a broad stratum of Middle Eastern mythology and ritual practice, explicitly thrust aside what it saw as the metaphysical clamps of later doctrinal 'orthodoxy' in search of a more direct, 'existential' response of faith. This, after all, was the hallmark of Bultmann's Heideggerian theology. As a result, and as we have just seen, even though 'pre-existence' of a 'mythical' form was presumed in the interpretation of Philippians 2, the 'emptying' here was not seen to imply the *divesting* of some clearly defined set of divine characteristics, otherwise uniquely shared with the 'Father'. Rather, if anything, the docetism of the gnostic redeemer mythology still hung over its Pauline reworking: the Christ figure appeared only 'in the *form* of man', feigning human weakness for the purposes of salvific activity. This being the case, we can now see that Daphne Hampson's charge against *kenōsis* with which we opened (as a masculinist ploy, beset by conscience), does not clearly score at all against this form of New Testament interpretation of Philippians 2. That is, precisely because the later 'two natures' gloss on pre-existence has, for theological or ideological reasons, been rejected by this school of thinking from the outset, so too it never considers the kind of compensatory 'emptying' that Hampson is attacking.[12] If anything, the quasi-gnostic redeemer of the pre-Pauline hymn merely pretends to abandon his divine powers, rather than actually doing so.

So Hampson's critique does not really touch this form of New

Testament analysis; but even less, significantly, does it bite against the alternative, 'ethical' reading favoured by a different school of New Testament scholarship. For here, if I am right, an even more far-reaching questioning of later Nicene or Chalcedonian 'orthodoxy' may be driving the theological direction taken. If, that is, substantial pre-existence of *no* sort is found in the Pauline text, then there is no clear charter here for later Nicene 'orthodoxy', and no full range of divine characteristics to be abandoned or otherwise.[13] So once again Hampson's criticisms are deflected.

If, on the other hand, another variant of the 'ethical' interpretation is preferred, as suggested by C. F. D. Moule, then more far-reaching metaphysical implications are involved, though not the ones normally associated with Chalcedonian 'orthodoxy'. On this 'ethical' view Jesus' 'emptying' is seen not just as the blueprint for a perfect human moral response, but as revelatory of the 'humility' of the *divine* nature. As Moule puts it: '... Jesus displayed the self-giving humility which is the *essence of divinity*'.[14] Moule's interpretation, we note, involves a strange combination of factors. Unlike other interpreters of our 'ethical' type, he appears to take Christ's pre-existence, and certainly his full divinity, as given in the passage; but *like* other 'ethical' readings he finds the 'emptying' not to refer to an effect on either of these, nor to his incarnation, but rather to his humanly 'humble' and 'non-grasping' nature – which, however, he then casts as the distinctively *divine* characteristic. Thus Moule combines a remaining 'orthodox' commitment to pre-existence and incarnation with a significant relocation of the attribute of 'humility'. This (new) metaphysical gloss was one taken up more systematically by Moule's Cambridge colleague, J. A. T. Robinson, and we shall return to consider its coherence a little later. The point to be made for our immediate purposes here is how *complex* is the entanglement of hermeneutical and dogmatic questions where this passage is concerned, even when questions of christological speculation in the patristic mode have ostensibly been abandoned (and that, too, before we get to the subtler issues of gender subtext). What is at stake is nothing less than our fundamental presumptions about divine and human nature, and the possibility, or otherwise, of their complete concurrence. In Moule's artful reworking of the 'ethical' interpretation, we note, Hampson's critique of *kenōsis* is again averted, but this time in yet another (and third) way: Jesus' 'emptying' involves no compensatory loss of 'masculinist' divine powers, because his example shows us that divinity is 'humble' *rather than* 'powerful' (whatever this means). His way to the cross is the revelation of an unchanging, but consistently 'humble', divinity. Thus, Moule's interpretation is somewhat closer to what Ruether seems to mean by *kenōsis* when she asserts that Jesus' message and example represent 'patriarchy's' *kenōsis*: that is (or so I read her), Jesus promoted values quite different from those of *machismo* or worldly power. In his ethical example patriarchy was emptied out (not, we note, Christ himself emptied out).

We come away from the New Testament debate, then, with a host of questions, only partially resolved. All commentators (or nearly all) concur that it is an anachronism to see Paul or his source expressing anything like the 'two nature' Christology of later 'orthodoxy'; yet disagreements about the original context, religious genre, and aims of the Christic hymn of Philippians 2 still lead to different (implicit) dogmatic conclusions about the normative relation of divine 'powers' to the human here expressed. Let us consider the range of possibilities we have already generated. Is the christological blueprint of Philippians 2 a matter of: (1) temporarily *relinquishing* divine powers which are Christ's by right (as cosmic redeemer); or (2) *pretending* to relinquish divine powers whilst actually retaining them (as gnostic redeemer); or (3) choosing *never to have* certain (false and worldly) forms of power – forms sometimes wrongly construed as 'divine'; or (4) *revealing* 'divine power' to be intrinsically 'humble' rather than 'grasping'? Of these four alternatives already in play, Hampson would presumably only regard (1) – or possibly also (2) – as falling under her critique of masculinist *kenōsis*; and I have argued that even they, if framed in the terms of the 'history of religions' approach, are less obviously subject to her criticism than if they had been formulated on the presumptions of later patristic categories. For my own part, for the reasons sketched above, I am more convinced by the third interpretation than the others (at least as far the New Testament debate is concerned), and I shall return to this option again when I regather my systematic conclusions at the end of the essay. Hampson, however, might justifiably here object that she had none of this New Testament complexity in mind when she made her charge. Rather, her target is the much later form of speculative 'kenoticism' devised by early twentieth-century British theologians of privileged backgrounds, exercising their (perhaps guilty) social consciences. In this she is right; but in order to see how we get from the New Testament to these exponents, some interim historical material is worthy of review. Again, as we shall see, ironic results arise from trying to bring different notions of *kenōsis* into consistent focus, especially where a feminist analysis is concerned. But at least we are beginning to see why Hampson and Ruether do not agree: it is because, in all this historical and semantic complexity over *kenōsis*, their views do not even properly *connect*. Ruether is promoting a view of *kenōsis* that Hampson does not seriously consider.

II

The patristic exegesis of Philippians 2, and of the term *kenōsis* in particular, makes very different hermeneutical and philosophical presumptions from those of the modern New Testament discussions we have just surveyed. Yet, strangely – as shown in a now-classic coverage of the patristic material by Friedrich Loofs[15] – the range of options presented (from 'ethical' to 'incarnational', with various stopping-points or combinations in between), is uncannily similar to the modern-day alternatives endlessly rejigged by New Testament scholars with (often) very little knowledge of 'pre-critical' exegesis. I do not, however, here want to focus on the 'ethical' (or what Loofs terms the 'Pelagian') variant, which in any case did not ultimately emerge as regnant in the patristic period. Rather, what I wish to underscore is the *irony* of the reversal of presumptions about *kenōsis* between the time of Paul and the triumph of Chalcedonian 'orthodoxy' in the fifth century – an orthodoxy highly influenced by the demanding paradoxes of the Christology of Cyril of Alexandria (d. 444).

Whereas Paul's views on *kenōsis*, as we have seen, were largely non-'speculative', non-'dogmatic', and arguably not even asserting substantial pre-existence at all, the formative christological discussions of the fourth and fifth centuries (in the wake of the hard-won battles over the Council of Nicaea) take Christ's substantial pre-existence and essential divinity *for granted*. The problem then resides in explicating what 'emptying' can *mean* in Philippians 2, assuming now that it is somehow coextensive with the event of incarnation, but granted that characteristics such as omniscience and omnipotence are taken (unquestioningly) to be unchanging aspects of the divine nature.[16] Thus Hilary of Poitiers, in the fourth century, could talk rather daringly – and indeed confusingly – of an 'evacuation of the form of God', whilst yet denying that Christ's divinity had been dislodged in any sense; while Cyril of Alexandria, in the fifth century, went on to make Philippians 2 the narrative focus of his entire Logos Christology, clarifying that the pre-existent divine Logos was – albeit paradoxically – also the personal or 'hypostatic' subject of Christ's human states, but without any impairment or restriction of the divine attributes.[17] For Cyril, then, the word *kenōsis* signified no loss or abnegation, but simply the so-called 'abasements' involved in the taking of flesh. He was finally at a loss how to *explain* how this assumption of flesh could occur without detriment or change to the divine ✳ Logos; it led him, for instance, to glory in such famously paradoxical expressions about Christ's passion as 'He suffered unsufferingly'.[18] But he achieved his theological goals by seeing the *kenōsis* of incarnation not as loss, but rather as an addition of human flesh and blood to the abiding and unchanging characteristics of divinity. As he writes: 'The Only begotten Word ... came down for the sake of our salvation and abased Himself into emptying [*eis kenōsin*] and was incarnate ... not indeed casting off what He was, but even though He became Man by the assumption of flesh and blood He still remained God in nature [*physis*] and in truth.'[19]

Now, if we again adjust the hermeneutical lens in a feminist direction, we immediately see the further ironies – for a feminist critique such as Hampson's – of the shift out of the New Testament discussion into the patristic one. For in Cyril's theology of *kenōsis* there is no question of any aspects of unchanging divinity being abandoned, restricted, or never taken up in the incarnation; whatever else one may accuse Cyril of, it cannot be that his vision of *kenōsis* signifies a compensatory exercise of masculinist guilt. Far as his metaphysical presumptions may be from Paul's in Philippians 2, then, his deflection of Hampson's charge is as complete: no *actual* 'self-emptying' can occur in Christ, since none of his pre-existent divine attributes could, by definition, be surrendered or modified. Whilst some feminists might wish to question the very construction of divine 'omnipotence' which Cyril is assuming (a point to which I shall return),[20] his theory of *kenōsis* scarcely suffers from squirmings of 'self-abnegation'. Cyril's Christ abandons no 'power' whatever. Thus, to our four-point list of possible interpretations of *kenōsis* gleaned from the New Testament discussion above, we must now add a fifth, and classically 'Alexandrian', one of very different presumptions. The meaning is indeed in straightforward contradiction with some of our earlier definitions, for here *kenōsis* connotes: (5) the divine Logos's *taking on* of human flesh in the incarnation, but without loss, impairment, or restriction of divine powers.

The christological paradoxes heightened thus by Cyril, and to some ill-defined extent taken over into Chalcedonian 'orthodoxy' a little later,[21] arguably achieved a form of theological coherence at the cost of some strained credulity about the form of Christ's earthly life, and certainly left many points of christological detail unanswered. We shall attempt to show in the remainder of this

essay how these points have direct or indirect feminist implications. In particular, the idea of Cyril and others that, in virtue of
the union of natures in Christ's *hypostasis* ('person'), one could
appropriately 'predicate' attributes of one nature to the other (the
so-called *communicatio idomatum*),[22] left question marks about
how, precisely and metaphysically, the all-too-human states of
anxiety, weakness and ignorance occasionally displayed by Jesus
in the gospel narratives could be explained. What effect, if any,
should these have on one's perception of the nature of divinity?
Could the classical notions of divine omniscience or omnipotence
really remain unimpaired? (We note how the particular problems
of *kenōsis* here become problems about the nature of incarnation
in general.) This last, and radical, question was one not adequately
faced at all in the patristic, or even scholastic, discussion.[23] Indeed
Cyril's solution, as we have intimated, hovered uncomfortably
close to our second definition of *kenōsis* given above (though he
would doubtless have rigorously denied any suggestion of
docetism): that is, Christ, he said, at 'times' in the incarnation
'*permitted* his own flesh to experience its proper affections, [and]
permitted [his human] soul to experience its proper affections';[24]
but this was a 'permission' operated all along, it seems, from the
unshakeable base of the Logos's unchanging divinity. Thus, since
no revision of the notion of divinity was envisaged in the light of
the gospel narrative on these points (or in the light of the
'attributed' *communicatio*), and no substantial change to the idea
of humanity either, it was hard to see how these manifestations of
the so-called *kenōsis* were not, in effect, only an *appearance* in the
human nature, and that somewhat sporadic. As christological
thought was further developed in the patristic East after Cyril and
Chalcedon, a clarification was achieved (by the eighth-century
Greek theologian John of Damascus, most significantly) about the
metaphysical implications of the *communicatio*. If anything,
however, it heightened the quasi-docetic tendencies of Cyril's
views: the 'communication' was now explicitly said to operate
only *one way* (from the divine to the human), the divine fully
permeating the human nature of Christ by an act of 'coinherence'
(*perichōrēsis*). What space, then, for those dimensions of Christ's
passion most poignantly demonstrating human anxiety, weakness
and desolation? Were those to be obliterated by the invasive
leakage of divine power into Christ's human nature? If so, the
kenotic act of the incarnation could now only signify 'emptying' in
the most Pickwickian sense: 'a condescension *inexpressible and
inconceivable*', as John of Damascus put it in one of his more
revealingly tortured sentences on the matter.[25] Whilst many

christological commentators have remarked on the discomforts of this position for the integrity of Christ's human nature *tout court*, our own more pressing (and novel) concerns in this essay are over the implications for a gender analysis of normative human–divine relations. The spectre raised here of a divine force that takes on humanity by controlling and partly *obliterating* it (and all, seductively, in the name of '*kenōsis*') is thus the issue that should properly concern us where the further outworkings of the 'Alexandrian' tradition are concerned: it is a matter of how divine 'power' is construed in relation to the human, and how this could insidiously fuel masculinist purposes, masculinist visions of the subduing of the weaker by the stronger. Thus, while we are still far away from Hampson's initial critique of (one meaning of) *kenōsis*, we may nonetheless here be facing a philosophical issue of more fundamental import. How, that is, are Christian feminists to construe the *hypostatic* 'concurrence' of the human and the divine in Christ (if indeed they wish to defend the Chalcedonian tradition at all) without endorsing a vision of divine power as forceful obliteration?

III

This matter was to take some new turns within early Protestantism. Many centuries later than John of Damascus, in the aftermath of the Lutheran reform in Germany, the question of the *communicatio idiomatum* again became contentious in the light of the interpretation of Philippians 2. This time the issue of the *precise* form of interpenetration between the natures, and especially the implications for expounding the significance of the human nature of Christ with integrity, could no longer be kept at bay. Luther's Christology stressed the extreme vulnerability of Christ on the cross; but at the same time he gave new reinforcement (for reasons to do with his defence of the 'real presence' of Christ in the eucharist) to the doctrine of the *communicatio idiomatum*: the divine had to permeate the human in Christ sufficiently to allow his 'real' (not merely spiritual) presence in multitudinous – and simultaneous – celebrations of the Lord's Supper. But how, then, could Christ's *divinity* be said to be operative in, for instance, his cry of despair at death?

Once this question was pressed, the main European Reformers fell into different camps on the issue, correlated to their divergent views on the Eucharist. Zwingli saw the 'communication' of attributes as no more than a hyperbolic figure of speech; Calvin (in the tradition of the school of Antioch and many of the western Scholastics) saw the attributes of the natures communicating in the *person* of the Saviour, but not interpenetrating directly; whilst the Lutherans, in the Formula of Concord (1577), clarified their preference for the Greek tradition of John of Damascus, insisting that attributes of divinity such as omnipresence and omnipotence fully pervaded the human nature of Christ. But the Lutheran position was still clearly problematic; to arrive back at an 'Alexandrian' solution of the *communicatio* (dictated by the needs of a high eucharistic theology) was merely to beg the question of Christ's human brokenness with which Luther had begun.

A school of seventeenth-century Lutherans from Giessen later proposed a solution which returned to Philippians 2 with a slightly novel twist,[26] and one that I wish to suggest might have some life in it as far as a feminist reconstruction is concerned. These theologians suggested that Christ's ostensible weaknesses could be explained in terms of a *kenōsis* operative on his *human* nature, whilst his divine nature retained its powers. The position was thus subtly, though importantly, different from the much earlier Cyrilline one, granted the relocation of the site of 'emptying': whilst Cyril and his Greek successors saw no actual loss in the so-called 'abasements' of incarnation (a *kenōsis* only in name), the Giessen school proposed that the *human* nature of Christ was in effect 'empty' of the possession of such divine attributes as omnipresence and omnipotence during the incarnation – though they added that in virtue of the *union* of the natures there remained the 'possibility' of their reactivation. This last admission was not of course a very happy one (*was* the human nature 'emptied' or not?); and one might well argue that this whole Lutheran debate was being propelled by its unfortunate earlier decision to opt for an interpretation of the *communicatio* that allowed total permeation of the human nature by the divine in the first place (here partially revoked).[27] But one can nonetheless see the good *intentions* of the Giessen school. They were grappling with the crisis of explanation both of Christ's human psychological growth and of his weakness and anxiety in the face of death (a crisis that could only become the more intense with the emergence of modern historiography); and they were doing so within the constraints of a broadly 'Alexandrian' reading of Christology, one that, as we have seen, always teetered towards the 'docetic' in its assumption that the ultimate point of personal identity in Christ could be *identified* with the pre-existent divine Logos. Thus we may perhaps see the Giessen school's vision of *kenōsis* as a variant on our third definition, above (Christ choosing *never to have* certain forms of power in his incarnate life, never to 'grasp'), the difference being that this approach is now linked to a 'two natures'

Christology and the 'emptying' applied to the human nature *alone*. That this solution fitted uneasily into its presumed 'Alexandrian' framework we have just indicated; but the possibility raised here of a vision of christological *kenōsis* uniting human 'vulnerability' with authentic divine power (as opposed to worldly or 'patriarchal' visions of power), and uniting them such that the human was wholly translucent to the divine, is I believe of some continuing relevance to Christian feminism, and an issue to which I shall return shortly. For the meantime, let us note that we have at last reached one version, at least, of what Hampson may be rejecting when she accuses 'kenoticism' of being a 'male problem'. That is, if we take something like the Giessen form of *kenōsis* as read, is the 'abandonment' of certain forms of control or power seen here in Christ's human realm to be regarded as of imitative spiritual significance only to *men*? Is Hampson objecting to 'self-emptying', 'vulnerability', or surrendering of 'control' featuring in *any* form in her vision of women's spiritual flourishing?[28]

Perhaps we can answer this with full clarity only when we have the final version of (nineteenth- and twentieth-century) *kenōsis* also in mind. For here I think is Hampson's real butt: not the relatively obscure post-Reformation reflections on the *communicatio* and the union of the two natures, but the much more daring – and distinctively modern – idea that even the pre-existent *divine* Logos is 'emptied' (in some sense) in the incarnation, actually relinquishing or 'retracting' certain attributes of divinity such as omnipotence or omniscience. It was another Lutheran (the late nineteenth-century Gottfried Thomasius) who took this bold step, and so tackled the remaining difficulties of the *communicatio* head on. As he acutely saw, they were rendered more problematic by the evolving disciplines of biblical criticism and developmental psychology. Did Jesus develop ordinarily as a human child? Was he aware of a pre-existent divine life? Thomasius felt unable to hold on to the orthodox notion of a personal unity of the divine and human in Christ 'without the supposition of a *self-limitation of the divine Logos* coincident with the Incarnation'.[29]

This, then, was a real *novum*: the idea of a self-limitation of the *divine* realm; but the attempt to express it without incoherence, within a broadly 'Alexandrian' reading of Chalcedon, was to prove at least as difficult (and I believe ultimately more difficult) than the earlier efforts to explicate the 'kenotic' act of incarnation. According to Thomasius, certain divine properties (omnipotence, omniscience, omnipresence) were in Christ shown to be only 'relative' divine characteristics, withdrawn to a condition of

'potency' during the incarnate life of Jesus. This position is
somewhat close to our first definition of *kenōsis* given above (the
temporary *relinquishing* of divine powers in the incarnation); and
yet to say it was a straightforward version of this type would
clearly be to mislead: to withdraw *some* divine properties into
'potency' for a while (leaving aside for the moment whether this
idea is cogent or not), is clearly not the same thing as a *total* –
albeit temporary – relinquishing of divine powers. The distinction
is significant, for it has proved useful to a number of distinguished
critics of this modern form of *kenōsis* to tar it with the brush of
complete, if temporary, abandonment of divine powers (or even of
the divine nature),[30] thus mightily confusing this already convoluted problem of definition. In order to avoid this muddle, we
shall need to generate a sixth definition of *kenōsis* for Thomasius
and his ilk, thus: (6) a temporary retracting (or withdrawing into
'potency') of *certain* characteristics of divinity during the incarnate
life. We are now in a position to consider the feminist implications
of this development.

IV

The challenge of expressing views like Thomasius' in pictorial
imagery vivid to minds of the time was taken up by a range of
British kenoticists in the early part of this century. It is surely these
writers that Hampson has in mind when she launches her attack
on *kenōsis* as a 'male' expression of compensatory need or guilt;
and she is certainly right to suggest that a gender analysis of their
work is long overdue. Frank Weston's *The One Christ*, for
instance (originally published in 1907), employs a revealing set of
analogies in order to express the 'law of self-restraint' that the Son
imposed upon his own divinity in the incarnation. Christ was like
'St Francis de Sales', first, acting in a professional role as priest and
confessor to his parents (a role seen here as restricted), but in
another, wider, role as their son. (We note how, for the purposes
of this analogy, the position of 'priest' is seen as involving partial
'limitation' and restriction of knowledge. This is a far cry from the
debates between the sexes over priestly powers in this century;
Weston can take a certain form of male priestly authority for
granted, but then focus on the professional 'limitation' that the
confessional imposes.) The next analogy utilized by Weston
(Canon of Zanzibar Cathedral at the time) is of an 'African king'
who is reduced to slavery; another is of a 'favourite son of a
commanding officer', who has to exercise pretence or filial
restraint when he is transferred to his father's own regiment; and
the final suggestion is the analogy of a 'king's son' who leaves his

palace and 'dwell[s] a workman amongst workmen ... [passing] through all the troubles and vicissitudes of the life of a manual labourer...'[31] *Autres temps, autres moeurs*: one can hardly suppress a smirk of embarrassment at this catalogue of class and gender assumptions. As Hampson indicates, the privileged male can afford to seek some compensatory 'loss' in such ways (though, tellingly, only the 'African king' seems to lose out substantially in these heart-warming tales of noble self-abnegation). To be fair, Weston is well aware of the fallibility and partiality of his analogues; but far from his mind – naturally enough – is the social and sexual subtext of what he proposes.[32]

In the slightly earlier writing of Charles Gore, the kenotic analogy was (not much more reassuringly, perhaps, to a feminist) that of empathetic identification with the circumstances of an 'inferior': the child, the uneducated, or the 'savage'. Again, as in Weston, Gore's christological analysis in *The Incarnation of the Son of God* (1891) and *Dissertations on Subjects Connected with the Incarnation* (1895) is both intricate and profound: there is no denying the originality and sophistication of these writers, for all the (new) problems of coherence they present. Yet Gore, rather bemusingly, could hardly be called a consistent 'kenoticist' according to the sixth definition we have just generated. Despite his fairly imprecise talk here about 'abandonment' of divine powers in the act of 'empathy', his work elsewhere suggests a retention of all divine characteristics, according to a 'two levels of consciousness' model (ironically the one now promulgated by analytic defenders of high Chalcedonian 'orthodoxy').[33] If a bishop understands an 'uneducated' [woman?] or a 'savage', then, he does so without any final ontological change to his privileged make-up.

In the writings of P.T. Forsyth, however (significantly the only non-Conformist of this group of British kenoticists), the tone is somewhat different. *The Person and Place of Jesus Christ* (1909) presents us with a range of analogies to the 'kenotic' act which involve much greater and more permanent loss than those rehearsed by Gore and Weston (so much so that Forsyth's position veers closer to our first definition of *kenōsis* than our sixth); but the analogies are no less embedded in the presumptions of male social and intellectual superiority. Here we have a 'venerable vizier' who takes poison in the place of a 'foolish young Sultan', and suffers consequent debilitation; a Russian concert violinist who is so committed to the poor (in pre-Revolutionary times) that he undergoes exile and loss of his musical career; and a promising philosophy student who sets aside an academic career to support his family, and so submits to 'drudgery' in 'modern industrial conditions' (which of course blunts his intellectual brilliance!). Forsyth's point, and it is movingly and even persuasively argued, is that a restriction on human freedom, consciously and resolutely accepted by an act of 'supernatural' will, can in due course be seen as a means of glory.[34] But what of those (women, 'workmen', 'African slaves') who arguably do not enjoy the capacity of 'supernatural' freedom in the first place? As with Gore and Weston, the extent to which the assumed 'masculinism' of the vital imagery employed affects the *cogency* or *coherence* of the theological picture is a nice point. The issue of the technical coherence of divine *kenōsis* might seem to be one removed from the precise evocations of a particular thought experiment, to be a matter merely of logic and consistency. Yet it is sometimes only when a range of controlling images or 'intuition pumps' break down (often for reasons beyond those of pure logic) that we realize that we have been obsessed with the wrong questions.[35]

The early twentieth-century kenoticists, as we have shown, struggled to express divine self-limitation within an 'Alexandrian' reading of Chalcedon. It never occurred to them to question, more radically, whether that particular gloss on Chalcedon (which located the personal identity of Christ undifferentiatedly in the pre-existent divine life of the Logos) was either theologically necessary or textually obvious; just as it never occurred to them to reflect on the gender and class evocations of their analogies (which just as clearly started from a presumption of possessed power and influence). Yet these are the very assumptions we shall shortly wish to question. Oddly, however, Daphne Hampson's critique of *kenōsis* also appears to make some similar gender presumptions. Thus, for her, 'males' (all males, including 'workmen' and 'slaves'?) need to compensate for their tendency to 'dominate' by means of an act of self-emptying; whereas 'women' (all women, including university professors?) do not. The question that now presses, therefore, is whether Hampson may not, in her perceptive critique of early twentieth-century kenoticists, have fallen into the trap of her own gender stereotypes. Has she not assumed, that is, that 'vulnerability' or 'self-effacement' are prescriptively 'female' (though regrettably so), and thus only 'helpful' as a secondary or compensatory addition to 'male' power and dominance; whereas such ('male') power ought now *rightly* to be pursued (also by way of compensation) by feminist women? But why should we continue with these outworn gender presumptions in the first place? Is there not, we might ask, a more creative theological way through our dilemma via a *reformulation* of the very notion of divine 'power' and its relation to the human?

Since Gore, Weston and Forsyth, the discussion of *kenōsis* has taken one more twist – in my view a misleading twist – which may nonetheless help us confront this question more directly and clearly. This is the form of 'kenoticism' aligned to the 'ethical' interpretation of Philippians 2 favoured by C.F.D. Moule (discussed above), but then given a more overt philosophical expression which was to undercut the 'two natures' structure still implicitly retained by Moule. Moule, we recall, spoke of the 'form of the servant' actually revealing the 'nature of God': 'the self-giving humility which *is* the *essence of divinity*'.[36] In line with this kind of exegesis of Philippians 2, John Robinson was to develop a more metaphysically enunciated notion of *kenōsis as 'plērōsis'*.[37] Instead, that is, of presuming a substantial pre-existence for Christ and then wondering how a 'human nature' could be compatible with it (the 'Alexandrian' problem, as we have seen, from the start), Robinson proposed a reversal of the traditional directionality of the *communicatio*, and thus a radical seepage of the *human* characteristics into the *divine* – such, indeed, as to collapse the apparatus of the 'two natures' doctrine altogether. Thus the human limitations of Jesus were seen as a positive expression of his divinity rather than as a curtailment of it. In somewhat similar mode, John Macquarrie has written of a 'new-style kenoticism', in which 'the self-emptying of Jesus Christ has not only opened up the depth of a true humanity, but has made known to us the final reality as likewise self-emptying, self-giving and self-limiting'.[38]

Now, it is important to underscore the radicality of what has occurred here. We are no longer speculating about the paradoxical *relationship* of human and divine 'natures' (and then arguing about the possible accommodations necessary when bringing them into 'concurrence'). Rather, it is being urged that the 'limitations' of Jesus' human life are in some sense directly *equatable* with what it is to be 'God'. But can we make coherent sense of this? It is obviously the final philosophical terminus of the 'Thomasian' road; but it goes far beyond anything Thomasius himself envisaged or desired – the *identification* of 'God' as permanently 'limited'. Does this not then also make God intrinsically non-omnipotent and non-omniscient (as opposed to temporally non-omnipotent and non-omniscient under the conditions of incarnation)? And how, then, could such a being be 'God'?

Interestingly, one of the rare *analytic* philosophers of religion to favour kenoticism today, S.T. Davis, seemingly takes these implications to follow from a 'kenotic' approach to Christology too,

and in exploring this avenue of approach he parts company with
most of his colleagues in the discourse of analytic religious philosophy. His reflections are therefore worthy of some comment.
Unlike Robinson, Davis maintains the Chalcedonian structure of
pre-existence and the 'two natures' doctrine, but argues that, if the
incarnate Christ as depicted in the biblical narrative shows signs of
non-omniscience, then an implication may be that omniscience is
not, after all, an *essential* property of the divine.[39] But then Davis
wavers on this point: it seems he is not familiar with the history of
the doctrine of the *communicatio idiomatum*, and which form of it
he wishes to espouse. Insofar as he considers allowing this permanent revelatory status for the human life of Christ as a window
onto the divine, he is joining hands with Robinson and the other
'new kenoticists' (who embrace the fourth definition of *kenōsis*
given above); but insofar as he also talks of Christ's failure in
omniscience as only 'temporary' (like a 'skilled tennis player
[choosing] to play a game with their weak hand'![40]), he is closer to
our first definition of *kenōsis*, where divine characteristics are only
briefly set aside for the purposes of the incarnation. The result is
not a very happy compromise, and only questionably coherent.[41]
Yet the 'new kenoticists', in contrast, seem in even deeper waters
metaphysically, as we have intimated. Perhaps it is they, after all,
who represent the final outworkings of the liberal 'masculinist'
guilt derided by Hampson? Their God, it seems, becomes intrinsically devoid of omniscience and omnipotence (at least in
anything like the traditional definitions). Yet it is one thing, of
course, to *redefine* divine 'power' creatively, another to shear God
down to human size, to make God intrinsically power*less*,
incapable of sustaining the creation in being.[42]

But how then does this recent, or 'new', kenoticism throw light
on our feminist agendas? What one sees so interestingly in writers
such as Moule, Robinson (and to some degree in Davis) is a
primary commitment to the given *narrative* of the New
Testament, and especially of the gospel accounts of Jesus' life; and
this takes precedence even over philosophical questions of
apparent coherence, or of traditional *a priori* assumptions about
the unchanging divine attributes. Such narrative commitment is a
feature of post-war theology in general (especially continental
theology), and indeed could be said to be the point at which
contemporary theology and analytic philosophy of religion divide
most painfully in their fundamental assumptions. What for
Barthian theologians, for instance, is seen as the inexplicable and
'absolute paradox' of the incarnation *given* in the irreducible
narrative of the biblical text, is for most analytic philosophers of

religion (bar, here, in some respects, Davis) instead a matter of the *logical* demonstration of the coherence of the traditional christological formulae, granted certain *a priori* presumptions about the nature of God and humanity.[43] Where the question of gender then insidiously inserts itself into this scholarly divide is in the willingness, or otherwise, to construe forms of 'weakness', 'passivity' or 'vulnerability' (all traditionally demerits for the 'male', but manifestly present in Jesus' passion) as either normatively human or even revelatorily divine. Most philosophers of religion would resist both of these options; some theologians, as we have shown, would consider one or both. If either of the latter positions is sustained, however (and I have already intimated that I prefer the former), then a traditional gender stereotype starts to crumble. That is, if Jesus' 'vulnerability' is a primary narrative given, rather than a philosophical embarrassment to explain away, then precisely the question is raised whether 'vulnerability' *need* be seen as a 'female' weakness rather than a (special sort of) 'human' strength. As in Ruether's standpoint, so here: Jesus may be the male messenger to *empty* 'patriarchal' values.

V

Such narrative commitment amongst theologians is thus in striking contrast to the general assumptions of mainstream analytical philosophy of religion (with which, as we have shown, Stephen Davis is in somewhat problematic conversation). Here it tends to be assumed that we know, either *a priori* or else via the authority of tradition, what 'God' must look like, as possessing a certain form of omniscience, omnipotence, omnipresence, immutability and perfect goodness.[44] It also tends to be assumed (especially where the problem of evil dictates the terms of the discussion), that a normatively 'human' trait is the possession of 'libertarian' freedom, that is, a sovereign self-possession and autonomy that is capable of rising above the weaknesses and distractions of human desires and human tragedy.[45] On this view, then, as in the patristic discussion, the gospel stories of Jesus' vulnerability and anxiety in the face of the cross present a problem to be negotiated, not a narrative prototype to be philosophically explained. But the christological difficulties are, I believe, here sharpened even beyond what Cyril and his ilk confronted. For the sovereignly-free 'individualism' of the Enlightenment 'man of reason',[46] is, when smuggled into christological construction, even more hard to square with the assumed notion of divinity inherited from the 'classical' tradition than the understandings of 'humanity' with which the Fathers themselves operated. Indeed, even the supposedly 'classical' view of

God just mentioned shows suspicious signs of bearing the masculinist projections of writers already committed to an Enlightenment view of 'man'. He, too, is another 'individual', a *very large*
disembodied spirit with ultimate directive power and freedom.[47]
How can the natures of *two* such 'individuals' concur christolog-
ically?

This point deserves a little more explication, because it shows
how gender presumptions and anxieties are, I believe, lurking in
the staunchly conservative – and for the most part staunchly anti-
'kenotic' – defence of Chalcedonian orthodoxy found in recent
analytical philosophy of religion. (I think here especially of the
work of Thomas V. Morris, David Brown and Richard Swinburne.[48]) The first point to note is the defensive resistance to any
form of feminist critique evident in the discourse of analytic
philosophy of religion in general. With striking disregard for
the developments of feminist theology, analytic philosophers of
religion have shown almost no cognizance of the profound critique
of 'masculinist' notions of God which is now almost taken for
granted in theological discussions. Nor have they heeded the
rigorous challenges of feminist philosophy, where a complex
debate has grown up about the construal of the self and of
'human' freedom in post-Enlightenment philosophy, and the
extent to which the notion of either a disembodied soul, or a
sovereignly 'free individual', may be masculinist abstractions with
little regard for bodily life, feelings or imagination – much less the
lessons of child psychology or the formative matrix of primary
family relationships.[49] So far, then, analytic philosophy of religion
has been remarkable for its resistance to feminist questionings.
The silence, we might say, is deafening.

But it is precisely in christological discussion that we can see
these basic philosophical assumptions made by analytic philosophy of religion beginning to come under strain. S.T. Davis's
probing, if uncertain, questionings about *kenōsis* are one sign;
another (as with the early twentieth-century 'kenoticists' we discussed earlier) is the revealing analogues that analytic 'anti-
kenoticists' bring to bear in their attempt to give clear expression
to the humanity and divinity in Christ. Their favourite, significantly, is the analogy of the Freudian 'divided mind'.[50] The
idea is that, as in modern psychoanalytic accounts of the self,
unconscious forces may be operating – even operating more
powerfully – than conscious forces, so too in Christ we may hold
up an image of an 'individual' with not one, but two 'centres of
consciousness' – one, however (the divine) more powerful and all-
encompassing than the other. Thomas Morris talks of an

'asymmetric accessing relation' between 'two minds', the divine encompassing the human; Richard Swinburne of 'two systems of belief to some extent independent of one another'; David Brown, rather differently, of a 'dialogue between ... conscious and sub-conscious selves'.[51] However, this basic analogue is a revealing one for a number of reasons. For a start, the very invocation here of the unconscious (or 'subconscious': they are not clearly dis-tinguished), let alone the appeal to Freud, with his messages of deep sexual motivations,[52] is a sign that the more normative 'Enlightenment man' of analytic philosophy of religion is wading out of his depth. For analytic philosophy of religion *properly* to take on Freudian issues of the unconscious or the dream-world, of primary parental relations and of sexuality, would I suspect be to transform its discourse about 'man' and 'God' almost out of all recognition; certainly it would drive it much more closely towards appreciation of feminist theological and philosophical critiques of its basic assumptions. (Contemporary continental philosophy's assimilation of Freud into its categories of discussion is a clear witness to that.[53])

But there are other uneasy aspects of this newly constructed 'orthodox' Christology.[54] For the resistance to raising previously held views about 'God' and 'man' in the light of the gospel passion narratives still shows itself in a number of ways. As in Cyril, we do not *start* from the constraints of the gospel story. Thus, since the dominating idea is that the divine pre-existent Logos must be able to *control* a (possibly resistant?) human nature, there is sometimes a covert 'Apollinarianism' lurking in the discussion, that is, the suggestion that there is a ready-made 'individual' who is the Logos and who, *qua* 'soul', simply has to join with, or take over, a human body. This kind of talk fits ill with the *two* 'centres of consciousness' otherwise promoted.[55] In Morris's work, too, there is a strange mixture, in his account of the two 'wills' in Christ, of a remaining commitment to a 'libertarian' view of human freedom, combined with an underlying concept of the divine as wholly *controlling* it.[56] Thus, as a feminist, I am not particularly consoled or inspired by the thought that Jesus' unique human–divine sin-lessness was perhaps rather like a man 'Jones', who, unbeknownst to him, has electrodes implanted in his brain by a big-brother figure, which can then prevent him from doing things that he ought not to do. In fact, however, the electrodes do not have to be operated if Jones does what he should on his own account. This rather chilling parallel is meant to give us an idea of how Jesus could be truly 'free' in a libertarian sense but at the same time 'necessarily good, unable to sin'.[57] Instead, to me as a feminist commentator, the Morrisian fantasy of one who achieves complete 'control' over someone else without that person even realizing it summons up every sort of political and sexual nightmare.

Another sign of strain to these prevalent analytic assumptions about the 'human' emerges in Richard Swinburne's insistence that human and divine natures be kept somewhat 'separate' in Christ (a strangely un-Chalcedonian form of expression[58]), lest the divine nature permeate the human in such a way as to undermine its integrity. The soteriological motivation for this point is admirable, of course, and fully in line with what we have argued above about the dangers of an eastern (or Lutheran) perception of the *communicatio idiomatum* inviting 'obliteration' of the human. What is more revealing in Swinburne's case, however, is his assumption that any sign of minor ignorance, frailty or 'desire' in Jesus is an indication of his *less*-than-perfect 'humanity'. (Indeed, this is perhaps the more profound reason why Swinburne wants to keep Jesus' humanity 'separate' from his divinity.) Thus events like Gethsemane and Golgotha seem to show Jesus' humanity, according to Swinburne, as in some sense *defective* from its true, heavenly norm.[59] But what, we may ask, if the frailty, vulnerability and 'self-effacement' of these narratives *is* what shows us 'perfect humanity'? The resistance to such a possibility is itself, I suggest, one shot through with gender implications; for to admit such would be to start to cut away the ground on which the 'man of reason' stands. But then analytic philosophy of religion is hardly noted, as we have seen, for its positive attention to states of 'passivity', 'vulnerability' or the ceding of 'control' – states, one suspects, that could normally be delegated to the subordinate (and wholly unmentioned) 'female'.[60]

Let me now sum up the results of this complex account of historic debates about *kenōsis* and its gender inflections. What we should underscore, first, about our recent comparative discussion of 'new' (theological) 'kenoticism' on the one hand, and analytic (philosophical) 'anti-kenoticism' on the other, is that both have severe – though very different – drawbacks from a feminist perspective. Whereas the 'new kenoticism' appears to make 'God' both limited and weak (by a process of direct transference from Jesus' human life to the divine), and so endanger the very capacity for divine transformative 'power', the analytic 'orthodoxy' clings ferociously to a vision of divine 'omnipotence' and 'control' which is merely the counterpart of the sexist 'man' made in his (libertarian) image. One model seems propelled by masculinist guilt; the other by unexamined masculinist assumptions. Neither considers – any more than does Hampson – the possibility of a 'strength made perfect *in* (human) weakness' (2 Corinthians 12.9), of the normative concurrence in Christ of non-bullying divine 'power' *with* 'self-effaced' humanity. It is here that the remaining potential of the third definition of *kenōsis* given earlier in our New Testament discussion (a choosing *never to have* 'worldly' forms of power), may yet, I suggest, join hands with the Giessen school's insight that *kenōsis* pertains appropriately to the *human* in a 'two natures' model. Yet we still have to confront the problems, both philosophical and feminist, that we have highlighted about the dominance of the 'Alexandrian' reading of Chalcedon, and to these issues we must now return in our final section. Can we after all locate a systematic alternative, both christological and spiritual, which finds an appropriate place for human *kenōsis* without merely reinforcing gender stereotype or sexist compliance?

As Stephen Sykes has well observed, the lessons of what he calls 'the strange persistence of kenotic christology' are mainly about failures in *anthropomorphism*.[61] What we tend (unwittingly, often) to read on to God from our human perspective will surely be revealed when we start to think about questions of *kenōsis*. And hence the extraordinary complexity of this historical tale I have just told, and the entanglement of gender themes with metaphysical and semantic choices. Before going on to explicate a feminist version of *kenōsis* which will, I believe, show a way beyond the Ruether–Hampson exchange (and also retrieve those strands in the story which are capable of contemporary application), it may therefore be worth pausing to recapitulate some of the ironies and confusions that have been laid bare in this account.

By distinguishing six different meanings of *kenōsis*, and highlighting the lack of clear interconnections between different discourses on the matter, we have demonstrated how various exponents of *kenōsis* can disagree on even such basic matters as: whether *kenōsis* involves pre-existence (or not); whether it implies a temporary loss of all or some divine characteristics (or neither); whether the 'emptying' applies to the divine nature or the human (or alternatively rejects 'two natures' Christology altogether); and whether the effects of *kenōsis* pass to the eternal nature of the Godhead (or not). Thus, further, when charges of 'kenoticism' are levelled by such as oppose it, they may often turn out to be shadow-boxing, to be attributing to the 'enemy' a position she or he never occupied (the total, if temporary, loss of the divine nature, for instance);[62] and, conversely, someone who (like Gore) embraces the *title* 'kenoticist' may actually hold a position on 'two centres of consciousness' almost indistinguishable from an 'anti-kenotic' defender of Chalcedon.[63]

As if this complexity were not enough, we have attempted to weave into it a thoroughgoing feminist analysis of the different options. What we now see even more clearly, I trust, is that Hampson's critique scores only against relatively modern forms of *kenōsis*, and in particular those where the 'emptying' is regarded as compensating for an existing set of gender presumptions that might be called 'masculinist'.[64] Thus in the course of our discussion we have detected two fundamental problems with the generalizing tone of Hampson's original criticism of *kenōsis*. First, it does not apply to notions of human *kenōsis* where 'masculinist' (or 'worldly', bullying) forms of power are eschewed *from the outset* by Jesus (and this, it seems, is closer to Ruether's position); and second, it appears to presume the very questions it is begging about gender stereotypes: the alignment of 'males' with achieved, worldly power, and women with lack of it. The presumption is that women *need* 'power' – but of what sort? How are they to avoid aping the 'masculinism' they criticize? In taking up these two points in my closing section I want to sketch out an alternative that Hampson seems not to have considered. For what – as I have hinted several times – if true divine 'empowerment' occurs most unimpededly in the context of a *special* form of human 'vulnerability'?

VI

But what form should this human vulnerability take? It is no secret why 'vulnerability' has been such a taboo subject in Christian feminist writing up till now.[65] The (rightful) concentration in the literature on the profound, and continuing, damage to women from sexual and physical abuse, even in 'Christian' families and churches, and on the seeming legitimation of this by men otherwise committed to disciplined religious practice and the rhetoric of cruciform redemption,[66] shows what a perilous path we are treading here. An undiscriminating adulation of 'vulnerability' might appear to condone, or even invite, such evils. I do not in any way underestimate these difficulties; nor do I wish to make a straightforward *identification* between 'vulnerability' in general (often a dangerous or regrettable state) and the particular notion of spiritual *kenōsis* here under discussion. But what I am suggesting is that there is another, and longer-term, danger to Christian feminism in the *repression* of all forms of 'vulnerability', and in a concomitant failure to confront issues of fragility, suffering or 'self-emptying' except in terms of victimology. And that is ultimately the failure to embrace a feminist reconceptualizing of the power of the cross and resurrection. Only, I suggest, by facing – and giving new expression to – the paradoxes of 'losing one's life in order to save it', can feminists hope to construct a vision of the Christic 'self' that transcends the gender stereotypes we are seeking to up-end.

But what can I mean by this? I know of no better way to express it than by reflection on the practice of prayer, and especially worldless prayer or 'contemplation'.[67] This is to take a few leaps beyond the notion of *kenōsis* as a speculative christological theory about the incarnate life of Jesus; but if the majority of New Testament commentators are correct, then the 'hymn' of Philippians 2 was, from the start, an invitation to enter into Christ's extended life in the church, not just to speculate dispassionately on his nature.[68] The 'spiritual' extension of Christic *kenōsis*, then (if we can now favour our third definition from above, that is, the avoidance of all 'snatching' from the outset), involves an ascetical commitment of some subtlety, a regular and willed *practice* of ceding and responding to the divine. The rhythm of this *askēsis* is already inscribed ritually and symbolically in the sacraments of baptism and eucharist; but in prayer (especially the defenceless prayer of silent waiting on God) it is 'internalized' over time in a peculiarly demanding and transformative fashion. If I am asked, then, what Christian feminism must do to avoid emulating the very forms of 'worldly' power we criticize in 'masculinism', I point to this *askēsis*. It might be objected (by an extension of Hampson's original argument, though not one she herself applies), that such a danger is not one confronted by women less fortunate, less affluent and less 'powerful' than such as me. But I do wonder about this. Foucault has shown us that we all wield 'power' in *some* area,[69] however insignificant it may appear to the outside world (power over our children, our aged dependants, even our domestic animals). If 'abusive' human power is thus always potentially within our grasp, how can we best approach the healing resources of a non-abusive divine power? How can we hope to invite and channel it, if not by a patient opening of the self to its transformation?

What I have elsewhere called the 'paradox of power and vulnerability'[70] is I believe uniquely focused in this act of silent waiting on the divine in prayer. This is because we can only be properly 'empowered' here if we cease to set the agenda, if we 'make space' for God to be God. Prayer which makes this 'space' may take a variety of forms, and should not be conceived in an élitist way; indeed, the debarring of 'ordinary' Christians from

'contemplation' has been one of the most sophisticated – and
spiritually mischievous – ways of keeping lay women (and men)
from exercising religious influence in the western church.[71] Such
prayer may use a repeated phrase to ward off distractions, or be
wholly silent; it may be simple Quaker attentiveness, or take a
charismatic expression (such as the use of quiet rhythmic
'tongues'). What is sure, however, is that engaging in any such
regular and repeated 'waiting on the divine' will involve great
personal commitment and great personal risk; to put it in psychological terms, the dangers of a too-sudden uprush of material
from the unconscious, too immediate a contact of the thus-
disarmed self with God, are not inconsiderable. To this extent the
careful driving of wedges – which began to appear in the western
church from the twelfth century on – between 'meditation'
(discursive reflection on Scripture) and 'contemplation' (this more
vulnerable activity of 'space-making'), were not all cynical in their
attempts to keep contemplation 'special'.[72] But whilst risky, this
practice is profoundly transformative, 'empowering' in a mysterious 'Christic' sense; for it is a feature of the *special* 'self-effacement' of this gentle space-making – this yielding to divine power
which is no worldly power – that it marks one's willed engagement in the pattern of cross and resurrection, one's deeper rooting
and grafting into the 'body of Christ'. 'Have *this* mind in you',
wrote Paul, 'which was also in Christ Jesus'; the meaning of that
elliptical phrase in Greek still remains obscure, but I am far from
being the first to interpret it in this spiritual sense, as a 'hidden
self-emptying of the heart'.[73]

If, then, these traditions of Christian 'contemplation' are to be
trusted, this rather special form of 'vulnerability' is not an invitation to be battered; nor is its silence a silenc*ing*. (If anything, it
builds one in the courage to give prophetic voice.) By choosing to
'make space' in this way, one 'practises' the 'presence of God' –
the subtle but enabling presence of a God who neither shouts nor
forces, let alone 'obliterates'. No one can *make* one 'contemplate'
(though the grace of God invites it); but it is the simplest thing in
the world *not* to 'contemplate', to turn away from that grace.
Thus the 'vulnerability' that is its human condition is not about
asking for unnecessary and unjust suffering (though increased self-
knowledge can indeed be painful); nor is it (in Hampson's words)
a 'self-abnegation'. On the contrary, this special 'self-emptying' is
not a negation of self, but the place of the self's transformation
and expansion into God.

To make such claims as these is clearly to beg many questions,
and I cannot answer them all in the brief compass of this essay. A

number of possible misunderstandings (that this prayer is élitist, or the luxury of a leisured class, or an invitation to abuse, or a recipe for political passivity) I have already tried to avert. The 'mystics' of the church have often been from surprising backgrounds, and their messages rightly construed as subversive; their insights have regularly chafed at the edges of doctrinal 'orthodoxy', and they have rejoiced in the coining of startling (sometimes erotically startling) new metaphors to describe their experiences of God. Those who have appealed to a 'dark' knowing beyond speech have thus challenged the smugness of accepted anthropomorphisms for God, have probed (to use the language of contemporary French feminism) to the subversive place of the 'semiotic'.[74]

But no human, contemplative or otherwise, is beyond the reach of either self-deception or manipulation by others; and the spiritual literature of the Christian tradition is rife with examples of male directors who have chosen to confuse this special contemplative 'vulnerability' to the divine with enforced female submission to priestly authority, or to undeserved and unnecessary physical and mental suffering.[75] These problems and dangers can only be confronted, however, by the making of fine, but important, distinctions: between this 'right' vulnerability and mere invitation to abuse;[76] between this contemplative 'self-effacement' and self-destruction or self-repression;[77] between the productive suffering of self-disclosure and the decentring torture of pain for pain's sake.[78] That the making of these 'crucial' distinctions (and I use the word advisedly) is itself powerful,[79] is a lesson only gradually being learned in white feminist theology – such has been the repression of a productive 'theology of the cross' in the face of continuing disclosures of women's abuse in the *name* of the 'cross'. It is striking, indeed, how much less coy is Black womanist theology about naming the 'difference' between abusive 'suffering' on the one hand, and a productive or empowering form of 'pain' on the other;[80] for Black theology has necessarily never evaded the theological problems of undeserved suffering.

Where, then, finally, does gender find its place in the 'contemplative' reception to the divine I have tried to describe? The answer is in one sense obvious: is not such willed 'passivity' a traditionally 'female' trait? Is not this precisely why 'mystical' literature has so greatly emphasized the huge psychic reversals for men engaged in such 'submission' to the divine? And hence, is not the obvious danger here the one with which we started, that is, Hampson's charge that *kenōsis* may only be 'useful' to men, as a complement to their masculinism? But I have already tried to hint at a way in which I believe the contemplative exercise may take us beyond such existing gender stereotypes, up-ending them in its gradual undermining of *all* previous certainties and dogmatisms. Here, if I am right, is 'power-in-vulnerability', the willed efface-ment to a gentle omnipotence which, far from 'complementing' masculinism, acts as its undoing. And whilst spiritual *kenōsis*, thus construed, may, in our current cultural climate, be easy for men to avoid altogether, and even easier, perhaps, for women seriously to misconstrue (as 'appropriate' sexual submission), we cannot rest while such implied 'essentialist' visions of gender still exercise us. When Hampson talks of the 'male' God I fear she is thus resting.

If, moreover, the more speculative christological counterpart of this appeal to *kenōsis* is to be laid bare, it must, as I have hinted, take a form not radically dissimilar from that of the Giessen theologians of the seventeenth century, that is, a form in which the 'emptying' applies to Christ's human nature rather than to the divine. To choose otherwise would be to fall into the manifold incoherencies and difficulties of Thomasius and his descendents, or, with the 'new kenoticists', to reduce God's 'power' to an inherent powerlessness. Yet if we are to avoid the lurking 'docetism' of the Alexandrian tradition, we shall also have to embrace a reading of Chalcedon that owes more to the Christology of the rival school of Antioch, that is, one in which Christ's personal identity (his *hypostasis*) is *confected out* of the 'concurrence' of the human and the divine, not already *identified with* the invulnerable pre-existent Logos.[81] In other words, what Christ on this view instantiates is the very 'mind' that we ourselves enact, or enter into, in prayer: the unique intersection of vulner-able, 'non-grasping' humanity and authentic divine power, itself 'made perfect in weakness'.

Ultimately, of course, Christian virtue is known by its 'fruits'. Perhaps this is the only final and safe test of 'contemplation', in which activity – I freely admit – so much self-deception, and so much bewilderment and uncertainty, can attend even faithful and regular practice. Strangely, I think this – my practical conclusion about 'fruits' – is the point at which Hampson is most likely to agree with me: our theological conceptions and institutional commitments diverge at many points, but our sense of what feminism aims to gain and display is curiously convergent. What then do we seek in feminist *discretio spirituum*? Love, joy, peace – yes, and all the other Pauline spiritual fruits and gifts; but espec-ially we must add to these: personal empowerment, prophetic resistance, courage in the face of oppression, and the destruction of false idolatry. What Hampson and other post-Christians do not believe in any more, however, is the importance of what we may call the narrative 'gap', the *hiatus* of expectant waiting, that is the precondition of our assimilation of Christ's 'kenotic' cross and resurrection. That this form of waiting often brings bewilderment and pain as the new 'self' struggles to birth, I cannot deny; that it is also transformative and empowering, I affirm; that Christian feminism ignores it at its peril, I have here tried to suggest; and that it is what finally keeps me a Christian as well as a feminist, it has been the task of this paper to explore.[82]

7
RESPONSE: *Daphne Hampson*

It has been agreed that I should be allowed more space for response as so much of the debate is directed at my thought. But where should I commence? The answer is in a sense obvious: with the gross misunderstanding of my work which occurs in Janet's piece. So much else – my response to what else Janet has to say, to Julie, Jane and Nicola and even in part to Sarah's very different essay – follows from what I must respond to Janet.

There is a confusion about the word 'particularity'. Janet writes: 'It is that aspect which Daphne Hampson finds most estranging in traditional Christianity to which I find myself continuously drawn – its particularity' (p. 31). Particularity in what sense? If we are talking about the fact that Christianity looks to the particular (which is what Janet with half of herself seems to mean), that it concerns the life and works of a particular man, that he told edifying parables which concerned concrete life situations of particular people, then in *that* sense I have no problems at all with Christianity concentrating on the particular. Quite the contrary. I find myself much attracted, for example, to so-called 'virtue ethics' precisely because it looks to the particular circumstances within which a group of moral agents are placed. Again, in relation to spirituality, I must surely start in a Quaker meeting from the beauty of the bowl of flowers on the table, or in prayer from the needs of my particular friend. I am precisely attracted to so much women's thought, whether Carol Gilligan's contention that we take our ethical decisions in relation to particular concrete circumstances, or the concentration on the particular in the ethical writing of Iris Murdoch or Martha Nussbaum (who would not necessarily call themselves 'feminists') because of its particularity. Nothing could be further from the case than the supposition, half implied, that I am interested in vague or abstract theories.

What I cannot believe in is particularity in the sense in which this was ruled out in the eighteenth century. That is to say I do not think that there can be one-off examples in nature or interruptions in the causal nexus of history (such as a bodily resurrection *par excellence* would imply). Newton in the early eighteenth century (even he) thought, when his mathematics did not work out, that this was the hand of God who every so often put the planets back on course. Then Neptune was discovered! The mathematics worked. Perhaps such an intervention is what Janet would understand under her term 'Wizard-of-Oz' interventions. But if you do not believe in Wizard-of-Oz interventions, then in what sort of intervention, in what sort of particularity, do you believe Janet? For me Christianity has become not credible because I cannot believe that one human being, and one alone, could have a second and divine nature (particularity); or that there could be one, and only one, example of resurrection. I should have thought that this was the basic problem with which Christians have been confronted since the Enlightenment?

Thus I want to unpack, Janet, your comment that 'we are not the first generation to find the particularity of the Christian faith scandalous, nor the first to be acquainted with belief systems of a more abstract and universal appeal'. You proceed then to instance that Augustine might well have been alienated by 'the unedifying tales of an unimportant provincial people like the Jews'. It seems to me that you have muddled two different meanings given to particularity here and that your remarks lack a historical perspective. Of course, since the eighteenth century at least, Christians have had to proclaim 'the scandal of particularity': they knew that what they had to confess was incommensurate with the rest of human knowledge. (I have already said that it is not that the only other possibility is to move, for example, to some abstract deism: one can concentrate on the particular, while not believing, as a modern person, that there could be particularity in the sense of a break in the causal nexus of nature or history.) My problem is then not what you state Augustine's problem to be; that one might think unedifying the tales of a provincial people. The particularity of Christianity in that sense does not bother me. But Augustine, I must insist, as a man living in the fifth century, did not have our post-Enlightenment sense that there could not be particular one-off events which broke the causal nexus. Christianity may always have been scandalous (note St Paul's words, to the Greeks a scandal) in the sense of not being abstract. But its claim to particularity looks quite different in the modern world. (Indeed I would want to say that the beliefs which grew up around Jesus – for example, that he had been resurrected – could only have grown up because people in the ancient world did not comprehend what we now know about the regularity of nature.)

Nor from all I am able to grasp – and I have now talked with various people involved in modern physics who know about quantum mechanics, or who are philosophers of science – is there anything about our current understanding of the universe which essentially makes possible what became known to be impossible in the eighteenth century. Thus quantum mechanics does indeed make conceivably thinkable – though it is one chance in so many million as not to bear thinking about – that my body could be transported outside the room in which I sit at my computer. But this does not help with resurrections; with a person coming back from the dead. Again, it is a great confusion to think that, because we now believe the basis of matter to be in some way random (there is an 'uncertainty principle' built into it), this should help the Christian cause. It is not that, at some point in history, say 1120 for the sake of argument, there suddenly came to be randomness at the basis of reality. (That would be equivalent to the kind of particularity which Christians proclaim in saying that God was differently related to one man or one tradition than to all other persons or traditions.) The basis of reality has always been whatever it is; and we may not yet have gone through all the revolutions we shall undergo in our ever greater approximations to what is the case. But whatever it is like, we should presumably say that reality has not changed. The particularity which Christians must needs, in some form, credit is no more possible than was seen to be the case in the eighteenth century.

That Christians must believe in particularity in *this* sense, in a way that contravenes what we thought we knew about the nature of the world, seems to be clear. A Christian is surely – as I am for ever saying – someone who believes Jesus to have been the Christ; who feels obliged to confess his uniqueness. (That there have been different ways of expressing this uniqueness in different periods of Christian history is of course the case; we can take a much broader definition of Christian than the bounds of Chalcedonian orthodoxy.) A number of my colleagues in this book seem to me to be unclear about this, but let me respond to Janet for the moment. You write Janet (p. 18) that Christianity is 'capable of being the good news for women'. Now I don't doubt for a minute that much of Jesus' teaching may be appropriated by women. Again, I don't doubt that, were it the case that Christianity were true (for example that there was a resurrection), this might be counted good news by women as well as men. But I do question (as I think you do) that Christianity is simply a 'message'. It is also a statement of faith in things which I cannot credit as having possibly been the case. Again, you tell me that Christians are always rereading their stories; that they look forward to a future realization of their ideals through the eschaton or the building of the kingdom of heaven on earth (p. 29). Once again I do not doubt that this is the case. (Incidentally all sorts of people, including atheists, Marxists and feminists may want to bring in a utopia.) But the fact that Christians reread their stories and look forward to the realization of their ideals does not touch the issue as to whether Christianity is true. For Christianity does not just consist in ethics or in parable. It makes a claim about the uniqueness of Jesus as the Christ.

I am then in complete agreement with you Janet when you state, of liberal Protestantism, that, if that is all that Christianity is about (Jesus in a very fine human being deeply in tune with God) then the feminist may well ask (as I have) why then look to this particular person? Let me put it this way: the claim that Jesus rose from the dead, if true, is not some minor fact, which can take its place in world history alongside all other events. If true, it would show that everything which I (and we may say the whole post-Enlightenment world) think to be the case, is false. The nature of what is the case, or of what is possible, would be wholly different. I understand then how it is that you Janet must think in terms of a triune God which is ultimate reality. As my theological teacher Arthur McGill used to say: either Christ is nothing – viz. just a human – or world shattering. What he is not, is what Kierkegaard contended Christians had made him into, a divine Uncle George. But now we come unstuck in our mutual comprehension at another point. Comparing the resurrection to the Big Bang, you contend that, if the latter was possible why not the former? (Your other example, prayer, is beside the point: if prayer is powerful, then it is powerful in every age. We may have to extend any narrow eighteenth-century sense as to what can be the case. But if it is so that prayer is powerful then that is part of what reality is like and no particularity – in the sense which I am contending impossible – is implied.) But the Big Bang is not an intervention, not a breaking of the laws of this universe (whatever they may be) in the way in which a resurrection would be.

Again on another tack I would ask this. Your argument seems to be that nothing has changed since the eighteenth century in relation to the question of the credibility of a resurrection, or presumably 'God sending his Son'. Of course I agree: Hume's arguments against particularity and against an argument from design for the existence of God are as applicable now as they then were. Nevertheless the scale of things has certainly changed; and I am wondering when a quantitative change becomes also in some sense a qualitative change? We now know that our solar system is part way out in one arm of a galaxy called 'the milky way', and galaxies themselves, it is coming to be thought, form clusters (such that there are clusters of galaxies). What do you mean that God 'sent his Son' to planet earth? I must ask the same question as the sceptic of the eighteenth century, who asked it in a different context than someone in the first century who thought the earth at the centre of the universe. I would suggest however that in our age there has been yet another leap, such that the context of this question comes to be differently placed.

So then to the question of the 'turning' of symbols. Of course I agree entirely that symbols are multivalent. They assume a particular meaning within a social context in which they are given that meaning. Your examples of the dreaming spires of Oxford and the eucharistic bread being understood differently by different people are fine. I have no reason to doubt that biblical stories can be read from a new perspective; look at the flowering of liberation theology, which has precisely so reread. But I do not believe that any of this is of much help to feminists. In the first place (as I have said), I do not think that there could be a 'particularity' such as that which Christianity claims, so that we have an especial reason to look to events surrounding Jesus of Nazareth two thousand years ago. I think our spirituality must start in the present, drawing on the past as we will. (That is to say, in terms of my article in this book, I think our religion must be autonomous and not display the heteronomy which Christianity must necessarily have through its situatedness in a past era of history.)

But secondly, although one might be able to reread a particular biblical story, or fill a particular symbol with new meaning, the problem for feminists in relation to Christianity is that the *whole context* is patriarchal. Thus the Bible overwhelmingly concerns male characters (whether in the recitation of history or the examples given in parable), God is understood as 'male', Jesus who is the Christ is central to the story and (most problematic of all perhaps) women are largely placed in roles decreed for them by patriarchy. Nor is there a Christian feminist scholar present in every pulpit, writing every school Scripture lesson, standing by every crib in a shop window at Christmas saying: 'You've got it wrong. Your reading is a wholly patriarchal view of the world. You must reread these symbols so that they do not demean women.' Such a rewriting is surely impossible. We should have lost the story and the symbols. The part of the Bible untainted by sexism, as has truly been said, could be written if not on a postage stamp then on a postcard. It seems to me Janet that you are not taking seriously that Christianity is an ideology; it has been that ideology which, supremely, has served to legitimize patriarchy in the West.

Having responded thus to Janet I can in short compass respond to Jane, Julie, Nicola, and say something of that which I wish to respond to Sarah. To turn to Jane's essay first. Yes, Jane, I don't doubt but that what you call the 'gospel message' has been freeing to many women; to women in seventeenth-century England and to black women today. Moreover I don't doubt that it has been read and appropriated differently by women in these different contexts. Your give-way sentence is however (p. 51), referring to the idea that there could be such a thing as 'Christianity' or 'feminism': 'it implies that there is one Christian message'. Christianity is not, I must insist, just a message (nor multiple messages). Christianity *minimally* must consist in some belief in Jesus as the Christ. (Otherwise we might as well look to the message of many people, seers and saints down the ages.) It is this that I am saying I cannot credit (for I do not think that there could be such a particularity); and which I am contending makes Christianity sexist, for Christians cannot but refer to a past period of history in which this particularity is held to have been situated (and that history is patriarchal). So it helps me not one whit to hear that some women have found the Christian message freeing: no doubt.

Again I must say this. I think we must have some *minimal* definition of feminism, when considering whether Christianity and feminism are compatible. I would have thought that that minimal definition was the 'equality of women and men' with all that that implies. I am contending that a religion based on this past patriarchal history and these patriarchal symbols, though it may be freeing in some respects (witness the gospel message which might be about human equality), cannot actually promote equality as long as it is based on this history and retains the symbols for God which arose out of that context. Maybe some black women today, as also women in the seventeenth century, are not yet living in a situation in which they could envision equality. Maybe Christianity is the best that can be hoped for in the oppression of Latin American society. But in modern Europe today (perhaps more so than in 'Christian' America) it is simply not the case that we have no other possibility than to reinterpret our situation within the framework of this myth. We can start thinking what a spirituality would be like which actually did allow for equality; and that, I am saying, would mean dropping the Christian myth.

In regard to poststructuralism I would simply comment that one should note that, particularly in its Derridean, deconstructionist, form, it makes Christianity impossible. For Christianity claims what Derrida will call 'presence': that there is a uniqueness to

Christian claims, a God beyond the world, a point at which there is truth. Deconstruction does not make Christianity more possible; it declares there to be no such absoluteness (a claim which has been fundamental to western theism). (It is the same argument, in different form, about particularity, but it extends that to any metaphysical absolute one might say.) Post-structuralism may help feminists in enabling diverse readings of texts. (Though I should want to ask what a reading of a biblical text which did not make women secondary would look like?) But we have already said that Christianity cannot simply consist in different more liberative reading of texts, or a proclamation of other versions of the gospel message. Christianity makes a truth claim, and a truth claim of a type which at least Derridean deconstruction sets out to deny.

So then we suddenly hear – p. 65 in Jane's essay – that God so loved the world that he sent his only begotten Son. Oh? Where does this come from? What status does this claim have? I had supposed that the 'gospel message' was about the overturning of an unjust society, treating women as equals etc. If God sending his Son is just 'mythological language' then I should want to say one is not yet making a Christian claim; for Christians believe there to be uniqueness, however that may be expressed. (I should then, if it is mythological language, want to ask whether it is the most helpful mythology for a feminist to employ.) If however it is metaphorical language, used because one has nothing but metaphor when it comes to ultimate things, but the metaphor is intended to be a metaphor *for something* and a claim for uniqueness is being made, then your position, Jane, is indeed Christian. I should want to question you however as to how there could be any such uniqueness?

I turn then to Julie's essay and I think that the response which I must make will already be evident. Julie tells us that: 'God is the One who acts to save in history and in creation. God, who liberated the Hebrew slaves from Egypt, revealed his identity to Moses ...' etc. (p. 77). What status, I ask myself, does such a statement have? What does it mean that 'God acts', as opposed to 'human beings believed God to have acted'? I read further with this question in mind. Liberation theologians, I am told, refuse 'to separate the sphere of profane history from the revelation of salvation history'. (It sounds, incidentally, rather like Pannenberg; which alerts me to the fact that such a historiography will not necessarily lead to the left-wing political practice of which Julie, and I, would approve.) 'This type of theology', Julie continues, 'places God in the centre of socio-economic life.' So we are talking about God are we? 'God is incarnate and embodied', Julie contends. What does this mean? Is it a metaphor? Does Julie believe in the incarnation? We read further: 'Certainly an embodied and suffering God was the original message of Christianity.' Certainly it was. But though the early Christians may have proclaimed something like this, I cannot believe in the incarnation. Then we learn: 'The only thing we know for certain is that his [Jesus'] name has been connected with a belief; namely that God was revealed in history through a radical prophet ... that three days later some women and men disciples witnessed him alive and ... they began to preach a new religion'. Yes: I suppose that that is what they believed and what they proclaimed. How credulous they were! Or perhaps they were just speaking mythologically?! It still remains open what it is that Julie believes to be the case. Then we find: 'This is a powerful and radically disturbing *symbolic story* ...' (italics mine). Ahha! And again: 'I shall only be convinced it is time for Christian women to give up this myth [sic] when I can be persuaded that another myth can better satisfy ...' etc.[1]

So why is it helpful to have a myth; a myth which one does not think to be true to what is in fact the case (for one cannot actually believe Jesus to have risen from the dead etc.)? Personally I could not live my life on the basis of a lie, or a 'mythological lie' should we say. Absolutely fundamental to me is a kind of integrity – intellectual and personal – which would not allow this. As a feminist, if I did want to hold to a myth, a sacred story, I should not choose one about God (conceived in male terms), sending his Son, who took my sins, etc. Nor am I clear that we need such myths that we may be inspired to radical political action. Nor that such a myth could be empowering if one knew it to be just that; a myth. If however Julie should want to back-pedal and say no I do not mean that it is a myth, I hold that it is true, then I should want to ask all the questions as to the possibility of the truth of this myth: the questions about particularity and the possibility of intervention and events which at the macro level break the causal nexus.

Julie finally speaks of Christianity as a 'spiritual and social path to the transcendent dimension of life'. I am not quite sure what she means, but is this perhaps what I intend when I speak of 'another dimension of reality' which we call God? If so let me point out that one by no means needs to be Christian in order to think that there is such a dimension: Buddhists may be said to hold this, western theists such as myself may hold this, etc.

I turn then to Nicola's essay, and my comments are becoming

almost predictable. Nicola tells me that: 'A Christian is one who lives in creative, fruitful relation to the Jesus-story, rather than one who believes certain doctrines about Jesus as the Christ.' OK, fine (except that I think that something more would have to be said than this for someone to be a Christian, but let us look at it). Presumably then, according to Nicola's definition, if I should find other stories more fruitful, I am free to discard the Christian story? A Christian is one who just happens to find this particular story fruitful? I think it most probable that I can indeed find other stories which could acquire greater symbolic significance in my life. But then Nicola quotes, seemingly with approval, Stephen Barton's words to the effect that if it could be shown that Jesus was irredeemably sexist 'this would constitute a serious problem for those in the Church today who wish discrimination against women to end'. But why? If to be a Christian is simply to find a story fruitful, why not use the Christian story insofar as one finds it to be fruitful and discard it insofar as one finds Jesus (if one does so find) to be misogynist like the rest of his generation. The story can have no authority over us given Nicola's stance.

Barton however clearly intends something very different: the story has authority over us and we have a heteronomous relation towards it; such that, were it to be shown that Jesus was sexist, this would constitute a 'serious problem' in the way of inaugurating a non-sexist regime in the church today. That is to say, what Christians are to do in the church today, is to be in some way dependent on what a certain Jew, who lived in a patriarchal society, subject to a patriarchal religion, did or said, two thousand years ago. Heteronomy we may say with a vengeance! Women are left hanging (on the results of biblical scholarship perhaps). Their dignity, rights and integrity are to be dependent on the words and actions of this man (or we might say this person, for it is immaterial which sex he was). Now if Jesus is the Christ, the incarnate Son of God, then his words and actions might be important. (One can see why, for Barton, if they are misogynist this constitutes a 'serious problem'.) But if no such truth claims are being made (as Nicola seems not to want to make) then there is no earthly reason to give that story significance. Personally I chose not to.

And so to Sarah's essay. In the first place one could make some comments in parallel to those which I have made in response to Janet, to Jane, to Julie and to Nicola. Is there present in Sarah's essay a belief that there is a Trinity, of which the second person became incarnate through a *kenōsis*; or alternatively that the man Jesus lived a life which was a *kenōsis* of patriarchy which acquires significance because he was the Son of God (or however Sarah would express his uniqueness)? If it is 'just a metaphor' this is confusing, since people have for generations believed it to be a metaphor which conforms to a truth. If you yourself Sarah think the latter to be the case, well then Christians are placed in a heteronomous situation in relation to something which they are, are they, supposed to emulate; which 'happened' in whatever sense (I am not sure what!).

But further, it surprises me Sarah that you should think that there is a Hampson–Ruether debate over *kenōsis*. I had thought that at least in this Rosemary Ruether and I thought alike. It was she who suggested to me the idea of *kenōsis* as a critique of patriarchy (and I cite her).[2] While she (in the course of reviewing *Theology and Feminism*) picking up specifically on my discussion of *kenōsis* (as relevant to men but not to women), comments: 'With these kinds of criticisms of the patriarchal character of traditional Christian theology and Christology *I am totally in agreement. Indeed in describing these criticisms I have added some of the language which I typically use to analyse these same issues.*'[3] No divergence here of which I know?

I turn however to the substance of the matter. I wish to make two points, which are interrelated. Firstly, it strikes me that, in commending *kenōsis* to women, you, Sarah, are continuing to move within the alternatives present in a dichotomous, 'male', paradigm. I wish to jump right outside that paradigm. Through not envisaging this, you misconstrue where I am or what I could mean. Secondly, I want to question the appropriateness of sexual metaphors for depicting the human relation to God.

To turn to the first of these: the alternatives, restrictive as they seem to me, present in the dichotomy within which you move. You write: 'is the "abandonment" of certain forms of control or power seen here in Christ's human realm to be regarded as of imitative spiritual significance only to *men*? Is Hampson objecting to "self-emptying", "vulnerability", or surrendering of "control" featuring in *any* form in her vision of women's spiritual flourishing?'[4] That is to say you, Sarah, seem to be working within a dichotomy; a dichotomy which would seem to me to be peculiarly masculinist. *Either* one is in control, one has power, and given what else you have to say I think we may add, one is complete in oneself in the sense of being self-enclosed; *or* one lets go, one becomes 'vulnerable', open, and 'defenceless'. This dichotomy has been written into Christianity with its talk of God as powerful on the one hand, and as giving up on power in the *kenōsis* of the incarnation on the other. (I discuss this further in my article 'On Power and Gender'.)[5] I refuse the alternatives. Let me recall the

definition I gave in the opening lines of the essay which I contribute to this volume, on the subject of what it means to be a self:
'It is only as I am treated as an equal, and conceive of myself as
such, that I shall be able to be fully present to others. Our goal
must be that persons are centred in themselves and open to one
another.' That is it. I think one must live in easy intercourse with
others: both centred and open. (Indeed, as I suggest in my essay,
able so to be open because one has a centredness, and acquiring
that centredness precisely through the relation with others.) I do
not think then that it is either for us to be 'in control', having
power and self-sufficiency; or, on the other hand, therefore
needing to be broken open, vulnerable and defenceless, inviting the
invasion of others. I think that the male paradigm of *kenōsis*, as I
have indicated, is a correction (and a needed correction) to the
male conception of power and self-enclosure (which men have
then predicated of God). But not starting with such a view of the
self (or of God), I refuse the corrective. I wish, as a feminist not
least, to overcome this dichotomy.

Thus your further comments Sarah such as 'Has she [myself]
not assumed ... that ... such ("male") power ought now *rightly* to
be pursued (also by way of compensation) by feminist women?'
strike me as quite beside the point. Feminist women, as I understand it, are wanting to 'deconstruct' the dichotomy of power and
powerlessness. As Derrida would say, they are wishing to introduce a third term which should jam the machinery of the
dichotomy as it is has previously been construed. Thus in my
article 'On Power and Gender' which I mention, I suggest that the
feminist paradigm is not powerfulness, nor that of the self-
divestment of power which is *kenōsis*, but rather (what is not
envisaged within the masculinist dichotomy), the mutual
empowerment of persons. To say it again: I think we are both
centred and relational, each of these enabling the other.

To turn then to the second matter which I should like to discuss,
the sexual overtones, or undertones, of your writing. I think it is
fascinating. You have subverted what have been the male ways,
present in their theology for two thousand years, of writing their
sexuality into their theological models. In my forthcoming *After
Christianity* I suggest, for example, that the out-pouring of love as
it is found in the doctrine of the Trinity is predicated upon the
nature of male genitality. Why should not women, equally, who
are Christians (as you wish to be), write a female sexuality into
their depiction of the human relation with God? Note the extent to
which you do this. (I do not know whether it was your intention
that one should read with a Freudian pair of eyes.) You speak of

'vulnerability', of 'surrendering of control', more worryingly one might think of 'self-effacement', of 'passivity', of 'a regular and willed practice of ceding ... to the divine', of 'defenceless' prayer. Perhaps in some sense you do intend this and you want to walk a tightrope between such language being acceptable (apparently) when conceptualizing (or experiencing?) the relation to God, and its misuse in the hands of men so that it should legitimize abuse of women.

I am however left with questions. In the first place the corollary of this deeply sexual language is that God, if God is to be what it must mean to be God and if God is understood metaphorically as 'male', must necessarily be construed to be 'masculine', while the believer (whether a woman or, I suppose, a man) must take up the 'feminine' position in relation to the 'male' God. You use the word 'passive'. One confirms, rather than undermines, these sexual stereotypes. (Incidentally you have before now accused me – coming from what you surmise is my Protestant background – of conceptualizing the Christian God as a powerful 'male'; a God which I have, consequently, needed to reject. But tell me: could this God of whom you speak in these terms be conceived of as anything other than 'male'?) Moreover I must ask this. Given that one thinks that it has been hugely problematic that, throughout western history, men have had a propensity to substitute, for a down-to-earth relation with a woman, a mystical 'sexual' relation to an ethereal God, can it be helpful that women should do this? You speak of 'a God who neither shouts nor forces'. And again: 'this rather special form of "vulnerability" is not an invitation to be battered; nor is its silence a silenc*ing*.' God has become the good lover.

Furthermore, I find myself wondering about the understanding of the self implicit in your writing. You speak of a 'disarmed self', of the 'great personal risk' of 'yielding to divine power'. It sounds as though one is such an enclosed self that to be so open to God is an ordeal! I wish to see the self as formed by relatedness; and, being centred, able to relate. Luce Irigaray impresses me by her use, philosophically, of markedly erotic imagery for describing, in her case, the relations between the sexes which she would have. But hers is a language of mutual exchange, through which each is empowered. That is very different. Perhaps such language is not available if God (who must remain God) is to be conceived of anthropomorphically?

I have no problem with 'vulnerability' *per se*. It is because we (women in particular you suggest) are vulnerable that we have material with which to work, that we may become a complex self enjoying tensile strength. As Nietzsche famously said (and Victor Frankl, extraordinarily, repeated to the inmates of the concentration camp in which he was placed), 'was uns nicht umbringt, macht uns stärker': what does not kill you, strengthens you. The enclosed self, often understood as 'male', which keeps others at a distance through creating barriers against them, is not actually strong but brittle. Sheer vulnerability however, untransformed, is likely to lead in effect to the exploitation of others. You suggest crucifixion to be an extension of incarnation. What I should admire about Jesus is not vulnerability, but the capacity, even in that extremity, to retain a measure of self-integrity.

The time of silence which I keep each day (your contemplative prayer) I do believe enables me to come to 'myself' again. God, hence, must be understood not as one to whom I am related heteronomously, but as one through whom I am centred. Such a God must be conceived non-anthropomorphically.

8
RESPONSE: *Janet Martin Soskice*

Christian feminism had its origins in a concern for justice, truth and the full dignity of all persons. Unless (preached) Christianity preached this message, and insofar as it underwrote inferiority and subordination for some, it could not be the gospel. Detestation of idolatry and invocation of precedents of prophetic resistance have been the hallmarks of feminist theology, and are evident in the essays here. Yet the feminist who is a Christian has also to answer this question: Shouldn't the first step for someone concerned with the full dignity of women be to run a million miles from Christianity? This is where I think Daphne Hampson's arguments are at their strongest. She has thrown down the gauntlet not merely (or even principally) to the churches, but to her fellow feminist Christians, and her message is simply 'why stay?' It is not merely the structures or current administration of the churches that are flawed, Christinity's whole cloth is 'bad for women'. Its sacred texts, its developed theological traditions, its symbolisms, all, to her mind, not only marginalize but negate women. 'As far ... as a feminist is concerned,' Hampson says, 'Christianity is a fishbone which must stick in her throat.' And she says (using language more directive than her own praise of autonomy and criticism of 'authority' might lead us to expect) it 'should not be swallowed'.

I find her challenge both cogent and salutary. Certainly one can reinvent Christianity almost entirely if one so desires – remake the canon, make Jesus a peripheral figure. Daphne's point is not that these would be 'bad' or unorthodox things to do, but, just, why bother?

As it has transpired, Daphne is the only one of the contributors to this collection who regards herself as 'post'-Christian. You could say that this is not surprising, that most women who have discarded Christianity do not pause to meditate on their reasons for having done so. I think, however, this is only part of an answer. What should surprise us more than it does is the strength and number of feminist women who continue to be Christians, who feel, as do a number of us here, that their Christianity compels them to their feminist positions. And this not just amongst theologians but amongst many women who continue to live somewhat vexed lives in the body of the mainstream churches.

You could say these women are deluded, or too fragile to break away from a structure intent on crushing them, but this is not my perception. Such women do not have an easy time. They are not always well regarded either by their churches or by secular feminist sisters. More than this, sometimes these women have the audacity to believe, as does Sarah Coakley, that Christian feminism is not just a 'tag along' but has something distinctive to offer the feminist movement as a whole.

It is interesting to see that while Daphne speaks of Christianity as a historical religion and of that history exercising, by various means, control over the contemporary Christian, all the other essays speak in one way or another of the story of Jesus and of what it is to live within this story. For Daphne, Christianity is rooted in a particular history, a patriarchal history, which makes a particular revelation at a particular historical moment normative. Despite her overall liberalism, there is a residual propositionalist flavour to these remarks, as though revelation were a set of truths laid down at this certain time. It is true that Christianity involves not only openness to the teachings of Jesus, but also acceptance of some beliefs about him. One of these, traditionally, is that in Jesus Christ we find God incarnate. But belief in the incarnation is as much a metaphysical belief as a historical one, and as such precisely does not tie God to one historical moment. Here, dramatically, is an extension of the conviction that 'God is with' the people of Israel, God is present to human history, not merely in the first years CE, but in and at all times. Nicola Slee, as concerned as Daphne with Jesus and history, sees the incarnation, with its insistence on God's entry into human history, as a means by which we can understand our time as God's time. To say that Christianity is a historical religion is not to say that it is fixed in the past, but to say it grows and is shaped as those who live by and within the story of Jesus grow and are shaped. Like the parables, this is a story which works by continual breaking and reforging of expectations, a story which must avoid, as she says, final closure. I particularly like Nicola's largely unstated presupposition that it is not texts, even biblical ones, which are sexist (a position which seems to trade on now suspect theories of 'authorial meaning'), but readings of texts which are, and that what women need now are new readings of the story of Jesus.

Jane Shaw brings to the fore some of the challenges post-Enlightenment/postmodernism brings for feminists. For instance, if everyone else is getting rid of the 'autonomous, Enlightenment self', ought women, who never really shared in this free-wheeling self-hood (any more than did most poor or non-western men) hang on to it? Daphne, clearly, is hanging on to the self in her insistence that feminists believe in 'autonomy with a vengeance', but how, after Wittenstein and Foucault and any number of others, can we enunciate this? We now understand ourselves as profoundly linguistic and social creatures. We learn, with our language, certain dispositions and biases that may be so deep within us as to be unnoticed by us. I am not saying we are slaves of this cultural inheritance, but rather suggesting we hesitate before claiming that we have fully discarded our society's deeply androcentric past orientation. We may unwittingly retain more of it than we would wish to admit.

To what extent must all versions of feminism be deeply children of the Enlightenment with its aspirations for freedom, truth and the pursuit of happiness and/or autonomy? And if a child of the Enlightenment then what might post-Englightenment feminism be? These of course are problems for a whole generation of feminist theorists and not for resolution here, but I presume they lie behind Jane's question as to how it is possible for women to be 'theologians' in the accepted meaning of the term.

Julie Hopkins, too, aspires to develop a new 'female historical subjectivity' – although how this can be done by moving 'beyond structures and images', if that means moving beyond such things entirely, is not clear to me. Julie's rejection of 'the eternal Father, Lord, King and static Judge' has echoes in both Daphne's paper and my own, although Daphne seems to think such a potentate is who (or what?) Christianity has always honoured, whereas I think 'He' (for clearly this 'god' is male) is largely a deist invention of western modernity and bears little resemblance to the trinitarian God of Christian orthodoxy. Strangely, Julie's position, perhaps the nearest to Daphne's own in seeing Jesus as one possible messianic role model, is the one which is most vulnerable to Daphne's criticism – why hang on to this symbolic story out of the many others? The liberation theologians whom Julie and we all admire, and the African women Mercy Amba Oduyoye invokes, may, when they read the stories of Exodus, 'feel their liberation directly', but white and western feminists seem obliged to feel increasingly estranged from the symbols and narratives that historically have fed the faith. Can we claim solidarity with those others who 'inhabit' Scripture newly without doing so ourselves?

Sarah Coakley has taken Daphne to task on some very fine and important points to do with power, autonomy and *kenōsis*. I have already suggested that I doubt whether the kind of 'autonomy' which Daphne invokes is possible. Sarah doubts whether it is desirable. As Sarah repeatedly remarks, she is on delicate ground here, for praise of 'powerlessness' has been hideously abused and women are right to be wary. Yet I think she is right in seeing a corrective to much worldly thought in the suggestion that 'true divine "empowerment" occurs most unimpededly in the context of a *special* form of human "vulnerability"'.

Feminist theology, if it is to be a vital movement, must move beyond its origins as a largely reactionary movement (reacting, that is, against a *status quo*) towards a constructive, theological vision of wholeness and holiness. Sarah's essay shows us how difficult a matter this may be.

Here is one of the real difficulties I see for a feminist theologian today, if such a creature can exist. Sarah has given us a fine piece of salvage (or salvation?) by scholarship. The tale of *kenōsis*, she has argued, is much more complex and diverse than Daphne's account suggests. And the same is true of any number of Christian doctrines which Sarah does not discuss: atonement, Trinity, salvation and sin. The question is 'to salvage or not to salvage?' Daphne and Julie reject the picture of God as Lord, King and static Judge, but then so do Aquinas, Athanasius, Augustine, and Schleiermacher. But even if the feminist theologian thinks that Christianity has had, and has now, much better visions to offer than what has been dished out 'from a million pulpits', should she expend her energy refiguring teachings and institutions which have shown themselves so capable of taking a negative warp? Should she be an exploratory archaeologist, speaking newly of the past, or an anarchic architect of an as yet unimaginable future? I suppose it is impossible not to be both. Change is not possible without there being some prior state as the basis for change. We cannot speak from nowhere, any more than we can discard the past: to fail to acknowledge our own embedding in history is to be in danger of unwitting enslavement to it.

Yet to look to the past is not simply heteronomous. It may also be to have regard for a rather old-fashioned thing which Christians invoke in the creeds – the communion of saints. In my understanding this means, amongst other things, a sense of union with many nameless people who, despite the limitations to which all of us are prey, went before and worked for the coming of a reign of love and justice such as neither they, nor we, nor secular feminists can conceive.

9
RESPONSE: *Nicola Slee*

Rather than discuss each of the essays separately, I intend in this response to focus on a few themes which emerge as salient throughout the collection as a whole. While my main intention is to consider the *content* of the essays, I want first to reflect on the *process* of making this book, and to consider what this might suggest for the feminist theological enterprise. Next, I want to focus on the issue of autonomy and its right understanding within both feminism and Christianity. Finally, I shall raise some questions about various understandings of historical particularity represented in the essays and the relation between this and the feminist theological enterprise to which most, but not all, of us are committed in this volume, namely, the reappropriation of Christian story, symbol and belief.

Reflecting on the process, I am conscious, as we all must be, of how difficult and protracted a task it has proved to be for each of us to write our pieces for this collection. What initially seemed a straightforward and appealing project – to state clearly our positions, as feminists, in relation to Christianity, and to engage in dialogue with one another – turned out to be an arduous, even tortuous, venture, as we each, to greater or lesser degree, struggled against paralysis, uncertainty and evasion to commit to paper our convictions. The difficulties, sometimes acute, experienced in the writing of our essays, seem to me significant in the dialogue we wish to engage with one another, because they indicate something of the present struggle and vulnerability involved in seeking to maintain and explicate a feminist theological commitment. At the present time when, as Julie Hopkins suggests, Christianity is undergoing a profound 'epistemological break' with established forms of culture and belief, and 'the old western paradigm of patriarchy' is breaking down, we experience 'a time of tension, a shifting of the paradigm' (p. 68) which makes it difficult to find one's bearings. In addition, as Jane Shaw argues, women experience particular difficulties in inhabiting the theological realm, since what has been culturally and historically associated with

female identity, namely bodiliness, emotion and mystical awareness, are the very aspects of human experience which have been
systematically expelled from theological enquiry. I have found
Jane's essay particularly illuminating of the personal difficulties I
experienced in attempting to 'incorporate and embrace ... the
spiritual, the intellectual, and embodied religious experience'
(p. 59) in the writing of my piece; and if I now feel, some two years
since writing it, that I did not entirely succeed, I can see more
clearly why. On top of all this, there is so much at stake in this
enterprise, and the weight of such an awareness can be felt as
oppressive rather than liberating. It is not so much the sense of
one's own academic or professional status being put at risk by the
statement of one's convictions (though there *is* this), as the larger
awareness of one's moral responsibility towards all those women,
both inside and outside the churches, for whom the interpretation
of the Christian tradition is not simply a matter of intellectual
curiosity or even spiritual sustenance but, as Janet Martin Soskice
so compellingly urges, a matter of life and death (pp. 23–4).

Nevertheless, and despite moments of heartily wishing that I
had never committed myself to this project, I am glad that we all
persevered, and deeply grateful to each of the other contributors
for what they have written. As so often happens, the insights,
convictions and arguments articulated by others in a community
of mutual respect, affection and common commitment, enable one
the more clearly to shape one's own, and to recognize both their
strengths and their shortcomings. It seems to me that the *methodology* of this collection of essays signifies something profoundly
important about the feminist theological enterprise; namely, that it
is a characteristically collaborative venture, rooted in female
friendship, within which difference is celebrated and engaged
creatively as well as vigorously, where respectful dialogue rather
than combative parleying is the model of exchange. Yet the
process of making this book has severely tested those values, and I
would be interested in hearing reflections from the other essayists
on the reasons for this and what we might learn from it.

The struggle to give authoritative voice to our convictions which
many of us have experienced in the process of writing this book is
reflected in the theme of autonomy which emerges as a central yet
problematic feminist goal in the collection. In particular, the
nature and scope of autonomy is thrown into sharp relief by the
contrast between Daphne Hampson's essay, on the one hand, in
which autonomy is elevated to the centre of a feminist spirituality,
and Sarah Coakley's, on the other, where autonomy is critiqued

and relativized from a perspective of *kenōsis*. Reading Daphne's essay in the light of the others, several important questions are formulated. Whilst autonomy is a laudable feminist goal, what *kind* of autonomy will enable the flourishing of authentic human community and the pursuit of justice on the earth? Daphne's vision of autonomy follows in that majestic, but deeply flawed, tradition of Enlightenment rationality which other essays in the volume – especially Jane's and Sarah's – tellingly critique. Indeed, she suggests that feminism itself 'might well be understood as the natural working out of the Enlightenment' (p. 1). Yet one does not need to look far to see some of the damaging results of the Enlightenment elevation of autonomous (male) reason over nature, women and 'foreigners': spiralling ecological crisis, as well as the poverty of the southern hemisphere and the oppression of women world-wide are its fruits no less than scientific progress and intellectual freedom (for some). Feminist models of autonomy need to overcome the limitations of the Enlightenment ideal. The rooting of the pursuit of female self-actualization within the community of those who are committed to the story of Jesus, I have tried to suggest, offers a creative challenge to historical patterns of female dependency, but also sets necessary boundaries to personal autonomy by its insistence that self-actualization is achieved precisely in the radical commitment to the freedom of others and the earth itself, not in distinction from them. In Daphne's vision, I would like to understand more how she sees the relation between the autonomy of the individual and the claim of the other, and in what these two poles are rooted.

Sarah's careful and nuanced discussion of *kenōsis* as a potentially fruitful model for feminist self-understanding raises equally compelling questions. In her attempt to read vulnerability as normatively human and therefore to reclaim it positively for feminists, Sarah recognizes that fine distinctions need to be made, and begins to articulate what some of these might be (p. 83). In order to understand more fully what she sees as the difference between a 'right' vulnerability and less authentic versions, I want to ask her how she understands the relation between such ('right') vulnerability and those virtues she adduces as central to feminist spirituality, viz, 'personal empowerment, prophetic resistance, courage in the face of oppression, and the destruction of false idolatry' (p. 110). I would also (or perhaps this is the same thing) like some help in seeing how the model of 'power-in-vulnerability' might extend to other experiences beyond that of contemplative prayer which Sarah offers as the paradigmatic experience within which we may catch a glimpse of vulnerability, not as 'negation of self, but the place of the self's transformation and expansion into God' (p. 108). Whilst I find this analysis of silent prayer suggestive, Jane's and Julie's essays sharpen for me the need to integrate the mystical with the intellectual and the political realms in women's search for authentic becoming. How does Sarah understand the interrelation between these various dimensions of the feminist quest? And how does Jane respond to Sarah's reading of contemplative prayer in the light of her own critique of female mysticism?

A further key issue for me in the essays revolves around the theme of historical particularity and its relation to the hermeneutical task of reclaiming or reworking Christian stories, symbols and beliefs by feminists. One of the central planks in Daphne's rejection of Christianity is its historical particularity, read by her as a radical limitation of the past on the potential development of the future, a curtailment of feminists' freedom to take responsibility for their own present. For the rest of us, Christianity's historical particularity is read differently and positively, as a guarantee of an embodied, concrete, and prophetic spirituality. Historical particularity is not to be read as the past dictating what may happen in the future but as the paradigmatic sign of the immanence of God in *all* history and the openness of the present to grace. As Janet puts it: 'It is in this sense that Christianity is a historical religion: not by endorsing the values of one place and period for all time to come, but in being a teleological or eschatological faith, always renewing itself as it longs for and works for the "coming of the kingdom"' (p. 29). Yet, though we share such a positive reading of Christianity's particularity, there is a great deal of divergence between us when it comes to the relation between such particularity and doctrinal belief. Janet, for example, seems to require nothing less than adherence to a fully-blown, classical pre-existent Christology in order to guarantee the presence of God in our own history. 'Unless Jesus is the Christ, God incarnate, then the whole thing is a waste of time' (p. 22). Though Sarah's position is less overtly stated, or, at least, is situated more narrowly in relation to the concept of *kenōsis*, her detailed development of her argument in close relation to the authoritative texts of Christian orthodoxy implies the necessity at least for close dialogue with, if not for committed adherence to, these texts and traditions. Julie, on the other hand, stands much closer to my position, as I read it, in which the primary commitment is to the cluster of stories and symbols inherited from the tradition and to the community of those inspired by them, but where adherence to received understandings of these stories and symbols is less vital to the renewal of the tradition in our time. Whilst classical doctrines of incarnation, Trinity and so on, may well be creatively reappropriated by feminists, it is not these doctrines, *per se*, which guarantee either the vitality or the salvific potential of the Christian tradition. As Julie puts it, it is the 'powerful and radically disturbing symbolic story which continues to inspire messianic movements, cosmic dreams and personal mysticism' (p. 80), rather than a particular set of beliefs *about* this story.

The questions arising for me out of our different placings of ourselves in relation to the shared tradition are these. How far is the continuity of Christian identity dependent on doctrinal consensus? I have tried to suggest, in my essay, that it is not so much doctrinal agreement which constitutes the heart of Christian identity as the lived relation to the story in community with others who are similarly committed to it. Julie has suggested that, if we take seriously the Christian paradigm of a concrete, historical understanding of lived truth, then ortho*praxy* rather than orthodoxy, becomes the crucial test of Christian identity. Jane alerts attention to the ways in which 'the exercise of power is deeply implicated in the holding and "exercise" of knowledge' (p. 56), and invites us to bring to bear a hermeneutics of suspicion against all orthodoxies, representing, as they generally do, the triumph of the politically powerful over the vanquished or marginalized, usually including women. The celebration of multiple truths, then, such as Jane and I call for, is a political commitment as much as a philosophical one. If I have read Julie and Jane aright, they share with me the conviction that Christianity permits, even requires, a far greater degree of doctrinal creativity and flexibility than the church has ever, in the past, been prepared to allow. I would like to know what Janet and Sarah, in particular, make of this, and why, for them, a much closer adherence to classical (Chalcedonian?) orthodoxy appears to be required. Are historical particularity, embodied and holistic spirituality, the presence of God in history and the prophetic imperative to justice put at risk if orthodox belief is abandoned? Is it not possible to 'turn the symbols', to use Janet's phrase, in creative and redemptive ways, without adhering so closely to doctrinal understandings worked out in a past age and according to cultural norms no longer shared? And to Jane and Julie (and this is a question for me too!): are there limits to the creative reworking of Christian symbols and stories, and, if so, what are they? Are these limits properly *theological* ones, or, as Jane suggests, of a rather different order, rooted in the moral and political realm (p. 53) – or elsewhere? If adherence to the Christian paradigm through its stories, symbols and rituals is not dependent on a particular doctrinal commitment, what are the boundaries of Christian belonging?

10
RESPONSE: *Jane Shaw*

When we are asked whether feminism and Christianity are compatible or not, the issue is often presented in terms of the challenge of feminism to Christianity. Such a formulation sets up Christianity as flawed in the light of a *coherent* feminism without allowing for varying forms of feminism – or feminism's possible flaws. In my response to the articles in this book, I shall concentrate on the varieties of feminism at play in our arguments as a way of trying to understand the reasons for our differences.

For Daphne Hampson, of course, feminism does present a challenge to Christianity. She give us a view of feminism as being about autonomy, which for her means that feminism stands in direct opposition to the heteronomous character of Christianity. She states that feminism consists in 'women coming into their own and not having to bow to authority', whereas 'Christianity, by definition, is not a religion which can allow for full human autonomy' (p. 2).

Her argument also relies upon a further set of oppositions: namely, that feminism is free from history whereas Christianity is always tied to a historical moment of revelation and cannot therefore move beyond its traditional and hierarchical structures. She claims: 'Feminists have of recent years tried to inaugurate a way of being and of acting which is free of past authorities and in which hierarchical ways of acting do not prevail' (p. 14). She contends that in a feminist epistemology 'women do not start with some truth "external" to themselves which has authority ... There is no authority such as might deny that what she [each woman] thinks may be thought; nor yardstick by which she should measure what she thinks' (p. 14).

There are some problems here. First, if Daphne thinks that feminism is about autonomy, then surely *that* is the yardstick by which she would measure a woman's thoughts and words? This, of course, opens up many cans of worms. For example, if a woman's words and thoughts do not express a 'proper' kind of autonomy, according to a particular definition of autonomy, does that mean that she is not a 'proper' feminist? Second, Daphne's

definition of feminism is not as free from history as she might
wish: she herself makes the claim that 'Feminism might well be
understood as the natural working out of the Enlightenment'
(p. 1). Here Daphne wants to adopt for women a particular notion
of Enlightenment selfhood, and I have already written, in my
article, about the profound problems for women of unquestioningly adopting such an 'Enlightenment self'. Third, and this is a
related point, it must be stressed that we are always located in
history. We can never not start with some truth which is 'external'
to ourselves. We are subjects constructed in the cultures in which
we live. No one is the free self that the Enlightenment claimed was
possible.

   All of this means that Daphne is working with a very specific
notion of feminism which the rest of us writing in this book might
not share, even if we agree with some of her aims and ideals. There
is a danger that Daphne is setting up a certain kind of feminism as
a new authority which women must obey. For example, the
statement 'Feminists abhor, on the whole, special costumes which
set people apart' (p. 15) has striking echoes with the kind of
essentialism prevalent, say, in Mary Daly's work, especially *Pure
Lust*, whereby women who wear skirts and make-up are –
according to Daly – duped by false consciousness. I know that
Daphne is not saying precisely this, but she is dangerously close!
Similarly, in a statement such as 'feminists *normally* hold that in a
sense people bring the truth with them', the 'normally' functions in
contradictory ways. That is, its inclusion in the sentence is a
gesture which simultaneously suggests that some feminists do not
think this way *and* imposes a normal (that is, authoritative) way of
feminist thinking.

   Nicola Slee also asserts that feminism presents a challenge to
Christianity, and answers that she can remain a Christian only if
'Christian identity is understood to be open to continual renewal,
reformation and transformation; and only if feminism is permitted
to become an agent of Christianity's own transformation' (p. 33).
She does, however, suggest that both Christianity and feminism
'are fluid, complex and developing traditions whose identity is
constantly open to question and revision' (p. 33), but throughout
her article places her emphasis on the transformation of
Christianity 'which feminism requires of it' without necessarily
talking about the ways in which feminism itself might be transformed in that process. My question to Nicola, then, is whether
(and how) she sees her feminist identity evolving along with, and
in response to, her Christian identity.

   Immediately striking about the remaining contributors is that our expressions of feminism are thoroughly intertwined with our visions of Christianity. The two are not easily separable. My own experience is that I became a feminist because I was a Christian: central tenets of both seemed to resonate so strongly with each other that it made no sense not to be a Christian and therefore a feminist.

Julie Hopkins expresses how strongly the two are linked in presenting a vision of social salvation which lies at the heart of both her feminism and her Christianity. 'The vision of a *social* salvation is an integral part of all liberation theologies' (p. 9). Personal salvation is a part of this, but it is only a part of a larger picture. Women need to hear the good news 'on the personal level ... that they have a vocation to be special ... Each woman is a temple of the Holy Spirit and is a full member of the Body of Christ (in other words she can have a messianic function)' (p. 76). This knowledge that women have a messianic function leads to ways of seeking salvation for others *and* for the world. How do we build the kingdom of God on earth? This means that, for Julie, feminism goes beyond personal salvation and female autonomy. In her theology she rejects Protestant notions of individual salvation which pay little or no regard to social problems and thus social salvation. In her feminism she rejects notions of individual, personal empowerment which do not take into account the sufferings of other women and how we, as white, western women, for example, can contribute to the suffering of others, sometimes in the very process of our own empowerment. Hence she rejects the Enlightenment model of selfhood, partly through her experience of listening to women for whom such a model makes no sense whatsoever, and thus most certainly does not represent feminism. As she points out: 'Now that women theologians throughout the world are gaining the confidence to speak from their own contexts and cultures, the old western epistemology is in disarray. African women, for example, do not think of themselves dualistically or even individualistically' (p. 78). I have spent some time discussing Julie's ideas because I think they form such an interesting contrast with Daphne's position. My questions to both Julie and Daphne are, therefore: What forms of feminism might bind you together? Are your notions of feminism mutually exclusive?

My final question is to Sarah Coakley. Sarah's essay explores the ways in which we might think rather differently about female vulnerability as empowering, via the practice of contemplative prayer ('expectant waiting'). She engages in a careful rethinking of gender stereotypes through an examination of a particular strand in the Christian tradition (that of *kenōsis*), providing a stimulating example of just the kind of productive deconstruction of gendered notions of theology and spiritual practice that I have suggested is necessary, in my own essay. She writes that 'the contemplative exercise may take us beyond ... existing gender stereotypes, up-ending them in its gradual undermining of *all* previous certainties and dogmatisms. Here, if am I right, is "power-in-vulnerability", the willed effacement to a gentle omnipotence which, far from "complementing" masculinism, acts as its undoing' (pp. 109–10). This stands in some contrast to Daphne's notion of feminism as autonomy, and yet, while recognizing this, Sarah writes that in terms of 'fruits' or feminist practice, she and Daphne are quite likely to agree. She writes that 'our theological conceptions and institutional commitments diverge at many points, but our sense of what feminism aims to gain and display is curiously convergent' (p. 110). She numbers amongst these aims 'love, joy, peace ... personal empowerment, prophetic resistance, courage in the face of oppression, and the destruction of false idolatry' (p. 110). This suggestion of the ways in which she might agree with Daphne, despite rather different notions of the means to female empower-ment, comes rather briefly at the very end of her article. I would, then, like Sarah to comment at some greater length on the defini-tion of feminism she might provide which would be both sup-portive of (and produced by?) her own Christian feminist practice, and in some considerable agreement with Daphne's definition of feminism as presented in the article in this book.

11
RESPONSE: *Julie Hopkins*

Since Daphne Hampson and I have such divergent views, I wish to concentrate my debating space primarily upon her stimulating paper. Daphne's goal is that women 'come of age', take control of their own lives and develop a feminist religious sensibility. I share this hope but I do not understand why, for her, western theism should undermine this aim. It would appear that Daphne thinks that for women to believe in a God who is in some sense 'other' than themselves creates unhealthy dependency and passivity. I should like to take issue with her here. But before I proceed, I wish to make a comment about her following statement. She claims: 'for a feminist to be a Christian and also to be true to herself and to her feminist beliefs is ... not possible.' I do not understand what Daphne means for this is obviously not the case with several writers in this book – we are feminists and Christians – unless she wishes to imply that we are not integrated or honest persons. I am sure that she does not wish to say this, because such a position would suggest that only she knows how a woman should be true to herself! However, Daphne has shown in her book *Feminism and Theology* that she perceives the psychological and existential complexity of achieving a sense of genuine female subjectivity. We are all on this journey beyond the logocentric symbolic order but none of us is in a position to evaluate to what extent another woman has integrated all the emotional, behavioural, intellectual and spiritual dimensions of her conscious and unconscious self.

To return to my main question to Daphne: why has a sense of the otherness of God such a detrimental effect upon feminists? Daphne calls upon women to become 'complete' and 'live in the present' by throwing off the shackles of a transcendent God. But most people in the West, including feminists, are already secular and where has this brought us? Ninety per cent of modern Europeans are not practising Christians, Jews or Muslims, but sexism, racism and social injustice are still rife. Are the minority of monotheists to blame? Daphne's glowing appraisal of the Enlightenment with its sense of an autonomous humanity which 'does not have to look to anything outside itself as an authority' is

an unusually positive evaluation coming from a feminist. At the
end of the twentieth century feminist theorists, amongst others,
are claiming that the rationalistic anthropocentric hubris of
Enlightenment modernism has failed humanity and is endangering
the well-being of our planet. I share this view to the extent that I
do not regard living in this 'present' as a healthy, happy or morally
edifying experience. Secular western market economics has sucked
us into a sterile cultural, ideological and spiritual vacuum.

My point is that feminism, as a contemporary female emancipatory movement, shares with other cognitive minorites a critical
voice with regard to the arrogance of anthrocentric autonomy
thinking. Postmodern natural and social scientists, ecologists and
thinking women across the world are saying that we need to
rediscover a proper sense of our radical interdependency and to
cultivate a humility towards our planet before our species destroys
itself and countless others. For every molecule and organism is
radically interdependent; the energy exchange and transformation
which occurs between all animate and inanimate matter defy us to
speak of autonomous boundaries. For example, our human brains
consist of self-reflective matter formed of elements which came
into being in the universe billions of years ago. The energy which
drives the brain comes in the form of heat, light, radiation and
oxygen from interactive processes between our star the Sun and
the atmosphere and plant-life of our planet. Our brains in this
sense do not belong to autonomous humans but to the cosmos.
Most disturbing of all, our thoughts are not our own. Thought is a
product of language and (unconscious) desire. What we think
depends to a large extent upon the symbolic order of the language
we have learnt from our particular culture and upbringing. As
Jacques Derrida says, we humans are as much a text written by
culture as we are sovereign thinking individuals.

Once we realize how interdependent and yet contextually particular we are, the nature of our relationship with the 'other' who
is different becomes of central significance. In my opinion we need
to accept that there are other values, norms and truths than our
own, not only in order to promote a peaceful and socially just,
pluralistic co-existence, but also because the survival of our planet
depends upon the success of dialogue. Further, once we recognize
that truth is constructed by specific groups we are freed from the
tyranny of 'the Truth'. Discourse, meaning and ethics can be
changed if enough people reach a consensus as to a new symbolic
order. This is what I think Janet Soskice means by 'turning the
symbols'. So, for example, just as Enlightenment thinkers such as
Descartes and Kant constructed the autonomous rational male, so

may post-Christians such as Daphne construct the autonomous religious female. But respecting difference also means that the reconstructive work of Christian, Jewish and Muslim feminists should be taken seriously. Obviously some constructions are dangerous or evil because they absolutize truth for their own ideology or lust for power – think of the Nazi Aryan *Supermensch*. But our feminist and postmodern sensibility requires that our radical differences in sex, class, ethnicity, religion and sexual orientation be accorded utmost respect.

This brings me to the final point I should like to make to Daphne. If all language, discourse and meaning is socially constructed and therefore particular to specific cultures and groups, how can we avoid constructing God in the image of our own symbolic order unless God has the independent capacity of self-communication? If God is only myself or the power of healing that flows between feminist friends how can I/we avoid unconsciously projecting our desires and will to power on to God? Further, if God, who I too believe to be the immanent ground of being and becoming and the holy erotic power of Life, is not also in some sense an 'other' who transcends the givenness of our daily lives, how can we know God? I do not wish to argue that we cannot commune with God through nature, loving relationships or mystical experience; far from it. But my point is that monotheistic religions have stressed divine self-disclosure through the medium of prophetic revelation in order to stress the independent initiatives of God. I cannot have an authentic relationship with another person if that subject has fused into an unhealthy symbiotic relationship with myself. By analogy, the balance between difference and similarity is essential in our relationship with the divine.

It is of course the case that God speaks and acts in history through the medium of persons. Such women and men, whom I call prophets, believe themselves to be possessed by the Spirit of God. They still speak in particular and contextually bound language, but theists believe that the word of God has the capacity to deconstruct language and break it open revealing a multi-dimensional reality which transcends human control. Nicola Slee's excellent article on the metaphorical nature of the parables in the Gospels demonstrates this extraordinary capacity of prophetic language.

To believe that God reveals knowledge of God's Self to humans through historical prophets does not necessarily imply that we must slavishly obey the Bible or church hierarchies. Christians believe that every believer is a temple of the Holy Spirit who communicates to us the nature, will and power of the divine. In the Netherlands, where I live, many churches now use the feminine gender for the Spirit in their sermons, prayers and hymns. This is a welcome development, for the biblical *Hokmah* (Hebrew) or *Sophia* (Greek) is the female revelatory principle of the creative and immanent presence of God. She brings wisdom, social justice and spiritual maturity to those who seek her gifts. I realize that for Daphne the gender of God is irrelevant; she rejects anthropomorphic representations of the divine. I do not wish to return to the abstract God of the Platonists or Deists because the Christian understanding of the suffering, vulnerable and loving dimension of God requires for me a personal language. I do agree that the patriarchal construction of God the 'Almighty Father' who sits enthroned in the heavens to promulgate decrees and judgements is a totally irrelevant image of God for Christian feminists. However, in rejecting the otherness of God and the self-communicating nature of the divine, I feel that Daphne is in danger of deconstructing theism to the point where there is nothing to be said or believed.

In the limited space that I have left I wish to explore this theme of construction, the divine self-communication and female prophecy further by discussing with Jane Shaw her approach to the history of female mysticism and prophecy. For in her interesting article Jane tends to describe this history as a series of strategies by women who tried to exercise power whilst remaining within the cultural construction of the 'woman'. I have a problem with contemporary feminist research which gives a functionalist explanation for the religious experience and the behaviour of women from other historical eras or other cultural contexts. Such an approach, in Jane's case influenced by Foucault's analysis of knowledge as power, tends to reduce religious beliefs and actions to political and social motives. But do we feminist theologians and historians wish to imply that religious women did/do not have authentic experiences of God but rather manipulate and exploit the life of the Spirit for their own subversive ends? I agree that power is an important element in religion but surely women are capable of communing with the divine as an end in itself or in order to mediate the presence of God to others? If we do not allow for the possibility of the self-disclosure of the divine through prophetesses, we inauthenticate their voices and religious experience becomes just another construction.

With this in mind it is possible to add an ethical dimension to the recent discussion about female mysticism and prophecy in English social history. Instead of simply examining questions such as 'How did women exercise a public voice by using spirit possession?' we could ask 'Why and how were women finally denied their God-given right to prophesy?' For this is indeed what happened. In sectarian and institutional Christianity, women lost their public prophetic role at the same time that the witch hunts ended, around the year 1700. The rise of the empirical sciences and later Enlightenment rationalism, psychology and secularization shifted the construct of the 'woman'. She is no longer considered capable of publically mediating the Spirit of God. Modern western feminists tend to share this construct which is a great pity because in Africa, Asia, Latin America and amongst the Afro-Caribbean communities, Christian female prophetism still plays an important religious, social and political role.

In this context I very much welcome Sarah Coakley's understanding of kenotic spirituality as 'the willed effacement to a gentle omnipotence'. Contemplation in the sense of the practice of waiting on God is an important contribution of Christian female mystics from Teresa of Avila to Simone Weil. The women in this spiritual tradition combined mental and psychological discipline with radical social action and political prophetism. I question, however, Sarah's reliance on Antiochean Christology. Why is it necessary to assert that in Jesus, divine and human 'power-in-vulnerability' was essentially united in his 'mind', whereas we can only imitate him through prayer? Is Jesus then of a different ontological nature than us? In my opinion, if Jesus was not my human brother then I cannot be sure that divine love can be incarnated in human subjectivity.

It is impossible in such a short space to discuss in detail every article in this book. However, I wish to express my gratitude to my sister theologians for such an honest, stimulating and creative debate. It is clear from these essays that British feminist theology is coming of age in the sense that women theologians are beginning to refine their research and methodologies in the fields of history, theology, philosophy and of course women's studies. What also encourages me greatly is that these writers, whilst demonstrating a sophisticated awareness of contemporary hermeneutical and epistemological issues, have not forgotten their roots in spirituality and the feminist struggle for social justice. Finally, it is good to note that feminism does not have to be a killjoy; thank you, Janet, for the brilliant joke about baptizing a pigeon!

12
RESPONSE: *Sarah Coakley*

Since I have already devoted my own contribution to this book to an analysis of a crucial dimension of Daphne Hampson's own thinking from which I part company, I will take no further space in this response in debating her 'post-Christian' alternative. (This is not because we have not got more to say to one another – clearly our exchange could continue quite lengthily – but rather because I am more keen to see first how others perceive our divergence.) Instead, then, I shall focus here on some features of the other essays (from feminists who, like me, remain within the Christian churches), and try to draw out some underlying assumptions in their theological method which may be somewhat different from my own. I intend this not in a combative mood, but rather as a means of clarifying certain different options (in theory of knowledge, metaphysical claims about the nature of God, and theory of language) which may interestingly divide those of us who share the struggle to bring Christianity and feminism into some sort of alignment. Often these deeper epistemological, metaphysical and linguistic issues are not brought explicitly to the surface when feminist Christian writers expound their views to the wider public; but (in my view) it is highly important to be clear about them. To the extent that the cogency of a Christian feminist position rests on (non-feminist) theological and philosophical assumptions that could be regarded as weak, questionable or fallible, to the same extent is it exposed to a (masculinist) rebuttal that fails even to *confront* the explicitly feminist dimension of its argument.[1] Hence it is perhaps worth taking a little space to spell out what some of these deeper questions may involve, and how different sorts of Christian feminist theologians may diverge on them.

First, *'relativism'*, *'pragmatism'* and *'standpoint epistemology'*. Feminist theology, which, in its (white, middle-class, American) origins, was importantly enabled and supported by a form of 'liberal' theology which was its backcloth, has easily – and even unconsciously – taken on many of the deeper presumptions of that 'liberal' tradition. One of these presumptions, shared most obviously in this volume by Julie Hopkins (and used to make important feminist points), is a sensitivity to the 'contextually bound' nature of all religious and theological beliefs (Julie, p. 70 citing Ruether). Thus stated, this principle of 'contextualization' is pretty anodyne, even truistic (*of course* doctrines are forged in particular historical circumstances which they to some extent reflect); but the principle can clearly be used to aid a feminist critique of the tradition, to the extent that it now allows *women* to 'speak with their own voices out of *their own contexts* and experiences' (pp. 77–8, my emphasis, citing Schüssler Fiorenza). The matter becomes more contentious philosophically, however, if what is implied here is not merely some principle of historical 'contexualization' of doctrine, but a true case of 'relativism', that is, the view that theological (or other) truths only *are* 'true' in virtue of, or 'relative' to, some specific 'context' or (female?) epistemological framework.[2] And I am not wholly certain whether Julie (and indeed other contributors to this volume) wish to say this or not. If they do (and certain statements such as Julie's that 'the old western epistemology is in disarray' (p. 78, etc.) suggest that they do), then a further problem arises about *whose* 'context' or 'standpoint' our own feminist 'truths' should represent: can it really be 'women's' in general (so-called 'female subjectivity': see Julie, p. 66, and cp. Jane Shaw, p. 50), or does not the relativistic epistemological principle force us into ever more fragmented and incompatible 'standpoints' (see Julie, p. 78)? The issue is an important one, because it has bearing, as I think Julie realizes (p. 78), on our capacity (or otherwise) to respond to the 'female other' beyond the boundaries of the First World. 'Female solidarity', world-wide, would look pretty thin and bleak if our epistemic structures disallowed *any* commensurable meshing with those we seek to support.

Normally, it seems to me, the sort of feminist theology that Julie quotes and represents in her essay is content to be rather vague about the degree of relativism it wishes to espouse. This is because *on the one hand* it wants to cast a negative pall on 'objectivism', 'universalism' and 'realism', on the grounds that these have been the masculinist philosophical strategies of those seeking to 'dominate' and exclude women (Julie, p. 68, citing Welch); but *on the other hand* it needs to avoid an untrammelled relativism if any sense is to be made of supportive feminist commitment to women beyond our own cultural horizon. The result, theologically, is a rather embarrassed backing away from any 'realist' claims about God and the world, lest these too be seen as imperialist; instead, the pragmatic criterion of 'what satisfies [my? whose?] aspirations for salvation' (Julie, p. 80) becomes the touchstone of Christian 'truth'. (Is that *all*? Might not my secular aspirations – even my secular feminist aspirations – be seriously flawed? Might not they be challenged by my encounter with God? Note that the appeal to 'satisfaction' here is rather different from the test of spiritual 'fruits' that I make at the end of my own essay (p. 110).)

To be fair to Julie, her essay does make some attempt to confront these problems head-on when she writes: 'I cannot accept that ... an understanding of particularity and contextual truth relativizes Christianity to the point of absurdity' (p. 71), but that it is only from her own 'standpoint' that she can 'communicate or begin to share power with someone who is different'. I am left uncertain, however, what degree (or kind) of 'relativizing' *this* view of a feminist 'standpoint' involves, and how we would know when we had arrived at such a 'point of absurdity'.

I think the cluster of points I wish to raise under this first heading will now be clear. It may be obvious from my own essay that (unlike – I think – Julie, Nicola and Jane, but like Janet and, ironically, Daphne) I remain an impenitent 'realist' in my state-ments about God; and that, for me, the activity of prayer, and a conceptual analysis of it, would hold an important place in the justificatory argument I would have to develop were I to give a complete defence of this form of theological 'realism'.[3] And therefore I am dubious whether it is either good strategy politi-cally, or (more importantly) theologically 'deep', for Christian feminists to disown all appeals to the divine 'real'; if past such appeals have been used as a cover for masculinist 'domination' (as they manifestly have), it does not follow, surely, that this need be so? What people should have learned from those past mis-demeanors is the absolute necessity of prayerful attention to the 'other', not the obliteration of all epistemological confidence in that possibility.

It is a short step from here to another cluster of (related) topics: *'story', realism* and *metaphysics*. For I also note that the appeal to a 'story' about Jesus' life, death and resurrection (see Julie, pp. 66 and 80, and Nicola Slee's essay, *passim*, especially her reference to Cupitt, p. 47) can be a rhetorical way of fudging the issue of whether one is aiming to make any 'realist' claims about God and the world or not. Since this is a common ploy in non-feminist theological discourse, it may not strike the reader as especially noteworthy! But again it is a point at which I think feminist theologians need to be clear about what they are doing and why.

This point does not detract from my admiration, and endorsement, of Nicola's central thesis about the genius of the biblical narrative's flexibility and its capacity thereby for endlessly novel and creative applications (see esp. pp. 33 and 47). This narrative flexibility does indeed provide a toe-hold for feminist subversion and redirection (just as, somewhat differently, 'deconstruction' does for Jane, and 'contemplation' for me). I would also strongly support the perception in Nicola's essay about what might be called the 'primacy', or 'irreducibility', of the narrative mode in the Christian doctrinal task (indeed this is also a strand in my own paper). But I get nervous, theologically and philosophically, when Nicola goes on to utter a number of negative remarks about conceptual belief and exposition, *tout court*, for example that 'A Christian is one who lives in a creative, fruitful relation to the Jesus-story, *rather than* one who believes certain *doctrines* about Jesus as the Christ' (my emphasis, p. 37); or that 'a particular set of *beliefs* about the story' (my emphasis, p. 37) is not a 'defining characteristic' (p. 37) of the Christian. My nervousness increases when we are told (p. 37) that we have no 'secure' grounds for excluding 'any' particular redirection of the Christian narrative.

It will be clear that this avoidance of doctrinal precision, along with (I think) a tacitly non-'realist' metaphysic, is a useful way of backing off engagement with the weight of Christianity's androcentric *credal* heritage. Moreover, it coheres with a fashionable 'fideism' in theological circles, whereby we all (supposedly) get off the hook of apologetic and philosophical clarification of our doctrinal commitments by a quick leap of faith into the circle of the Christian 'narrative'-tellers. But again I do wonder whether this is a politic, let alone theologically profound, route for feminist theology to take in the long run. As Nicola herself admits (p. 37), the Christian story 'invites, indeed compels, theological reflection and articulation'; and it does not follow (at least not as far as I can see) that the very activities of 'reflection' and 'clarification' are *intrinsically* 'masculinist'. Rather, it is surely the job of a responsible feminist theologian to unfold, with some painstaking care, the ways in which our doctrinal (as well as our story-telling) heritage has been shot through with androcentric bias, and then attempt an equally painstaking reconstruction. That, at any rate, is how I perceive the task that is set before me.

I am especially concerned about two implications of Nicola's 'fideist' approach which emerge in the course of her essay. The first is the suggestion, already quoted (from p. 37), that we have no grounds for excluding '*any*' interpretation from the 'memory' of the Christian community. This sounds like good news for flexible feminist reinterpretation; but it should be noted that it leaves no

grounds on which to exclude masculinist, racist or fascist interpretations of the gospel either. Would these still be all right, then,
as long as people were happily ensconced in a 'community' that
shared such presuppositions, and were inspired by a 'narrative'
that supported them? (We see how the issues about relativism
from my earlier paragraph resurface here.) In other words, as soon
as we are up against difficult ethical or political dilemmas, the
'narrative flexibility' argument looks pretty feeble unless supple-
mented by other criteria of judgement. And these, I suggest,
feminist theologians and philosophers cannot afford to leave
unexpressed.

Similarly, and this time with an eye to metaphysical claims
about the nature of God, I am interested to see Nicola
'psychologizing' about Jesus' state of mind in the face of the cross
(p. 43), in a way that itself suggests rather radical metaphysical
implications for the relations between the 'Father' and the 'Son'.
Thus, Nicola writes, 'The cross threatens to shatter the normalcy
of Jesus' own horizons, especially the horizon of his relationship
with "the Father"'; and, 'In the cross, his trust in and intimacy
with the Father is broken, and he is confronted with the radical
challenge of his own fractured and subverted human story.' Such
statements are also fashionable theological fare, and should
occasion no surprise if one is familiar with the theologies of (say)
von Balthasar and Moltmann. But again I want to press the point
about doctrinal clarity and metaphysical implications, because
these really do have important consequences here. Does Nicola
want to say that in the cross Jesus' relation with the 'Father'
actually *was* broken in some sense, divinity set off against divinity?
(And if so, did the 'Father' intend some such 'break', inflicting
extra suffering on his 'Son' by design? And what are the metaphysical consequences of such a 'break'? Is the notion of divinity-
set-off-against-itself philosophically coherent? If so, on what –
perhaps Hegelian? – presumptions?) *Alternatively*, is it rather that
what Nicola wants to say is that Jesus *felt* (by virtue of his
'kenotic' humanity?) abandoned and cut off from his 'Father' in
the cross; but what was *actually* occurring, metaphysically
speaking, involved no such break, but rather a summation of
divine love for humanity?

It is not hard to see, I hope, that such metaphysical decisions
have huge bearing on matters of ethics and spirituality – where
gender issues are again never far from sight. If I endorse, for
instance, a vision of divinely sanctioned rupture of relations
through the application of torture and pain, I will have one sort
of vision of how families and marriages should operate – with

insidious implications for women in already dependent positions. But if I have another vision – of a God who *never* abandons us or directly wills our pain, but sustains us in love even through apparent human collapse – quite different implications will clearly follow. It is for reasons such as this, then, that I am suspicious of any 'anti-doctrinal' posturing in feminist theology; and why I myself expend such an enormous amount of energy on (apparently tedious and pedantic!) distinctions between different forms of christological claim.

Finally, I want to make one or two remarks about feminist theory of language, though I shall keep these brief in hopes that Janet Soskice may say more. (Her book *Metaphor and Religious Language* makes most of these points with elegance and clarity.[4]) The first point is that a rich perception of the operations of 'metaphor' in religious talk by no means rules out a 'realist' approach to God, as followers of Sallie McFague (cited with approval by Julie, p. 67, and Nicola, n. 2 p. 172) tend to presume. Religious metaphors, phenomenologically considered, are not by and large optional frills by which we 'construct' universes of our own choosing, or at whim. (It is only if we are antecedently committed to a wholly 'constructivist' vision of religious language that such a theory seems convincing.) And metaphors do not *invariably* subvert or surprise; they may do that when first coined (and we can only comprehend the surprise by considering the *context*), but over time they generally lose their 'edge' and become 'dead'.[5] So no convincing theory of 'metaphor', it seems to me, can fail to address this fluid, 'diachronic' dimension of a metaphor's life-and-death cycle; and no theory of 'metaphor', I have also come to believe, is wholly free of ideological (or theological) freight. By the same token, I am suspicious of any theory of 'parable' (as some sort of concatenation of metaphors, according to Nicola, p. 41, citing McFague) that magically 'subverts' on any occasion of its retelling. (I am afraid my cynical observation of church-goers attending to a Sunday Gospel in which a parable is read suggests otherwise!) So something else is needed: *of course* the biblical narratives can disturb and redirect our lives if the conditions are right; but what are these right conditions? My own suggestion has been that the sustained practice of 'contemplation' – a kind of regular and disciplined self-stripping before God – might be one of those possible existential conditions; but I am aware that there are other means also to feminist subversion and enlightenment, some of them illuminatingly discussed in this volume. After all, 'Whoever is not against us is for us' (Mark 9.40).

13
AFTERWORD: *Daphne Hampson*

I am somewhat stunned at the extent to which I could be misread. Let me try again.

For me, feminism consists in not simply accepting the male scenario and placing oneself within it, but in drawing the lines differently.

Hence I start by redefining autonomy. The word, I say, has been captured by patriarchy (no wonder it has had a 'bad press' among feminists). In fact it means 'auto-nomos' (self-rule) as opposed to 'hetero-nomos' (letting another rule one): that precisely for which feminists have striven. 'It need not imply conceiving of oneself as an isolated atom in competition with others. Indeed, that it has come to hold such connotations may tell us much about the male psyche within patriarchy.'

I wish, then, a conception of the self as coming to itself through relations with others (the only way in which one can come to oneself); and, having come to have such a centredness, able to be present to others. 'Our goal must be that persons are centred in themselves and open to one another.' Commensurately with this I describe practices (of non-hierarchical groups, in the peace movement, among Quakers) in which a relational self is formed. Competitive, isolated selves are weak and in their inadequacy dominate others. Nicola writes: 'Feminist models of autonomy need to overcome the limitations of the Enlightenment ideal.' Indeed.

It is precisely because I hold such an ideal for the self and, furthermore, believe in human equality and relationality, that I do not wish a 'God' who stands in clear contradiction to these. (Indeed I should have thought that it is as one does away with hierarchy and an isolated sense of self that one would be open to the relational understanding of God for which I am arguing.) But Christianity, through the fact that it is a religion of revelation, conceives of a God who in some way is other than and set over against humankind. God is not held simply to be known through the beauty of the world or within human relations. True, as I indicate and as Janet points out, there have been other conceptions of God present within the western tradition. Nevertheless, Christianity cannot evade some notion of God as 'Other'; and the biblical tradition, not least, is profoundly anthropomorphic and heteronomous.

Humankind must come into its own. Julie seems puzzled. Feminists should stand in that tradition, following Hegel's discussion of the 'unhappy consciousness', and taken up in their respective ways by Feuerbach, Marx, Nietzsche and Freud, which holds that we need to overcome the male, transcendent God if humanity is to gain maturity. (It does not follow that we have to substitute for such a God a man in his image.) It is only as we take responsibility for ourselves that we shall cease to dominate and needlessly exploit the rest of creation. (Thus a major factor in our current predicament is over-population, caused not least by human beings, heteronomously, obeying religious authorities which forbid the use of contraceptives.) Inter-relatedness must, of course, extend to the creation.

I do not doubt that in one respect feminism is a flowering of that model of human rights which was born in the Enlightenment. It led in time to the freeing of slaves and to universal human franchise. (Christianity incidentally had not accomplished these things; it was left to secularity.) We dare not go back on a discourse of rights. But again, that does not mean that we need to buy modern liberal democracy (one man, one vote) as the only form of social organization. I precisely describe consensus decision-making. True equality must mean that men will learn from women, not simply that women – as substitute men – should join a male world. As Janet says, women have never had a 'free-wheeling self-hood'. Would that men could learn relationality!

'Particularity' I have discussed in my Response. I repeat. I favour an ethics which looks to the particular. This however is a different issue than that there can be no break in the causal nexus of history and of nature (at the macro level at which we live), such that there could be a (one-off) example of a resurrection. I cannot conceive that it could be that one period of history, or one man, stands in a different relation to God than do all others.

I of course do not disagree with Janet that there is no need for Christianity to consist in 'a set of truths laid down at this certain time'; that Christianity is not 'fixed in the past', that it 'grows and is shaped' and that it must 'avoid ... final closure'. Christianity has developed and will continue to do so. But this does not change the fact that Christians believe in a *particular* revelation in history; and therefore regard that period and supremely the words of Jesus as in some way normative. Christians look to something *outside themselves* in considering, for example, moral questions (viz. they act heteronomously).

Christianity I must insist is 'historical' not simply in the sense that, like all other movements, it bears the marks of the time in which it arose. Christians read the Bible as 'Scripture'. What concerns me then is that literature which comes from a past age will continue to influence people, the more especially at a sub-conscious level, in regard for example to their understanding of relations between women and men. I do not dispute Jane's contention that 'the Christian gospel and values' may, in many respects, be commensurate with feminism. But Christianity is not simply a teaching, in the way that are Marxism or feminism. It is anchored in what is believed to have been a revelation in a particular (patriarchal) world.

I did not know that my thought was incompatible with Sarah's talk of vulnerability, as Nicola and others suppose. I think women, through their sensitivity, are often deeply vulnerable. It is through not being impervious that one can gain a maturity and an integration (and hence an integrity) in oneself. Simply to remain vulnerable however is probably, through an inability to see them other than in relation to oneself, to exploit other people. It is certainly to fail to have enough centredness in oneself to be present to them. When Sarah, quoted by Nicola, speaks of prayer as ' "the place of the self's transformation and expansion into God" ', I wonder whether this may not be translated into my sense that, in prayer or contemplation, one attains to an in-tuneness with all that is. (And hence gains one's true self.)

In a fine turn of phrase, Janet asks whether a feminist is an 'exploratory archaeologist' who speaks newly of the past, or an 'anarchic architect' of an as yet unimaginable future. I think one is both. I do not but doubt that we must have a regard for the 'wisdom, love and holiness' of those who have preceded us. Yet I believe that we shall need to conceptualize differently what it is that God may be. It is in advocating both this continuity and this discontinuity with the past that I name myself post-Christian.

Note: Since writing this, I have been in contact with Jacky Fleming, whom I did not previously know and whom I had suggested to SPCK should be asked to provide a cartoon for the cover. Jacky at first refused – on principle, though she has now been glad to do so once she understood that the book was a debate. She could have taken the words out of my mouth, writing (of her well known little girl): 'If I allowed her to ally herself to a specific religious creed she could no longer represent the autonomy which is fundamental to her integrity, nor the fierce irreverence needed to fly in the face of prevailing wisdom. Far from accepting historical precedent she would be the first to question it on the basis of her own experience.' It is this sense of autonomy – which seems to me so fundamental to feminism – which I intended to put across in my essay!

14
AFTERWORD:
Janet Martin Soskice

My Response makes many of the points I might otherwise make here, but let me reply to those questions directed especially to me by Nicola and by Daphne, for in some ways these are complementary.

Nicola invites us to comment on the process by which this volume came together. I recall the initial brief suggesting that we were to write in a relatively informal way – more personally than in most 'academic' articles, and this I tried to do. My piece accordingly is far more descriptive than prescriptive, as I try to reflect throughout what, for me, it is to be a Christian feminist. This was the point of mentioning the varieties of Christian and correlative post-Christian feminist positions. One part of my answer to Nicola's question, then, about my seeming to require a classical Christology is that in my own case I do. My Christian faith has been built around this, and were it to go I don't know if I would want to remain a Christian. In saying (and Nicola needs to quote me in full) that 'it has always seemed to me that unless Jesus is the Christ, God incarnate, then the whole thing is a waste of time', I intended to make a confessional statement and not a prescriptive one, for of course I have many friends who, feminism apart, do not share this conviction. I am trying then to say where I am, not where others must be. However, the wider context is that of Daphne's post-Christian arguments and I do think these cut sharpest against Christologies in which Jesus is not exceptional, other than by being a great teacher, prophet and inspiring focus of the Jesus movement – a point to which I will return.

As mentioned, for me feminism has for the most part deepened and enriched my understanding of Christian faith, and even some of its more intellectually opaque Christian doctrines. I want to try to refigure the doctrine of the Trinity and atonement, for example, not because I feel one must but because I feel one can – that indeed these doctrines are always and have always been refigured. (This may betray the sensibility of someone who is more attracted to the sonnet than to blank verse, but please note that the sonnet is no less creative in virtue of its apparently restrictive form.)

The doctrine of the Trinity is a good example, for its place has been contested in almost every century. Even Calvin asked if it was really necessary because, he considered, it was not self-evidently biblical. But in the end where Christians have wanted to pray to Christ as God, and God as God, and Spirit as God, and yet insist they are not tritheists, some version of trinitarian thought has emerged. Not just because Christians felt they had to keep it or were fearful for the consequences if they did not, because there were times, and particularly in post-Reformation debates, when it really might have been got rid of on pious grounds. Yet it is wrong to suggest that, because the doctrine of the Trinity has continued to have a place in the faith of Christians, one monolithic version of this teaching has always held sway and brooked no criticism. Even in the early church period, what Augustine has to say is decidedly different from Athanasius, and what Schleiermacher or Elizabeth Johnson might say is different again.[1] There is huge vigour and diversity in the texts of historical theology. Now, many women have, undoubtedly and destructively, in their church experience been presented with a picture of the Christian faith as monolithic and invariant, as though the 'old teaching' were unchanged, from CE 33 to the present. This is simply not the case, and part of my interest in refiguring the traditional doctrines is to remind people that Christianity is, and always was, alive.

I, too, fear interpretive closure – the assertion that only 'this' can be said. But in some feminist theology we get a good deal of negative closure (such and such cannot be believed by women) and this is just as totalizing. A negative universal is still a universal. I am concerned then not to say that everyone must accept classical Christology (if that is what we should call it), but I am interested to see if the symbol may be turned so that women/feminists can accept it, and still retain their dignity as women.

That being said, I must also confess that I find the following argument of Daphne's extremely compelling: if Jesus is not God but merely a man, if these stories are just useful myths, then why, as a feminist, waste any time with these particular stories, framed as they are by societies that were patriarchal and perhaps at times misogynistic? Why not start from somewhere else? Why waste any time on the community of women and men around Jesus? That they are part of our formative past does not seem to me sufficient for the attention we pay them.

Daphne makes a pincer movement in which we are offered an either/or. Either you believe that Jesus is the Christ, God incarnate, or you believe he was a great man who started a movement for justice and liberation, and about whose life a rich mythology has been spun. Now if the feminist believes the latter, according to Daphne, she collapses into undesirable heteronomy, for her life must be defined by a man not much different from any other, and these constitutive myths and stories of the Bible, even if modestly liberating of the human person in general, can only be destructive to women, couched, as they are, in the terms of reference of a patriarchal society. The remaining possibility, that Jesus is God incarnate, is discounted by Daphne not on feminist grounds, but on grounds familiar to any student of the eighteenth-century empiricist philosophers – the closed causal nexus, the improbability of the resurrection, and so on.

To turn then to Daphne's response, it is worth noting that her extensive questions to me have virtually nothing to do with feminism and instead go over ground familiar to philosophers of religion from Hume onwards. As such you might say the task of responding is outside the brief of the current book, especially since a huge literature exists on this topic, but I will try to sketch a response.

Particularity. I was not suggesting that, because I understand the incarnation to focus on particularity, those who are not Christians, including Daphne, are unable to have regard for particularity. Rather my emphasis is on a belief which Daphne would not share: that a high point of intimacy, of the at-oneing of God and creation, comes when God Godself becomes a human being, with human language and body, in Jesus. Now others can of course value particularity, but we in the West should not also underestimate the extent to which our formative concern for the individual and the particular, and, yes, even the body, has been shaped by the beliefs of the Christians and of the Jews in this regard. The drift of neo-Platonism, to take only one influential example, where the concrete, the bodily, the transient and the feminine were unwelcome distractions from the abstract purity of the form of the Good, was quite otherwise.[2]

Now Daphne 'cannot credit' the particularity of the incarnation, and nor can she believe that there has been one and only one resurrection. The resurrection, by the way, is not a particular focus of my own essay, but Daphne in bringing it out enables the argument to focus on the question of the possibility of a 'break in the causal nexus of nature or history'. Post-Enlightenment Christians know about this 'causal nexus' and must be troubled by it, Daphne suggests, in a way earlier Christians were not. Now, several things could be said here, one of which is that the medieval philosophers, or at least Aquinas, were certainly aware of what we would call the 'causal nexus', although they would have referred to it in other terms. Their point is not that God can 'cause breaks in the causal order' but that God as creator is creator of the causal order in all its complexities – some of which may not be known to us. Invocation of the Big Bang here is not simply to say that 'funny things happen', but also to point out that the idea of a stable 'causal nexus' breaks down at this point. For the Big Bang happens 'outside' all space and time. We cannot even speak of 'cause' here.[3] We cannot say that the 'cause' of the Big Bang is the same as anything else within the 'causal nexus', *except of course* it happened outside space and time. To say it happened outside space and time is to deny that any of our notions of causality *could* be applicable to it! So in that sense the Big Bang is a 'breaking of the laws of this universe', although most astrophysicists would not wish to speak in terms of fixed laws these days.

Now, the theological point is that, if God is Creator, God is Creator of the space–time continuum. God is not an actor in the world in the sense of pacing himself alongside it and intervening from time to time (a deist picture). God in God's eternity (which is not everlastingness) might bring into being a world in which resurrection took place, and this would not be inconsistent with the order of that creation, even though we might not see it as such.

Furthermore, neither the incarnation nor the resurrection is adequately thought of as a funny 'event' in the natural order. The resurrection of Jesus is not about 'a person coming back from the dead' (Daphne, p. 113) – otherwise earlier Christians would not have distinguished the resurrection of Christ from the raising of Lazarus. But Jesus, and not Lazarus, was raised not to die again or, in the words of piety, to eternal life. This sharing in God's own life is not, as I said, to be everlasting in relation to space and time but to be, in ways we cannot conceive, 'outside' (the spatial term is inadequate) space and time altogether. Similarly the incarnation is a divine event and not, as of course Daphne knows, something a biochemist might confirm by a cell sample demonstrating two natures. It is because these 'events' are not part of the space–time continuum that they cannot be critiqued as ruptures in a 'causal nexus'. As an event within the causal nexus the claim that 'God "sent his Son" to planet earth' (the Wizard of Oz meets Star Trek) would only be bizarre. As a statement of belief about the Creator of all that is, it is not obviously so.

Now Daphne need not, and probably will not, be convinced by all of this. But equally she must concede that many intelligent Christians, even post-eighteenth century, have not had the difficulties she has with the incarnation and even the resurrection, and nor were they simply credulous (Daphne, p. 115). I can allow her the integrity of her position – indeed her sense of integrity I admire above all in her work – but she must allow me mine.

Let me end, then, with a point on which (I think) we agree. Daphne finds herself centred by prayer and that God is the one through whom she is centred. This, she points out, is not the experience of a heteronomous Other over and against me. I agree. To be centred in God is not to cease to be centred in myself. That might be so if God were a 'thing amongst things' or a two-bit actor on the world stage. A 'thing' can only be so close to us – there is always distance – but the Godness of God who is 'no thing' is to be as close to us as life itself.

15
AFTERWORD: *Nicola Slee*

The sharpest critical comments raised about my essay emanate from Sarah, so I shall concentrate here on her remarks. Whilst sharing my commitment to the irreducibility of narrative in the theological task, Sarah is concerned by what she takes to be my 'fideist' approach to questions of truth, characterized by the avoidance of doctrinal precision, a negative approach to conceptual belief and a tacitly non-realist metaphysic. Before attempting to respond to Sarah's questions, it seems important to clarify what I see as a significant difference between the two of us concerning the focus of a contemporary Christian apologetics, which may go some way to explaining the difference of approach we have taken to our respective essays. For Sarah, the apologetic task appears to be conceived as a reasoned defence of Christian belief, conducted by painstaking engagement with the credal texts of the tradition. I conceive of the apologetic task (in which, I take it, we are engaged in this volume) rather differently, as the demonstration of the vitality and dynamism of the tradition *itself*, by the telling, the reworking and the metaphoric engagement with the Christian narrative as such. Unless the story *itself* can be reworked in ways which compel recognition and engagement from those to whom it is a strange tale, I do not see that any amount of philosophical precision avails. This is why, in my essay, I point to the work of novelists, poets, liturgists and artists as those who may revitalize Christian identity in our times. These are our primary apologists, because it is they who enter directly into the power of the narrative and incarnate it in word, symbol, sound or image, not at one remove, but with the immediacy of narrative knowing which, in human genesis, precedes our more sophisticated critical awareness.

Nevertheless, my espousing of a narrative religious identity should not be read as anti-intellectual. The model of living-in-relation to the Jesus story which I have proposed implies a fundamental commitment to critical and responsible dialogue amongst those who, in the community of the church, share adherence to this story and yet who read it in radically differing ways. The appeal to the primacy of the shared story over any doctrinal consensus about it should not be read as a tactic for foreshortening theological debate, but precisely as an invitation to renew it. Notwithstanding, I maintain that, both in terms of the coherence of Christian identity and in terms of the apologetic task, story has a logical and a chronological primacy over doctrine. Living the story constitutes the 'first act' of faith; reflecting upon it and explicating its meaning constitutes the 'second act' of theology. Both 'acts' are vital to the integrity of faith, yet there is a sense in which the story itself outlives every attempt at doctrinal explication and holds together those who make radically opposed readings of it. The dialogue between these differences matters profoundly; and for just the kinds of reasons which Sarah herself adduces. Yet the commitment to living in a community which continues to embrace profound and often unwelcome difference is, for me, primary. (Jane, this is one of the features of my Christian experience which I bring to my understanding of feminism and which offers a challenge and critique to feminist notions of 'sisterhood'.)

To hold that the commitment to the common story takes logical precedence over the search for shared understandings of it does not mean that there are no valid grounds on which to test diverse readings of that story. When I call for the welcome embrace of multiplicity, I am not advocating total relativism but a more critically discerning hermeneutics which recognizes the cultural, political and, indeed, gendered bias of all readings, including and perhaps especially ecclesiastically sanctioned ones. Such a hermeneutics must certainly be capable of discriminating between good and bad readings, but it will not do so by a naïve appeal to orthodoxy. There are no foolproof tests, but a range of criteria – such as coherence, comprehensiveness, ethical and social praxis, aesthetic appeal, relevance, and so on – which have to be held in critical tension. So, for example, any reading of the Jesus narrative which sought to legitimize violence against the vulnerable would fail not only on ethical grounds but in terms of consonance with a story whose focus is the bias of divine love towards the vulnerable and disenfranchized.

This brings me to Daphne's questions about the locus of authority and my understanding of truth in relation to the Jesus story. Daphne wants to know why I 'choose' to live my life in relation to the Jesus story rather than to some other, if I do not think it to be, in some sense, 'true'. I live in relation to this story because I have discovered, do discover, and trust that I will continue to discover, manifold and continually expanding potential within it for healing, liberation and renewal, not only of my own life but that of others and the world within which I live. But this discovery is a complex process of mediation. The authority of the story resides neither in the story *per se*, nor in some story-telling God who can be known over and against the story, nor, *à la* Hampson, solely in the autonomous choice of the individual, but rather in the lived relation to the story. I continue to vest authority in the story, without which commitment it would cease to *be* living, authoritative tradition; yet as I live it, I discover that it *is* 'true', that the story does indeed have potential to renew and re-create me in ways I could not have imagined except by putting it to the test. This does not mean that I simply 'construct' the truth of the story. My discovery that the story is 'true' is both rooted in and testimony to the conviction that there is a genuine consonance between my experience of the world and the Christian narrative. It is an article of faith that the story does indeed faithfully reflect the reality of God, the world and human community – but even to speak about it in these terms implies that one could step outside the story to test the 'match' between it and 'reality', whereas, in fact, there is no way of appropriating and living that reality except by and in relation to the story itself. To put this in traditional theological terms, God is to be known only as God is revealed in and through the life, death and resurrection of Jesus; there is no other God than the one we meet in the story of Jesus. I do not think this makes me a non-realist (even a tacit one!), but it does mean that I cannot speak of my experience of God or the world except in terms of the narrative in which that experience is embedded.

Finally, an attempt to respond to Sarah's christological query. Sarah wants me to state 'plainly' (i.e., non-metaphorically?) what seems to me only possible to grasp at by way of image and metaphor – and it is precisely because I share her and Janet's conviction that metaphor is genuinely cognitive that I do not attempt a 'literal' response. I have tried to argue, in my essay, that the Christian narrative is open to extraordinary flexibility and multiplicity of meaning, yet this is not infinite. It is able to hold rupture and reversal within a narrative which has an ultimate coherence, and this is, itself, a guarantee as well as a sign that chaos and severance are not the final realities, though they are crucial moments upon which the story may hinge. What this means for me in terms of Christology is that, whilst there is indeed radical rupture in Jesus' relationship with God on the cross, nevertheless, this dislocation is not the final reality, since there is narrative continuity between the God who acts 'before' and 'after' the cross. To speak of 'divinity against divinity' is to push the moment of rupture so far as to risk collapsing the coherence of the story.

16

AFTERWORD: *Jane Shaw*

In this Afterword, I will comment on three things: first, the cluster of questions, raised by Julie, Sarah and Nicola, about mystical experience, theology and the status of woman's 'voice'; second, Daphne's comments about my reading of poststructuralism *vis-à-vis* Christian claims; third, Nicola's call for each of us to relate something about our experience of the writing of this book.

Julie suggests that I have tended to describe the history of female mysticism and prophecy 'as a series of strategies by women who tried to exercise power whilst remaining within the cultural construction of the "woman"', and that this leads to 'a function-alistic explanation for the religious experience and behaviour of women from other historical eras or other cultural contexts'. She therefore suggests that I have reduced religious beliefs and actions to political and social motives. I agree with Julie that such func-tionalist explanations are very problematic, and if I have done this, then she is right to take me to task. Indeed, one of the reasons why I particularly admire Phyllis Mack's book on female prophets in seventeenth-century England (which I footnoted in my article) is that she is so aware of this problem. She both addresses and contextualizes the religious experience of those seventeenth-century women with considerable historical and theological sen-sitivity and yet always remains alert to the lines of power which shaped and defined what women said, and how, in their proph-ecies. In my article, I did not intend to suggest that 'women did/do not have authentic experiences of God', nor to suggest that they only 'manipulate ... the life of the Spirit for their own subversive ends' (I am quoting Julie here), but rather to ask *how* and by what means women have been able, within the Christian tradition, to speak and write about those authentic experiences of God. I wanted to ask, too, how scholars (historians and theologians, for example) have defined and marked women's theological reflections 'merely' as mystical experience, (especially, perhaps, in the post-Enlightenment world where religious experience has been end-lessly prodded, examined and categorized by philosophers, scientists, anthropologists and others), rather than as theology.

My intention was not to ascribe certain motives to the women I was discussing (though reading over my article again I can see that I get dangerously close to that sometimes), but rather to talk about the categorization of both women and religious experience which has prevented women's writings from being read as either theological or 'rational'.

Nicola asks: 'How does Jane respond to Sarah's reading of contemplative prayer in the light of her own critique of female mysticism?' My immediate response to Nicola's question is – given my comments above – to note that I did not intend to make a critique of female mysticism. Rather, I was pointing to the ways in which women's religious experiences and theological reflections have frequently been read *only* as mysticism or prophecy. My questions were (and remain): How can women forge our identities as people of faith who are gendered as female and think about God? How is this possible when our religious experiences and ideas have been read as mystical, as signs of possession or prophecy, as healing gifts, but not as theology? How do we *retain* all those vital elements of religious experience, profound components of our relationship with God, and at the same time write and speak theologically? My response to Sarah's reading of contemplative prayer is therefore positive. I am seeking to find ways in which women – and men – can embrace and integrate the spiritual, the intellectual and their embodied religious experience. It therefore seems to me entirely appropriate that Sarah's theology should be grounded in the practice of contemplative prayer, a practice which in turn grounds her political action. My own experience of contemplative prayer supports such an integration of these different elements of religious experience and human activity. But we should note that Sarah writes as a theologian who painstakingly and consistently engages with the Christian tradition to understand how the 'feminine' has been figured in certain Christian doctrines and practices; I would venture to suggest that Sarah is breaking new intellectual and spiritual ground by writing of doctrine and contemplative prayer in this way as a female theologian.

Let me turn now to Daphne's critique of my use of poststructuralism. Daphne claims that 'poststructuralism ... particularly in its Derridean, deconstructionist, form ... makes Christianity impossible. For Christianity claims what Derrida will call "presence": that there is a uniqueness to Christian claims, a God beyond the world, a point at which there is truth.' Daphne's reading of poststructuralism is accurate – if one takes poststructuralism to be a purely philosophical enterprise, concerned almost entirely with epistemology. This is the approach which a number of theologians have taken, including Don Cupitt and Mark Taylor whom I discuss briefly in my article. But, trained by Barbara Johnson in the *practice* of deconstruction, while I was a graduate student, I have since then always taken deconstruction to be primarily and most usefully a reading strategy. It enables us to read a text against itself; it is thus a productive tool rather than a nihilist philosophy. It takes some of us to the beginning of the practice of Christian theology rather than the end. Furthermore, I am deeply wary of any claim that the poststructuralists themselves succeed in freeing themselves of metaphysical absolutes. I retain the right to practise a certain hermeneutics of suspicion here! In this I was influenced by Alice Jardine's excellent work, *Gynesis*, in which she reads a series of male poststrucrualist thinkers to show how they retain the figure of 'the feminine' or 'woman' as a metaphysical category throughout much of their work. Indeed, one only has to read Jacques Lacan's writings on women, pleasure and mysticism to grasp Jardine's point.[1]

Finally, let me turn briefly to Nicola's invitation that we each comment on the methodology of this collection of essays. The process of commenting on each other's work has been both stimulating and very interesting. In that sense, I would consider it a collaborative venture of some success. It may, however, have been enhanced by more collaborative editing. This is not to decry the very fine job Daphne has done in this area (nor her patience with us all!), but rather to suggest that it would have been interesting to see what happened when we each took responsibility for editing one other person's article, along with all the tasks of goading and encouraging which editing involves. Would this have been a publisher's nightmare, or a constructive step towards more collaborative work, or both? Furthermore, as Nicola rightly says, these articles have been difficult to write both because it is hard to write a short, nuanced statement of one's religious convictions and because such a task bears with it intellectual, spiritual and moral responsibility of some weight. The difficulty of this task has meant that this book has been a long time in the making, which, in turn, has led to each of us being made acutely aware of the ways in which our theological positions have shifted with this passage of time. For my own part, a declaration of those shifts in thinking may have been more helpful than the coherence for which I strived. I remain somewhat suspicious, in fact, of poststructuralism, and yet deeply influenced by it; I am a Christian and yet often find myself unsure of my exact relationship to and with the church. I suspect that each one of us could tell such a tale of shifting ideas and practical questions.

17

AFTERWORD: *Julie Hopkins*

In every debate, having the last word often swings the vote in your favour. However, I do not want to adopt the strategy of saying a few beautiful or devastating lines and making a grand exit. I do not wish to get involved in scoring points, nor would I want readers to have the impression that we feminist theologians are simply playing the old theological game of criticizing one another and calling that sacred science. What I shall try to do is explain, particularly for the benefit of Sarah and Daphne, what I perhaps only implicitly address in my essay, namely my methodological presuppositions about spiritual practice and theological reflection.

I have always considered myself a theological 'realist' in the sense that I try to enter into a dialogue about religious experience with those who live around me. My work as a feminist theologian in a secular, individualistic and materialistic Europe is about engaging with those women who are seeking an ethical spirituality in the context of the current ideological and philosophical vacuum within and outside the churches. These encounters have taught me that contemporary western women are suspicious of any form of dogmatism because of their memories of extremism, nationalism and two world wars, and because they wish positively to affirm cultural pluralism in Europe. Further, European feminist theory is currently engaged in an epistemological debate with post-modernism about where to draw the line with respect to the deconstruction of rationalism. In particular, what does the deconstruction of rationalistic or normative 'truths' mean for feminist ethics? This is then the context in which I reflect upon the relationship between God and society.

As a Christian theologian I bring the tradition into my reflections but, as with all of us, that tradition is coloured by my confessional background. I come from non-conformist Baptist roots, therefore I have never ascribed to a written creed. We believe that the hermeneutical dialogue between our faith communities and the Jesus movement is a reality through the indwelling presence of the Holy Spirit.

Why then does Sarah call me a 'relativist'? Perhaps because I do

not automatically apportion revelatory status to the ecclesiastical
and conciliar formulation and handing on of the ecumenical
dogmas. My attitude towards dogma is one of suspicion, not only
because its content is sometimes idolatrous, misogynist, illogical
or irrelevant, but because it is dogma. I cannot accept that theologians, bishops or church councils, however holy or inspired,
could/can know the definitive 'truth' about God in God's Self. Of
course they can speculate in the realm of metaphysics, but then we
need to read such doctrines as poetry, not descriptions of God. For
surely, if God is God and not to be a construct of our wishes or
hubris there must be room for mystery, for the apophatic spring
into the unknown.

Christian theologians have always realized that God is not a
thing or a being but the One who transcends our conceptions of
transcendence and immanence. Yet they give the impression of
knowledge of the essential nature of God. I regard this as false
gnosis. Why do I think this? Because I try to accept my created-
ness. To put it in biblical language, I have received the divine
image and the life-breath of God as a gift not a possession. This is
a matter of wonder which calls forth a loving response. So whilst
my knowledge of God falls short, I can try and believe that God is
the source, ground and goal of individual, communal and planetary life. Such a faith is grounded in actions. For me there are two
forms of action, both of them equally necessary as methods for
doing feminist theology. These are prayer and justice-making, or
what Dorothee Soelle calls 'mysticism and resistance'. I cannot
imagine an engaged feminist theologian who does not practise
both these forms of spirituality; in that sense each of the writers in
this book shares a common praxis. However perhaps we do not all
share the same presuppositions about what this means for our
theologizing.

Here I wish to make two points which could be called the
'relativist' side of my 'realism'. First, when we pray, call upon the
dynamic power of the Sophia-Spirit, or contemplate, we still
cannot escape the limits of our creatureliness. By this I mean that
we have certain personality traits, and that we have also inherited
to a greater or lesser degree, through socialization, the symbolic
order of our language and unconscious desires and of course our
context as women in a particular culture, race and confession. So
however much we are lovers of God sharing the pain and joy of
the vulnerable divine presence in our world, we cannot claim to
know God in God's Self. It is not simply that our experience of
God is necessarily contextual, but also that the God we encounter
in prayer is always partially our own construct, made in our own

image. However far we are along the spiritual path towards full possession of the Spirit, deification, the beatific vision or whatever we wish to name it, we are and remain human subjects; we are not essentially merged into the divine Self. Revelation, grace and wisdom are always mediated through our experience and language which is contextually bound and ambiguous. So whilst prayer protects us from the abyss of nihilism or existential despair, it also relativizes our truth claims because in prayer we learn that we can only see in a mirror dimly.

Second, theological relativism teaches us to be genuinely self-critical and humble, prerequisites which are necessary if we are to allow the Spirit to guide us into the unknown future beyond deconstruction. No one can sit behind a computer and type up a new religion. Rather, we theologians are caught up in a critical process of exorcism, change and renewal as lovers of God seek a path of justice through the secular desert. If Christian women no longer understand or accept certain christological doctrines, which I have shown to be the case in my book,[1] then we need to reflect with them in their theological confusion and existential pain.

Finally, we white western feminist theologians have to develop ways of learning to listen with radical attention to women whose experience is fundamentally different. Why? Because the only peaceful future for a world-wide religion such as Christianity is within the horizon of religious and cultural pluralism. This does not make me feel insecure because I trust multiplicity as the expression of Being. When different women, usually by working together in a shared project for well-being and justice, come to trust and respect each other, they begin to tell each other the Divine Names which they cherish. These Names are slowly being built up into the patchwork quilt of a contemporary theological tradition and practical spirituality. For Christian feminists the story of Jesus is at the heart of the quilt, but it is not the quilt.

18
AFTERWORD: *Sarah Coakley*

The first thing I wish to say is that I am touched by the warmth of some of my co-contributors' responses to my views (even when they are raising points of criticism); in contrast, my own first response may have seemed to have adopted a rather crusty academic tone. However, I think my feminist friends will know me well enough not to take this amiss, and I want to say how much I have been illumined, and at points much moved, by their separate contributions. We have all been formed by slightly different intellectual and ecclesial heritages; and the divergent emphases we bring to our essays also reflect the problems and opportunities we now face in our particular places of work, and (bar Daphne) in our churches. The discerning reader will I think be able to perceive this.

I am also challenged by Nicola's important comments about the difficulties that we all encountered in writing our initial essays; and I know that for my part these were primarily auto-biographical. I was trying to write about the abiding significance of spiritual *kenōsis* at a uniquely difficult phase of my professional life which also called for feminist resistance and courage and strength (not to speak of political astuteness). To explain how these goals could be combined was a difficult and subtle matter, involving some fine distinctions and a good deal of historical delving, as well as a lot of moral nerve; and although I do not tackle head-on in my essay the way in which prayer and politics merge (one of Nicola's questions to me), I hope it may be clear that I do not see 'contemplation' as an *escape* from the political arena. Indeed, even in my limited and feeble experience, it seems that prayer of this sort causes one to engage at a *deeper* level with the ills and pains of the world – much more in fact than one would choose for comfort. It would be nice to escape, but in practice God does not let one! Julie helps me here in her comments about women like Teresa and Simone Weil *combining* prayer with 'radical social action'.

Julie's own queries to me I will try to answer succinctly. I think they probably rest on some misunderstandings, arising perhaps

from the rather gnomic Pauline phrase, 'Have this *mind* in you ...'
(Philippians 2.5). Whatever Paul meant in this verse (it is
somewhat disputed), later Chalcedonian Christology – here,
indeed, heeding 'Antiochene' concerns – affirmed the significance
of the *whole* humanity of Christ ('fully man'), and not just of his
'mind'. And so most emphatically do I. Also, I am not for a minute
claiming that Christ can be imitated '*only* in prayer'; I am making
the more circumscribed claim that a particular form of prayer may
give us special insights into the nature and relationship of his
'humanity' and 'divinity'. Finally, I do of course share Julie's
concern that if Jesus is not truly like us ('our brother') then he can
scarcely be a prototype for us of incarnate love. But Chalcedon
happily agrees with this ('like us in all things, apart from sin').
Thus it must be, I think, that Julie finds the very notion of a God/
man incongruous, or has other reasons (perhaps good Baptist
reasons!) for wishing to short-circuit patristic metaphysics. I can
here only underscore that for a Chalcedonian Christology (and
especially for the 'Antiochene' reading of Chalcedon I have tentatively proposed) Christ's 'ontological uniqueness' is not
perceived as *undermining* his human closeness to us, but rather as
enclosing us in his redeeming humanity. To force a choice between
these two seems to me to pose a false set of alternatives.[1]

Now finally I come to Daphne's comments. The first, ostensibly
rather pedantic, point concerns Daphne's apparent difference from
Rosemary Ruether on the matter of *kenōsis*. Daphne denies any
such difference. But I think it is a matter of context and definition.
In *Sexism and God-Talk* (pp. 137f., the passage in question),
Ruether is delineating the significance of Jesus and his message
(including the so-called '*kenōsis* of patriarchy') for both men and
women, 'the new humanity'. Indeed she goes so far as to say that
'the maleness of Jesus has no ultimate significance' (p. 137), and
that 'Christ is not necessarily male' (p. 138). There is no suggestion
that the significance of *kenōsis* (as understood here) might apply
only to men; rather this *kenōsis* is co-terminous with 'the over-
throw of the present world system' (p. 138). Hence my remarks
(p. 87) that on the view represented in *Sexism and God-Talk*, it is
not Christ who is emptied, but patriarchy. (In Ruether's review of
Daphne's book she does discuss *kenōsis* in Daphne's sense, with
an approbation that seems in some tension with her earlier
remarks; but this was not what I was commenting on in my essay.)

Now we come to the more substantial issues, in particular the
vexed question of the relation between 'sexuality' and God-
language. Here, on the one hand, Daphne tells us that 'male
genitality' has fixed the course of Christian trinitarian perceptions

of 'outpouring' love (and I take it this implies that women will be
exhibiting false consciousness if they show any appreciation of this
view of love). On the other hand, Daphne debars any 'female'
dependence on God (and apparently any use of sexual metaphor in
this area at all), because that would display a 'heteronomous'
acceptance of submission to 'male' authority.

In the small space left to me here I fear I can comment on this
only rather briefly and sharply, which I trust Daphne will not take
amiss. It is surely ironic that Daphne presents an argument in this
form having just accused me of a 'peculiarly masculinist' reliance
on dichotomous sexual stereotyping, a charge I find hard to
understand. Yet she herself relies on seemingly crude sexual
essentialisms in her critique of my position (and of the Christian
tradition she has rejected). As Daphne well knows, the argument
from male ejaculation (as outpouring love) has been used by tra-
ditionalists such as von Balthasar against the ordination of
women; the idea that one should *rely* on it in an attempt to rebut
an interlocutor in feminist debate is very strange. Moreover, the
view of love-making that lurks here is dismal indeed: the female is
passive and assaulted, the male dominating and 'powerful'. I
cannot see that this form of argumentation represents a positive
way forward, for Daphne or anyone else. It is seemingly only
because Daphne is unwilling to grasp what I explicitly write in my
essay, viz., that the special sort of 'vulnerability' I am discussing is
not to be specifically identified with the 'female', nor with powerlessness (indeed with the opposite), that she accuses me of such
sexual 'dichotomizing'. Recall what I wrote on p. 106, that 'true
divine "empowerment" occurs most unimpededly in the context of
a *special* form of human [not 'female'] "vulnerability"'. This
specialness arises from the *sui generis* nature of our relationship to
God.

For Daphne, it seems, *any* sort of 'dependence' on God, and any
kind of sexual metaphor used to evoke this dependence, can be
nothing but 'heteronomy'. Whereas for me, the *right* sort of
dependence on God is not only empowering but freeing.[2] For God
is no rapist, but the source of my very being; God is *closer* than
kissing (I am happy to put it thus, metaphorically); indeed God,
being God, is closer to me even than I am to myself.

NOTES

1. ON AUTONOMY AND HETERONOMY

1 Michèle Le Doeuff, *Hipparchia's Choice*, Oxford and Cambridge MA, Basil Blackwell, 1991, back cover.
2 Oxford and Cambridge MA, Basil Blackwell, 1990.
3 This theme is central to my forthcoming book, *After Christianity* (London, SCM Press, 1996).

2. TURNING THE SYMBOLS

1 There are many other factors, of course. For instance, if we were to consider the growth of interest in feminist theology amongst academic theologians we would want to consider the heightened interest in recent years in questions to do with interpretation and ideology, and so on.
2 Sandra M. Schneiders, *Beyond Patching: Faith and Feminism in the Catholic Church*, Mahwah NJ, Paulist Press, 1991.
3 Schneiders, *Beyond Patching*, p. 34.
4 For an excellent argument to this effect see Michael Buckley, *At the Origins of Modern Atheism* (New Haven, Yale University Press, 1987), p. 24.
5 Feminist theologians, of course, may make a more comprehensive study of the varieties of Christian feminism and find all wanting, as Daphne Hampson does in *Theology and Feminism* (Oxford, Basil Blackwell, 1990). But it is difficult to be genuinely 'inside' confessional positions that are not one's own. Catholic readers of Daphne's book, for instance, may find her dismissal of 'high Christologies' peremptory.
6 See Daphne Hampson in her debate with Rosemary Radford Ruether, 'Is There a Place for Feminists in a Christian Church?', *New Blackfriars*, vol. 68, 1987, p. 12. Note Hampson always uses He/Him, etc. when speaking of the male conception of God.
7 Athanasius' *Contra Gentes* is less sexist reading on this than many later theological treatises.
8 Hampson, *Theology and Feminism*, p. 41.
9 To caricature, this variant of liberalism is one that says the Bible gives us good stories about a great man, stories much embellished by the then current mythology. Space precludes a more positive account of 'myth' here.
10 Hampson and Ruether, 'Is There a Place for Feminists?', pp. 21–2.
11 Schneiders, *Beyond Patching*, p. 64.
12 Amartya Sen, 'More Than One Hundred Million Women are Missing', *New York Review of Books* (December 1990), p. 61.
13 For this discussion of so-called 'basic biological facts' see Manfred Hauke, *Women in the Priesthood? A Systematic Analysis in the Light of the Order of Creation*, San Francisco, Ignatius Press, 1988.

14 Athanasius, *De Incarnatione*, Section 9, tr. Robert W. Thomson (Oxford, Oxford University Press, 1971). The Greek noun here is *anthropos*.

15 Bernard Lonergan, 'Christology Today: Methodological Reflections, A Third Collection', ed. Frederick E. Crowe (Mahwah/London, Paulist Press, 1985), p. 78.

16 Paul Tillich, 'The Religious Symbol', *Myth and Symbol*, ed. F.W. Dillistone (London, SPCK, 1966), p. 16.

17 Gregory Baum, following Mannheim, makes a similar point in more formal terms:

> While society provides the common symbolic coordinates for perceiving the world, it is possible within this context to follow ideological symbols that protect the inherited order or to identify with utopian symbols that summon people to social change. Both the ideological and countervailing symbols are in some sense generated by the dominant social order and reflect its structure either by confirming or questioning it. It follows from this that even though consciousness is created by the society to which we belong, there is room within that setting for creative religious symbols which are related to the inherited mind-set as sacred legitimation or as sacred critique, or as a mixture of both.

Religion and Alienation (Mahwah NJ, Paulist Press, 1975), p. 248.

18 In 'Black and Reformed: Contradiction or Challenge?' *Black and Reformed: Apartheid, Liberation and the Calvinist Tradition* (Orbis Books, 1984), pp. 83–4.

19 John de Gruchy has written of the importance for black Calvinists of this 'revitalization of traditional symbols, the reconstruction of the symbolic universe of those who are deprived and oppressed, in order more adequately to interpret and transform reality'. In 'The Revitalization of Calvinism in South Africa: Some Reflections on Christian Belief, Theology, and Social Transformation', *Journal of Religious Ethics* (Spring 1986), p. 35.

20 Cited by de Gruchy, 'The Revitalization of Calvinism', p. 39.

21 *Texts of Terror* (Philadelphia PA, Fortress Press, 1984), pp. 2–3.

22 Hampson, *Theology and Feminism*, p. 2.

23 Hampson, *Theology and Feminism*, p. 41.

3. THE POWER TO RE-MEMBER

1 M. Rukeyser, 'Kathe Kollwitz', quoted in L. Bernikow (ed.), *The World Split Open: Women Poets 1552–1950* (London, Women's Press, 1974).

2 In developing this reading, I am drawing widely on the work of Sallie McFague, especially in *Metaphorical Theology: Models of God in Religious Language* (London, SCM Press, 1983) and *Models of God: Theology for an Ecological Nuclear Age* (London, SCM Press, 1987).

3 B. Swimme, 'The Resurgence of Cosmic Storytellers', *The Way*, vol. 29, no. 1 (1989), p. 27.

4 J. Navonne, *Towards a Theology of Story* (Slough, St Paul Publications, 1977), p. 18.

5 D. Cupitt, *What is a Story?* (London, SCM Press, 1991), p. 77.

6 E. A. Johnson, 'The Maleness of Christ', *Concilium*, 6 (1991), p. 108.

7 R. Page, *The Incarnation of Freedom and Love* (London, SCM Press, 1991), p. 80.

8 For a summary of the problems, see D. Hampson, *Theology and Feminism* (Oxford, Basil Blackwell, 1990), ch. 3.

9 E. Schüssler Fiorenza, *In Memory of Her: A Feminist Theological Reconstruction of Christian Origins* (London, SCM Press, 1983).

10 For a helpful discussion of the way in which the reader of the biblical texts is constructed as male, see S. Durber, 'The Female Reader of the Parables of the Lost', *Journal for the Study of the New Testament*, 45 (1992), pp. 59–78.

11 Again, for a summary, see Hampson, *Theology and Feminism*, ch. 2.

12 M. Daly, *Beyond God the Father: Towards a Philosophy of Women's Liberation* (London, Women's Press, 1986), p. 73.

13 This is not a new idea, but has been proposed by a range of theologians. See, for example, R. Funk, *Language, Hermeneutic and Word of God: The Problem of Language in the New Testament and Contemporary Theology* (New York, Harper & Row, 1966); J. D. Crossan, *In Parables: The Challenge of the Historical Jesus* (New York, Harper & Row, 1973); L. E. Keck, *A Future for the Historical Jesus: The Place of Jesus in Preaching and Theology* (Philadelphia, Fortress Press, 1981); and S. McFague, *Models of God*.

14 McFague, *Models of God*, p. 50.

15 McFague, *Models of God*, pp. 48ff.

16 N. Slee, 'Parables and Women's Experience', *Modern Churchman*, 26, No. 2 (1984), pp. 20–31.

17 McFague, *Models of God*, p. 53.

18 E. Moltmann-Wendel, *The Women Around Jesus* (London, SCM Press, 1982), p. 71.

19 S. C. Barton, 'Woman, Jesus and the Gospels' in R. Holloway, (ed.) *Who Needs Feminism? Men Respond to Sexism in the Church* (London, SPCK, 1991), p. 33.

20 R. R. Ruether, *Sexism and God-Talk* (London, SCM Press, 1983), ch. 5.

21 Cupitt, *What is a Story?*

22 Cupitt, *What is a Story?* pp. 102–3.

23 See, for example, M. Roberts, *The Wild Girl* (London, Methuen, 1984) and *The Book of Mrs Noah* (London, Methuen, 1987), and S. Maitland, 'Triptych' in *A Book of Spells* (London, Michael Joseph, 1987).

24 See, for example, Ruether, *Sexism and God-Talk*; I. Carter Heyward, *The Redemption of God* (Washington DC, University of America Press, 1982) and *Our Passion For Justice* (New York, Pilgrim Press, 1984); M. Grey, *Redeeming the Dream: Feminism, Redemption and Christian Tradition* (London, SPCK, 1989), and R. Nakashima Brock, *Journeys By Heart: A Christology of Erotic Power* (New York, Crossroad, 1988).

25 See, for example, J. Morley, *All Desires Known* (London, SPCK, 1992, 2nd edn) and M. T. Winter, *WomanWord: A Feminist Lectionary and Psalter: Women of the New Testament* (New York, Crossroad, 1990).

4. WOMEN, RATIONALITY AND THEOLOGY

1 Alessandra Lipucci, 'The Problem of the Subject', a talk given at the Critical Legal Studies/Fem Crits Conference, Harvard Law School, 1992.

2 'The Notion of Virginity in the Early Church' in *Christian Spirituality: Origins to the Twelfth Century*, ed. Bernard McGinn, John Meyendorff and Jean Leclerq (New York, Crossroad, 1989), p. 435.

3 See, for example, Daphne Hampson, *Theology and Feminism* (Oxford, Basil Blackwell, 1990), ch. 2.

4 Hampson, *Theology and Feminism*, p. 77.

5 Margaret R. Miles, *Carnal Knowing: Female Nakedness and Religious Meaning in the Christian West* (Boston, Beacon Press, 1989), p. 177.

6 Jacquelyn Grant, *White Women's Christ and Black Women's Jesus: Feminist Christology and Womanist Response* (Atlanta, Georgia, Scholars Press, 1989), pp. 212, 215.

7 'Truth and Power' (from *Power/Knowledge*), reprinted in *The Foucault Reader*, ed. Paul Rabinow (New York, Pantheon Books, 1984), p. 73.

8 For example, Deborah Valenze shows how the Primitive Methodists gave a prominence to women which the later, more 'respectable' Methodist Church did not. See her *Prophetic Sons and Daughters: Female Preaching and Popular Religion in Industrial England*, Princeton NJ, Princeton University Press, 1985.

9 For the tests put to Teresa's mystical visions, see her *Life*.

10 See Phyllis Mack, *Visionary Women: Ecstatic Prophecy in Seventeenth Century England*, Berkeley, University of California Press, 1993.

11 Alex Owen argues this in *The Darkened Room: Women, Power and Spiritualism in Late Victorian England*, London, Virago Press, 1989.

12 Thomas Laqueur writes of the ways in which people began to *seek* differences between the sexes, in the Enlightenment and into the modern period, even when scientific research did not necessarily support the idea that men and women were fundamentally different from each other. See his *Making Sex: Body and Gender from the Greeks to Freud*, Cambridge MA, Harvard University Press, 1990.

13 Genevieve Lloyd writes of the tensions between notions of 'woman' and rationality in western philosophy: 'There are not only practical reasons, but also conceptual ones, for the conflicts many women experience between Reason and femininity. The obstacles to female cultivation of Reason spring to a large extent from the fact that our ideals of Reason have historically incorporated an exclusion of the feminine, and that femininity itself has been partly constituted through such processes of exclusion.' See *The Man of Reason: 'Male' and 'Female' in Western Philosophy* (Minneapolis MN, University of Minnesota Press, 1984), p. x.

14 Roberta Bondi, 'Spirituality and Higher Learning: Thinking and Loving', *The Cresset* (June 1993), pp. 5, 8, 9, 10, 12.

15 For a lucid account of poststructuralism and its relationship to feminism, see Chris Weedon, *Feminist Practice and Poststructuralist Theory*, Oxford, Basil Blackwell, 1987.

16 See Linda J. Nicholson (ed.), *Feminism/Postmodernism* (New York/London, Routledge, 1990) and Seyla Benhabib, *Situating the Self: Gender,*

Community and Postmodernism in Contemporary Ethics (New York, Routledge, 1992).

17 Don Cupitt, *The Time Being* (London, SCM Press, 1992), p. 16. See also, Mark C. Taylor, *Deconstructing Theology*, New York, Crossroad/Chico CA, The Scholars Press, 1980.

18 The American literary critic, Barbara Johnson, writes of deconstruction as productive of, rather than destructive of, meanings: 'Deconstruction is not a form of textual vandalism designed to prove that meaning is impossible ... The deconstruction of a text does not proceed by random doubt or generalized skepticism, but by the careful teasing out of warring forces of signification within the text itself. If anything is destroyed in a deconstructive reading, it is not meaning but the claim to unequivocal domination of one mode of signifying over another.' 'Translator's Introduction' to Jacques Derrida, *Dissemination* (Chicago, University of Chicago Press, 1981), p. xiv.

5. RADICAL PASSION

1 Cf. 'Feminism and Patriarchal Religion: Principles of Ideological Critique of the Bible', *Journal for the Study of Religion* 22 (1982), pp. 56–72.

2 Cf. *Metaphorical Theology: Models of God in Religious Language*, London, SCM Press, 1983.

3 Cf. *Bread Not Stone: The Challenge of Feminist Biblical Interpretation*, Boston, Beacon Press, 1984.

4 Cf. *Communities of Resistance and Solidarity: A Feminist Theology of Liberation* (New York, Orbis Books, 1985), pp. 1–14.

5 Cf. *To Change the World: Christology and Cultural Criticism* (London, SCM Press, 1981), p. 43.

6 Cf. *Womanguides: Readings Towards a Feminist Theology* (Boston, Beacon Press, 1985), p. 195.

7 Cf. 'The Descent of Woman: Symbol and Social Condition', *New Woman, New Earth: Sexist Ideologies and Human Liberation* (New York, Seabury Press, 1975), pp. 3–35.

8 Cf. 1 Timothy 2.11–14. For an excellent discussion of Augustine's position see Kari Børrensen, *Subordination and Equivalence: The Nature and Role of Women in Augustine and Thomas Aquinas*, tr. C. H. Talbot (Washington DC, 1981), pp. 15–34.

9 Cf. Augustine, 'Opus Imperfectum Contra Julianum' which is cited and discussed by Elaine Pagels in *Adam, Eve and the Serpent* (London, Penguin, 1988), pp. 127–50.

10 For a discussion of Tertullian's 'De Cultu Feminarum' cf. Pagels, *Adam*, pp. 98ff.

11 Cf. Elisabeth Schüssler Fiorenza, *In Memory of Her: A Feminist Theological Reconstruction of Christian Origins* (London, SCM Press, 1983), pp. 53–6.

12 An example of this saying, as found in the Gospel of Thomas, is cited and discussed by Ruether in *Sexism and God-Talk* (London, SCM Press, 1983), p. 128.

13 Cf. Sallie McFague, *Models of God: Theology for an Ecological Nuclear*

Age (London, SCM Press, 1987); Ruether, *Sexism and God-Talk*; Grace Jantzen, *God's World God's Body* (London, Darton, Longman and Todd, 1984).

14 Cf. *The Redemption of God: A Theology of Mutual Relation*, Washington, University Press of America, 1982.

15 Cf. Valerie Saiving, 'The Human Situation: A Feminine View' in C. Christ and J. Plaskow (eds.), *Womanspirit Rising* (London, Harper and Row, 1979), pp. 25–42; J. Plaskow, *Sex, Sin and Grace: Women's Experience and the Theologies of Reinhold Niebuhr and Paul Tillich* (New York, University Press of America, 1980); Mary Grey, *Redeeming the Dream: Feminism, Redemption and Christian Tradition* (London, SPCK, 1989).

16 Saiving, 'The Human Situation', p. 37.

17 'Re-imaging Jesus: Power in Relation', *The Redemption of God*, pp. 25–72.

18 Cf. Schüssler Fiorenza, *Bread Not Stone*, pp. 43–63.

19 Cf. *Hearing and Knowing: Theological Reflections on Christianity in Africa*, New York, Orbis Books, 1989.

20 Cf. Schüssler Fiorenza, *In Memory of Her*, pp. 97–159.

21 Cf. Isabel Carter Heyward, *Our Passion for Justice: Images of Power, Sexuality and Liberation* (New York, Pilgrim Press, 1984) and Mary Hunt, 'Lovingly Lesbian: Toward a Feminist Theology of Friendship', in R. Nugent (ed.), *A Challenge to Love: Gay and Lesbian Catholics in the Church* (New York, 1984), pp. 135–55.

22 Grey, *Redeeming the Dream*, pp. 134–8.

6. KENŌSIS AND SUBVERSION

1 D. Hampson, *Theology and Feminism* (Oxford, Basil Blackwell, 1990), p. 155.

2 See R. R. Ruether, *Sexism and God-Talk* (London, SCM Press, 1983), pp. 137–8.

3 Hampson, *Theology and Feminism*, p. 155 (my emphasis).

4 It is important to underscore at the outset that I do not use this word in an élitist sense, but rather to denote any (relatively) wordless form of prayer in which discursive thought is reduced to the minimum. For more on this, and its centrality to the essay, see section VI below.

5 See E. Lohmeyer, *Kyrios Jesus: Eine Untersuchung zu Phil. 2, 5–11* (Heidelberg, C. Winter, 1961(1928)). Lohmeyer was, however, not the first to detect a strophic construction to the passage, and the debate continues on how to divide the *strophēs*: see (for example) J. Jeremias, 'Zu Phil. ii.7: *heauton ekenōsen*', *Novum Testamentum* 6 (1963), pp. 184–8, for a discussion and analysis of this problem, with criticism of earlier solutions.

6 See R. P. Martin, *Carmen Christi: Philippians ii.5–11 in Recent Interpretation and in the Setting of Early Christian Worship* (Cambridge, Cambridge University Press, 1967), pp. 74–84, 89–93, for a brief account of this theory as maintained by various members of the Bultmannian school. (Martin's book remains the best general introduction to the exegetical problems of Philippians 2.) M. Hengel, *The Son of God* (London, SCM Press, 1976), esp. pp. 1–2, represents the most impenitent recent

reassertion of the view that Philippians 2 is speaking of Christ's pre-existent *divinity*. As such, Hengel's exegesis falls outside the two major contemporary 'types' of interpretation I am here sketching.

7 E. Käsemann, *Exegetische Versuch und Besinnung: erste Band* (Göttingen, Vandenhoeck und Ruprecht, 1960), p. 70 (cited in Martin, *Carmen Christi*, p. 83).

8 See (for example) Jeremias, 'Zu Phil. ii.7' (by implication; and more fully in J. A. T. Robinson, *The Human Face of God* (London, SCM Press, 1973), pp. 162–6, and J. D. G. Dunn, *Christology in the Making* (London, SCM Press, 1980), pp. 114–21). Martin, *Carmen Christi*, pp. 68–74, provides a brief discussion of earlier twentieth-century exponents of this 'ethical example' interpretation.

9 See Dunn, *Christology*, ch. 4, *passim*, for this line of argument on Adam typology. (The matter is, however, not uncontentious: it is not *clear* from the original Hebrew text of Genesis 2 that being 'equal with God' is deemed to be either a 'snatching' or a 'sin'. I am grateful to Robert Murray sj for a number of illuminating discussions on this point.) N. T. Wright, *The Climax of the Covenant: Christ and the Law in Pauline Theology* (Minneapolis, Fortress Press, 1992), *passim* (see esp. the chart on p. 81 as résumé), contains an exhaustive survey of the possible meanings of *harpagmos* in this context.

10 So Jeremias, 'Zu Phil. ii.7', p. 187; Dunn, *Christology*, p. 118.

11 This is the conclusion of Wright's complex argument (*The Climax of the Covenant*, p. 97), which picks up some dimensions of an influential earlier article by C. F. D. Moule ('Further Reflexions on Philippians 2:5–11' in W. W. Gasque and R. P. Martin (eds.), *Apostolic History and the Gospels* (Grand Rapids, Eerdmans, 1970), pp. 264–76, see esp. pp. 264–5). I treat of Moule's position in some more detail below.

12 The one major exception to this rule would be Hengel, *Son of God*. See n. 6 above.

13 See again Dunn, *Christology*, pp. 114–21, for the clearest enunciation of these points.

14 Moule, 'Further Reflexions', p. 265 (my emphasis).

15 As presented in English in F. Loofs, 'Kenōsis', *Encyclopaedia of Religion and Ethics*, ed. J. Hastings, vol. VII (Edinburgh, T. & T. Clark, 1914), pp. 680–7.

16 A glance at the entry '*Kenōsis*' in G. W. H. Lampe, *A Patristic Greek Lexicon* (Oxford, Clarendon Press, 1961), with its various sub-categories, is revealing here, showing a prevalence of patristic discussions of Philippians 2 concerned to defend the unchanging nature of the divine essence in spite of the biblical language of 'emptying'.

17 There is a brief, but clarifying, discussion of Hilary of Poitier's position in W. Pannenberg, *Jesus – God and Man* (London, SCM Press, 1968), pp. 307–8. Cyril's distinctive approach to *kenōsis* is well charted in F. Young, *From Nicaea to Chalcedon* (London, SCM Press, 1983), pp. 260–3, drawing on an important earlier article by R. A. Norris, 'Christological Models in Cyril of Alexandria', *Studia Patristica* 13 (1975), pp. 255–68.

18 Again see the discussion and references in Young, *Nicaea to Chalcedon*, p. 261.

19 From Cyril's third letter to Nestorius, translated in T. H. Bindley and F. W. Green (eds.), *The Oecumenical Documents of the Faith* (London, Methuen, 1950), pp. 213–14. (This is also cited and helpfully discussed by S. W. Sykes in his article, 'The Strange Persistence of Kenotic Christology' in A. Kee and E. T. Long (eds.), *Being and Truth: Essays in Honour of John Macquarrie* (London, SCM Press, 1986), pp. 350–1.)

20 Thus Frankenberry's feminist analysis of different forms of theism rejects 'classical theism's' definition of God as hopelessly incoherent from the outset, even in advance of feminist critique (see N. Frankenberry, 'Classical Theism, Panentheism, and Pantheism: On the Relation Between God Construction and Gender Construction', *Zygon* 28 (1993), pp. 30–3). My own (feminist) view, whilst criticizing particular 'masculinist' thematizations of God's nature, is, for philosophical and theological reasons adumbrated in this essay, more accepting of the 'classical' divine attributes such as omnipotence, omniscience, immutability and timelessness (see below, section V).

21 The extent to which Cyril's 'Alexandrian' Christology is endorsed in the Chalcedonian Definition of 451 remains a matter for dispute. The Definition represented a compromise between the rival christological schools of Alexandria and Antioch; but it is also a subtle exegetical matter whether we should read it as straightforwardly *identifying* the pre-existent Logos with the *hypostasis* ('person') who unites divine and human 'natures'. Such would be a 'Cyrilline' reading; but it can be challenged. (See A. Baxter, 'Chalcedon, and the Subject in Christ', *Downside Review* 107 (1989), pp. 1–21, and see n. 81 below.) The *Tome* of Pope Leo, which was officially endorsed at Chalcedon, does contain a view of *kenōsis* (*exinanitio* in Latin) comparable to Cyril's, that is, the 'self-emptying' involved is not seen as implying any detraction from Christ's divine characteristics. (On this point, see Sykes, 'The Strange Persistence', p. 351.)

22 This is a common, if loose, definition of *communicatio idiomatum* (as given, for example, in Young, *Nicaea to Chalcedon*, p. 238), but it is not as technically precise as we might wish. Quite how the 'communication' is deemed to operate – in which direction (or both), whether only in virtue of the *hypostasis* or directly from one nature to the other, and if merely by verbal attribution or *in re* – were matters for later dispute (see, for example, Pannenberg, *Jesus*, pp. 296–307, and my further discussion below). None of the patristic authors, however, argued that *human* attributes could be directly attributed to the divine nature.

23 See below, section III, for the post-Reformation developments.

24 Cyril, *De recta fide* II.55, cited in Young, *Nicaea to Chalcedon*, p. 262 (my emphasis).

25 *De recta orthodoxa* III.1, cited in A. B. Bruce, *The Humiliation of Christ* (Edinburgh, T. & T. Clark, 1881), p. 73 (my emphasis).

26 There are brief discussions in English of this school's position in J. A. Dorner, *History of the Development of the Doctrine of the Person of*

Christ (Edinburgh, T. & T. Clark, 1870), II.2, pp. 282–6; Bruce, *Humiliation*, pp. 106–14; Sykes, 'The Strange Persistence', p. 352.

27 See the criticisms from a Reformed perspective in Bruce, *Humiliation*, Lecture III, esp. pp. 106–14.

28 Such would appear to be the clear implication of Hampson's adjunct essay 'On Power and Gender', *Modern Theology* 4 (1988), pp. 234–50, esp. p. 239: 'I want to suggest that this paradigm [the paradigm of self-giving to another], which men may have found useful, is inappropriate for women. Feminist women seemingly reject it with unanimity.' This is of course precisely the point I am questioning.

29 An extract from G. Thomasius, *Christi Person und Werk*, II (2nd edn, 1857), translated in C. Welch (ed.), *God and Incarnation in Mid-Nineteenth Century German Theology: G. Thomasius, I. A. Dorner, A. E. Biedermann* (New York, Oxford University Press, 1965), p. 89 (my emphasis).

30 So (misleadingly) J. M. Creed, in his essay 'Recent Tendencies in English Theology' in G. K. A. Bell and A. Deissmann (eds.), *Mysterium Christi* (London, Longman's Green, 1930), p. 133; Donald Baillie in *God Was In Christ* (London, Faber and Faber, 1948), pp. 94–5, 96–7; and David Brown in *The Divine Trinity* (London, Duckworth, 1985), p. 231.

31 See F. Weston, *The One Christ* (London, Longman's Green, 1914 (1907)), ch. 6, esp. (for these analogies) pp. 166–87. This quotation is from p. 182.

32 Weston admits the inadequacy of each of his analogies as he discusses them, and esp. on p. 185 of *The One Christ*: 'these analogies have not taken us very far . . .'. J. Hick, *The Metaphor of God Incarnate* (London, SCM Press, 1993), ch. 6, has recently presented a clear analysis of modern 'kenoticist' positions, with philosophical critique, but makes no remark on what I have here termed the 'social and sexual subtext' of their accounts.

33 For Gore's analogies for christological *kenōsis*, see C. Gore, *The Incarnation of the Son of God* (London, J. Murray, 1891), pp. 159–62 (and note the talk of 'real abandonment' of divine properties, p. 161). In C. Gore, *Dissertations on Subjects Connected with the Incarnation* (New York, C. Scribner's, 1895), p. 93, however, Gore adopts what is now called a 'two centres of consciousness' model, which denies any actual loss of 'divine and cosmic functions' during the incarnation. (R. Swinburne, *The Christian God* (Oxford, Clarendon Press, 1994), p. 230, n. 32, comments illuminatingly on the confusion caused by dubbing Gore's position straightforwardly 'kenotic'.) See section V, below, for further discussion of the contemporary 'two centres of consciousness' defence of Chalcedonianism, which is predominantly anti-'kenotic'.

34 See P. T. Forsyth, *The Person and Place of Jesus Christ* (London, Hodder & Stoughton, 1909), pp. 296–300.

35 This point is well made (in relation to the question of how misleading images may dominate philosophical discussion of free will) by D. C. Dennett in *Elbow Room: The Varieties of Free Will Worth Wanting* (Oxford, Clarendon Press, 1984), pp. 169–71.

36 See again Moule, 'Further Reflexions', p. 265 (my emphasis).

37 Robinson, *Human Face*, p. 208, citing Moule with approval: '*kenōsis* actually *is plērōsis*'.

38 See J. Macquarrie, 'Kenoticism Reconsidered', *Theology* 77 (1974), pp. 115–24; this quotation from p. 124.

39 See S. T. Davis, *Logic and the Nature of God* (Grand Rapids, Eerdmans, 1983), pp. 123–4.

40 Davis, *Logic*, p. 125. (Playing tennis with one's weak hand may be an analogy laudably free from *sexist* overtones, but it is scarcely calculated to inspire spiritually.)

41 For recent criticism of Davis's position on grounds of coherence, see Hick, *Metaphor of God*, ch. 7. Relevant comments on Davis in a mode more sympathetic to 'kenoticism' are to be found in R. J. Feenstra, 'Reconsidering Kenotic Christology' in R. J. Feenstra and C. Plantinga (eds.), *Trinity, Incarnation, and Atonement* (Notre Dame, Notre Dame Press, 1989), pp. 128–52.

42 See Sykes in Kee and Long (eds.), *Being and Truth*, pp. 358–60, for critical reflection on this point. (A 'process' view of theism would of course more willingly embrace these implications. See again Frankenberry, 'Classical Theism', pp. 34–9, for a view of Hartsthornian 'panentheism' that is read positively by her in terms of gender issues. The full case for my own maintenance of a more 'classical' perception of God is unfortunately impossible within the constraints of this essay, although some of the main lines of argument are sketched here.)

43 For one of the testier examples of the latter approach, see Morris, *Logic*, esp. ch. 3 and 4. Morris insists that 'the figure of the God-man is in no way at all even a paradox for faith' (p. 74).

44 See, for example, the much-quoted opening paragraph of R. Swinburne, *The Coherence of Theism* (Oxford, Clarendon Press, 1977), p. 1: 'By a theist I understand a man who believes that there is a God. By a "God" he understands something like a "person without a body (i.e. a spirit) who is eternal, free, able to do anything, knows everything, is perfectly good, is the proper object of human worship and obedience, the creator and sustainer of the universe".'

45 M. McC. Adams and R. M. Adams (eds.), *The Problem of Evil* (Oxford, Oxford University Press, 1990), esp. the editors' introduction, pp. 10–16, shows with clarity how problems of theodicy have propelled modern philosophers of religion (even Calvinists) towards a 'libertarian' view of freedom (since without such an explanation, the divine responsibility for appalling levels of evil in the world would appear impossible to square with the notion of perfect divine goodness). Adams and Adams do not discuss the question, raised here in my essay, of whether these Christian philosophers are already predisposed towards a 'libertarian' view of freedom on account of their Enlightenment heritage. (For what the masculinist implications of such a view might be, see Frankenberry, 'Classical Theism', pp. 33–4, who comments on the gender presumptions smuggled into discussions of divine power in current analytic philosophy of religion.)

46 For a discussion of the gendered nature of this Enlightenment figure, in his various forms, see G. Lloyd, *The Man of Reason: 'Male' and 'Female' in Western Philosophy* (Minneapolis, University of Minnesota Press, 1984), esp. ch. 3–5.

47 See again Swinburne, *Coherence* esp. pp. 1–7: God is a 'person' ... 'in the modern sense' (p. 1 and n. 1). The revised edition of the book (1993), more conscious of trinitarian issues, omits n. 1.

48 See Morris, *Logic*; Brown, *Divine Trinity*; Swinburne, *Christian God*.

49 For discussion of the potential importance of feminist and psychological considerations for contemporary epistemology, see N. Schemann, 'Individualism and Objects of Psychology', and J. Flax, 'Political Philosophy and the Patriarchal Unconscious: A Psychoanalytic Perspective on Epistemology and Metaphysics' in S. Harding and M. B. Hintikka (eds.), *Discovering Reality: Feminist Perspectives on Epistemology, Metaphysics, Methodology and Philosophy of Science* (Dordrecht, D. Reidel, 1983), pp. 225–44 and 245–81, respectively.

50 Utilized in a variety of ways by Brown, *Divine Trinity*; Morris, *Logic*; Swinburne in his article 'Could God Become Man?' in G. Vesey (ed.), *The Philosophy in Christianity* (Cambridge, Cambridge University Press, 1989), pp. 53–70; and (in somewhat revised form) Swinburne, *Christian God*.

51 See Morris, *Logic*, p. 103; Swinburne in Vesey (ed.), *Philosophy*, p. 65; Brown, *Divine Trinity*, p. 262.

52 For the most part the 'divided mind' christologians wholly ignore this dimension of their own analogy, though – if one pressed it – Freud's deeper sexual motivations would presumably have to be associated with the *divine* nature in Christ (i.e., that 'mind' kept somewhat in the background during Christ's earthly existence). Swinburne's brief exploration of the sexual analogy in Vesey (ed.), *Philosophy*, p. 62, however, sees sexual desire as a *human* temptation which some stronger dimension, analogous to the divine (i.e., the will), should overcome. Perhaps significantly, Swinburne omits this element of the 'two minds' analogy from his more recent (parallel) discussion: Swinburne, *Christian God*, ch. 9.

53 Thus contemporary French feminisms can build on an existing discussion in French postmodern philosophy of Freud and Lacan: see, by way of introduction, the useful discussion of French feminist writers in C. Weedon, *Feminist Practice and Post-Structuralist Theory*, Oxford, Basil Blackwell, 1987.

54 See Hick, *Metaphor*, ch. 5, for a clearly expressed critique (motivated *against* traditional Chalcedonianism).

55 See Swinburne in Vesey (ed.), *Philosophy*, p. 59 ('[Christ's] soul which is subsequently the human soul'), and, more clearly, p. 61 ('joining his [Christ's] soul to an unowned human body'). In Swinburne, *Christian God*, ch. 9, these phrases are repeated (pp. 194, 196), but the suggestion of quasi-Apollinarianism is corrected by a clarification that the 'reasonable [human] soul' of Christ (defended at Chalcedon against Apollinarianism) is not to be seen as an identifiable substance, like Christ's pre-existent divine soul, but rather as 'a human *way of thinking and*

acting' (p. 197, my emphasis). This adjustment is arguably still not very comfortable, however, importing as it does a Cartesian notion of 'soul' into the ('Alexandrian') reading of the pre-existent Logos as *identical* with Christ's *hypostasis*.

56 See Morris, *Logic*, pp. 150–3 (esp. pp. 151–2, drawing on a well-known thought-experiment devised by Harry Frankfurt).

57 Morris, *Logic*, p. 153.

58 Recall the injunctions of the Chalcedonian Definition: '... in two natures, without confusion, without change, without division, *without separation*...'.

59 See Swinburne, *Christian God*, p. 208: 'the "divided mind" view ... allows the human nature of Christ to be not a nature as perfect as a human nature could be', etc.

60 There are occasional, and interesting, exceptions to this rule in the discourses of analytic philosophy of religion. R. M. Adams's profound spiritual questioning of the 'lust for control of my own life and its circumstances', in *The Virtue of Faith and Other Essays in Philosophical Theology* (New York, Oxford University Press, 1987), pp. 18–20, is an important counter-instance (though, significantly, he remarks in a note, p. 1, that he owes this insight in large part to his wife). In a christological context, J. R. Lucas has argued (in 'Foreknowledge and the Vulnerability of God', Vesey, (ed.), *Philosophy*, pp. 119–28) that – *contra* Swinburne et al. – the 'Christian God' (as opposed to 'an impersonal Neoplatonist Absolute') is necessarily a 'suffering', 'fallible' and 'vulnerable' God. Ironically, these conclusions seem to arise less from a conviction of the priority of the New Testament narrative (though the passion is briefly mentioned in closing), than from an outworking of philosophical presumptions also shared by Swinburne (and *not* shared by 'classical theists' in the Thomist tradition): the 'libertarian' freewill of the individual, and the en-timed nature of the divine.

  Neither Adams nor Lucas, we might note, raises gender issues in making these points about 'vulnerability' and loss of 'control'.

61 See Sykes in Kee and Long (eds.), *Being and Truth*, p. 357. (Sykes is not, however, considering gendered anthropomorphism.)

62 See again n. 30, above.

63 See again n. 33, above.

64 I am aware of the regrettable looseness with which I have wielded the term 'masculinism' in this essay. In feminist writing the word tends to be used as a shorthand, to denote attitudes and actions derogatory to women and women's flourishing, but often encouraged or condoned in the population at large, especially amongst men. (Such a definition, however, begs many questions itself. For example: how are such attitudes promoted and sustained? Are women themselves immune from them? What *is* 'women's flourishing'?) For a clear, and critical, introduction to some philosophical issues encountered here, see J. Grimshaw, *Feminist Philosophers: Women's Perspectives on Philosophical Traditions* (London, Harvester Wheatsheaf, 1986), esp. ch. 2 and 7. I hope it will be clear from what I have written that I do not share Hampson's (apparently) essentialist and

universalizing views (expressed in Hampson, 'On Power and Gender' and *Theology and Feminism*) that there are fixed 'male' and 'female' approaches to God, human nature, 'power', etc.

65 It would be misleading to suggest it has been completely taboo; indeed, 'vulnerability' in 'mutual relation' (see I. C. Heyward, *The Redemption of God: A Theology of Mutual Relation* (Lanham MD, University Press of America, 1982); R. N. Brock, *Journeys by Heart: A Christology of Erotic Power* (New York, Crossroad, 1988), suffering as purposive (see D. Soelle, *Suffering* (Philadelphia, Fortress Press, 1975)) and ethical 'risk' (S. D. Welch, *A Feminist Ethic of Risk* (Minneapolis, Fortress Press, 1990) have been significant, though not dominant, themes in recent feminist theological writing. There has also been one specific discussion of *kenōsis* from a feminist dialogue with Buddhism: see C. Keller, 'Scoop Up the Water and the Moon in Your Hands: On Feminist Theology and Dynamic Self-Emptying' in J. B. Cobb and C. Ives (eds.), *The Emptying God: A Buddhist–Jewish–Christian Conversation* (Maryknoll NY, Orbis, 1990), pp. 102–15.

  Much more common in feminist literature, however, is the (wholly understandable) emphasis on 'vulnerability' as an opportunity for masculinist *abuse*: see, for example, M. P. Engel, 'Evil, Sin, and the Violation of the Vulnerable' in S. B. Thistlewaite and M. P. Engel (eds.), *Lift Every Voice: Constructing Christian Theologies from the Underside* (San Francisco, Harper & Row, 1990), pp. 152–64.

66 See the chilling cases of abusive Christian fathers documented in A. Imbens and I. Jonker, *Christianity and Incest* (London, Burns & Oates, 1992).

67 This dimension of my argument is spelled out in more detail in my forthcoming book on the Trinity, *God, Sexuality and the Self* (based on the Hulsean Lectures, Cambridge University, 1992).

68 This point is well made in Sykes' essay in Kee and Long (eds.), *Being and Truth*, esp. pp. 361–5, though Sykes applies it mainly to the practice of the sacraments.

69 See Foucault's late essays on power in M. Foucault, *Power/Knowledge* (Brighton, Harvester Press, 1980).

70 In Oxford Faculty Lectures, 1991 and 1992; further discussed in my forthcoming book *God, Sexuality and the Self*.

71 This is the theme of Tugwell's anti-élitist arguments in S. Tugwell, *Ways of Imperfection* (London, Darton, Longman & Todd, 1984), esp. ch. 9–11. Tugwell is not, however, especially interested in the gender dimensions of his subject-matter, and, whilst lauding Julian of Norwich's theology, is deeply scornful of Margery Kempe (see ch. 16 and pp. 109–10).

72 The word 'special' is used by the author of the fourteenth-century *The Cloud of Unknowing* (ed. J. Walsh (London, SPCK, 1981), p. 115) in this context of entry into 'contemplation'. The work of the sixteenth-century Carmelites, Teresa of Ávila and John of the Cross, is marked by a particular interest in charting the appropriate moment of transition from 'meditation' to 'contemplation'. On this, see my discussion in S. Coakley, 'Traditions of Spiritual Guidance: Dom John Chapman OSB (1865–1933),

The Way 30 (1990), pp. 246–53, which contains (p. 253) some preliminary remarks about the gendered dimension of the issue.

73 This phrase is from the opening sentence of the Syriac *Book of Steps* (fourth to fifth century), translated in S. Brock (ed.), *The Syriac Fathers on Prayer and the Spiritual Life* (Kalamazoo, Cistercian Publications, 1987), p. 45. I am grateful to Sebastian Brock for a helpful discussion of early Syriac treatments of Philippians 2.

74 For Kristeva's (Lacanian) appeal to a time preceding the development of language as a source of creativity and feminist subversion, see J. Kristeva, *Desire in Language: A Semiotic Approach to Literature and Art* (Oxford, Basil Blackwell, 1980), and T. Moi's helpful introduction to Kristeva, *The Kristeva Reader* (New York, Columbia University Press, 1986), esp. pp. 12–15.

75 See my discussion of this problem in relation to the spritual direction of J.-P. de Caussade, in ' "Femininity" and the Holy Spirit'; in M. Furlong (ed.), *Mirror to the Church: Reflections on Sexism* (London, SPCK, 1988), pp. 128–30.

76 See the discussion of this point by C. Keller in Cobb and Ives (eds.), *The Emptying God*, pp. 105–6.

77 See Soelle's attempt at this in relation to Eckhart's theology in her lecture 'Mysticism-Liberation-Feminism' in D. Soelle, *The Strength of the Weak: Toward a Christian Feminist Identity* (Philadelphia, Westminster Press, 1984), pp. 79–105.

78 For a perceptive – and politically astute – discussion of the deliberate destruction of both language and the personality in the act of torture (in distinction from other forms of productive and religiously motivated suffering), see E. Scarry, *The Body in Pain* (New York, Oxford University Press, 1985), esp. pp. 34–5.

79 This is a point made by Nussbaum in her discussion of 'fragility', 'vulnerability', and 'luck' in Greek thought. See M. C. Nussbaum, *The Fragility of Goodness* (Cambridge, Cambridge University Press, 1986), esp. p. xv: 'It occurred to me to ask whether the act of writing about the beauty of human vulnerability is not, paradoxically, a way of rendering oneself less vulnerable and more in control of the uncontrolled elements of life.'

80 On this point, see Townes' essay, 'Living in the New Jerusalem' in E. M. Townes (ed.), *A Troubling in My Soul: Womanist Perspectives on Evil and Suffering* (Maryknoll NY, Orbis, 1993), esp. pp. 83–6.

81 This is, I believe, a legitimate (though 'Antiochene') way of reading the Chalcedonian Definition, granted that the word *hypostasis* does not appear in the Definition until the phrase relating to the 'concurrence' of the natures, and is not explicitly identified with the pre-existent Logos. On the significance of this 'Antiochene' reading, see the important article by A. Baxter, 'Chalcedon, and the Subject in Christ', *Downside Review* 107 (1989), pp. 1–21. The full implications, philosophical and theological, of developing this interpretation of Chalcedon, can unfortunately not be spelled out here; but it is instructive to note that feminist writers on Christology have so far been divided on whether the 'Alexandrian' or

'Antiochene' traditions hold more promise for a feminist standpoint. See P. Wilson-Kastner, *Faith, Feminism, and the Christ* (Philadelphia, Fortress Press, 1983), esp. pp. 83–4, for a position sympathetic to the 'Alexandrian' reading of Chalcedon, and Heyward, *Redemption of God*, esp. pp. 189–92, for a champion of the 'Antiochene' school.

82 This essay was written during a sabbatical from Harvard as a Henry Luce III Fellow. I would like to acknowledge my gratitude to the Luce Foundation for this opportunity for research and writing.

7. RESPONSE: DAPHNE HAMPSON

1 It also seems to me that, in relation to a liberation theology, there are theodicy questions and questions as to the usefulness of speaking of God in (masculinist) terms as powerful (if powerful in saving the downtrodden), which need to be addressed from a feminist perspective and which I cannot tackle here. See my 'On Power and Gender', *Modern Theology*, vol. 4, no. 3 (April 1988), p. 237; to be anthologized in E. Stuart and A. Thatcher (eds.), *Christian Perspectives on Sexuality and Gender*, *Christian Perspectives* series (Leominster, Gracewing/Fowler Wright, 1996). Can one, as Audre Lorde will have it, ever destroy the master's house while using the master's tools; or does not feminism call for a much more radical kind of revolution which would do away with speaking of 'power over' (which kind of power incidentally also implies a God in relation to whom the human must exist in a heteronomous relation)?

2 Oxford and Cambridge MA, Basil Blackwell, 1990, p. 155, citing *Sexism and God-Talk* (Boston MA, Beacon Press and London, SCM Press, 1983), pp. 137–8.

3 'Is Feminism the End of Christianity? A Critique of Daphne Hampson's *Theology and Feminism*', *Scottish Journal of Theology*, vol. 43, p. 393. My italics.

4 On the question as to whether 'all' men and conversely 'all' women, see my 'On Power and Gender'. I agree that some men (slaves – Coakley p. 98) do not need to undergo a *kenōsis* of power and wealth; and that some women do. But I take it that in this discussion (with half of herself Coakley seems to be and my discussion certainly is) dealing with issues of 'self-enclosure' versus what Coakley names 'vulnerability'. I am unclear (see 'On Power and Gender') that men who are at the bottom of the male social hierarchy (I instance black men and Russian serfs) are any less apt to be self-enclosed (and to dominate others) than are white, privileged men.

5 See note 1.

12. RESPONSE: SARAH COAKLEY

1 These kinds of debunking strategies are well evident in Alvin E. Kimel (ed.), *Speaking the Christian God: The Holy Trinity and the Challenge of Feminism* (Grand Rapids MI, Eerdmans, 1992), a 'backlash' volume against feminist theology (which nonetheless bemusingly contains an essay by Janet Soskice).

2 I explored some of these epistemological distinctions at greater length in

an early article, 'Theology and Cultural Relativism: What is the Problem?', *Neue Zeitschrift für Systematische Theologie und Religions-philosophie* 21 (1979), pp. 223–43.

3 I do not wish to espouse either a 'naïve' realism or a 'classical foundationalism', though I am sometimes taken to be doing so.

4 Oxford, Clarendon Press, 1985.

5 This 'diachronic' dimension of metaphor is well discussed in Richard Swinburne, *Revelation* (Oxford, Clarendon Press, 1992), who strongly differs from Soskice, however, in his fundamental preference for literal speech for God over the use of tropes.

14. AFTERWORD: JANET MARTIN SOSKICE

1 And here I would like to go on record as saying, since Sarah brings the Kimmel book up in her footnotes, that I was told when asked to contribute that it would be a collection from diverse perspectives on feminism and the Trinity. When it appeared it was less 'diverse' than some of us might have wished.

2 On this, 'woman', and the texts of western philosophy see Luce Irigaray, *Speculum of the Other Woman*.

3 Or of 'inside', or 'outside', or 'before' or 'after', as in 'What was there before time began?' All this language is stretched.

16. AFTERWORD: JANE SHAW

1 Alice A. Jardine, *Gynesis: Configurations of Woman and Modernity* (Ithaca, Cornell University Press, 1985). For Lacan's writings on women, pleasure and mysticism see Jacques Lacan, 'God and the *Jouissance* of The Woman. A Love Letter' in *Feminine Sexuality*, ed. Juliet Mitchell and Jacqueline Rose (London, W. W. Norton and Company, 1988).

17. AFTERWORD: JULIE HOPKINS

1 *Towards a Feminist Christology*, (London, SPCK, 1995).

18. AFTERWORD: SARAH COAKLEY

1 I have myself discussed the manifold difficulties of reformulating a Chalcedonian Christology for today in *Christ Without Absolutes: A Study of the Christology of Ernst Troeltsch* (Oxford, 1988). The problem of how the Jesus of history can also be an 'archetypal' figure was central to Troeltch's concerns, as it also is to Julie's.

2 In my earlier article 'Creaturehood before God', *Theology* (September/October 1990), pp. 343–54, I attempted to distinguish different sorts of human dependency (some, I argued, inevitable features of the life-span) from the *sui generis* dependence that we have on God, whilst admitting how entangled these different forms may become in both our conscious and unconscious minds.

SPCK

The Society for Promoting Christian Knowledge (SPCK) has as its purpose three main tasks:

- **Communicating the Christian faith in its rich diversity**
- **Helping people to understand the Christian faith and to develop their personal faith**
- **Equipping Christians for mission and ministry**

SPCK Worldwide runs a substantial grant programme to support Christian literature and communication projects in over 100 countries. Special schemes also provide books for those training for ministry in many parts of the world. All gifts to SPCK are spent wholly on these grant programmes, without deductions.

SPCK Bookshops support the life of the Christian community by making available a full range of Christian literature and other resources, and by providing support to bookstalls and book agents throughout the UK. SPCK Bookshops' mail order department meets the needs of overseas customers and those unable to have access to local bookshops.

SPCK Publishing produces Christian books and resources, covering a wide range of inspirational, pastoral, practical and academic subjects. Authors are drawn from many different Christian traditions, and publications aim to meet the needs of a wide variety of readers in the UK and throughout the world.

The Society does not necessarily endorse the individual views contained in its publications, but hopes they stimulate readers to think about and further develop their Christian faith.

For further information about the Society, please write to: SPCK, Holy Trinity Church, Marylebone Road, London NW1 4DU, United Kingdom.
Telephone: 0171 387 5282